The German Library: Volume 96

Volkmar Sander, General Editor

CONTEMPORARY GERMAN PLAYS I

Rolf Hochhuth,
Heinar Kipphardt,
and Heiner Müller

Edited by
Margaret Herzfeld-Sander

CONTINUUM · NEW YORK

2001

The Continuum International Publishing Group Inc
370 Lexington Avenue, New York, NY 10017

The German Library
is published in cooperation with Deutsches Haus,
New York University.
This volume has been supported by Inter Nationes.

Printed in the United States of America

Library of Congress Cataloging-in-Publication Data

Contemporary German plays / edited by Margaret Herzfeld-Sander.
p.   cm. — (The German library ; v. 96–)
Contents: v. 1. The deputy / Rolf Hochhuth. In the matter of J. Robert
Oppenheimer / Heinar Kipphardt. Hamletmachine / Heiner Muller.
ISBN 0-8264-0972-5 (v. 1 : alk. paper). — ISBN 0-8264-0973-3
(pbk. : v. 1 : alk. paper)
1. German drama—20th century—Translations into English.
I. Herzfeld-Sander, Margaret.   II. Series.
PT1258.C66   2000
832'.91408—dc21   99-030830

Contents

Introduction

During the Hitler regime literary, artistic, and theatrical avant-garde achievements in Germany received a severe blow. It led to a fateful loss of talent and a drain on ingenuity. People of all walks of life, among them artists, writers, and critics had to leave the country, or even worse were sent to concentration camps.

The lively, innovative spirit of the 1920s and early 1930s was condemned; the aesthetic and substantive advances in the arts of the Weimar Republic were ridiculed, defamed, and eventually eliminated. At the end of World War II, the break with progressive forces had left a void that could be filled only gradually. It was the Swiss writers Max Frisch and Friedrich Dürrenmatt who gave a fresh impetus to the German theater after the war. Both writers, although from different viewpoints, exposed the causes of injustice, persecution, and violence on the stage and investigated the individual's place in the world, as well as his or her actions and responsibility in society.

However, in the 1960s Bertolt Brecht became the most decisive influence on German playwrights. His epic-dialectic theater brought the contradictory sociopolitical powers to the stage by exposing subject matter, incidents, and characters through a process of alienation.

When Erwin Piscator, the well-known director of Weimar Germany, who had founded the Actor's Studio in exile in New York City, returned to Berlin, the political theater and documentary technique were revived. German dramatic publications and productions increased, and so did the various dramatic devices and concepts of postwar drama. Theater as a public forum regained its position as a moral and emancipatory setting. There was not just one, homogenous dramatic genre, but many. Soon there existed side by side the paradoxical world of tragicomedy, the further development of the so-called epic theater, documentary drama, the theater of the absurd, the neorealism of folk plays, and finally the speak-ins and linguistic investigations of the up-and-coming postwar generation.

The three plays included in this volume must be understood within the immediate context of the German postwar era, the aftermath of the national-socialist dictatorship, and the shock experienced following the explosion of the atomic bomb. The urgency to accept the burdens of the past and to enlighten the present demanded a thorough knowledge of recent German history, which in turn led many writers to the study of documentary evidence: above all, the Holocaust. As a consequence, many German dramatists expressed a predilection for documentary theater in the 1960s and 1970s.

There is no single documentary genre, nevertheless, but a variety of approaches to what came to be called Documentary Theater. After 1960, there are playwrights such as Rolf Hochhuth, Heinar Kipphardt, Dieter Forte, Peter Weiss, Hans Magnus Enzensberger, Alexander Kluge, Günter Grass, and Tankred Dorst who employed documentary material in different fashions and subject matter as part of their dramas. Everyone in the theater also remembered Erwin Piscator and his famous staging of provocative texts in late 1920s' and 1930s' Berlin. As director of *Freie Volksbühne* in Berlin, he produced Hochhuth's *The Deputy* in 1963 and Peter Weiss's *The Investigation* (see The German Library, volume 92) in 1965. Both plays are about Auschwitz. Piscator had always pleaded for an epic, political theater and the assimilation of documentary aspects into the drama. The works that now appeared varied in theme, structure, style, and discourse. They moved from traditional, idealist Schillerian dramaturgy, as in *The Deputy,* to a laconic and unemotional discourse in the Brechtian manner, as in Heinar Kipphardt's *In the Matter of J. Robert Oppenheimer* (1964). There was a noticeable reduction of action and overwhelming pathos in Peter Weiss's *The Investigation,* and a sardonic, intelligent dialogic structure about art, politics, and rebellion in East Berlin in *The Plebeians Rehearse the Uprising,* 1966, by Günter Grass.

Yet in spite of the diversity of aesthetics and intellectual dimensions, these and other playwrights adhered to major premises. No one, for instance, would negate the dictum that the emancipatory elements of the documentary play should critically accompany the prevailing public discourse. Modern drama draws its strength from its dialogic structure and dispenses with psychological probings into the motivations of dramatic characters. A detached, almost scientific observation of sociopolitical conditions propels the dramaturgy of the plays. The text allows the writers to incorporate select newspaper report, protocols, trial records, files, letters, interviews, statistical data, annual reports of banks and corporations, photographs, as well as historic figures in order to lend persuasive authenticity to fictional representation. These playwrights also insist that the documentary play should *not* be understood as a political manifesto, and that it does not claim objectivity. The freedom to condense and arrange factual data and build it into the dramatic action permits the appearance of both historic and fictitious characters, combining actual quotations with invented monologues and dialogues. There never are raw facts, as some critics proclaimed at first, since documentaries are always subject to an artistic process. Authentic material enhances reality without destroying the aesthetic dimension of the play. The task remains that an important issue has to be communicated in order to stimulate and augment reflections on how to change sociopolitical reality.

Apart from the drama itself, theoretical discussions on the nature of documentaries abound. Virtually all plays are supplemented by explanatory notes. Peter Weiss writes extensively on documentary theater: its specifics and ramifications. (Cf. Peter Weiss's "Notes on the Contemporary Theater" in *Essays on German Theater,* The German Library, volume 83, pp. 294–301). Heinar Kipphardt, in the preface to *In the Case of J. Robert Oppenheimer,* relies on the documentary technique in order to lay bare the very essence of a historic moment. There are subject matters—such as trials—which cannot be treated in a more satisfactory way.

Several years later not only a particular epoch but Western history itself came under suspicion and dramatic scrutiny in many plays by Heiner Müller. So far, history had provided themes, conflicts, contradictions, and characters to analyze the human condition. For the poet-playwright-historian Friedrich Schiller (1759–1805), the entire realm of fantasy and history belongs to the jurisdiction of the stage. Georg Büchner (1813–37) censored the French Revolution and its Reign of Terror, and characterized the dramatist as "a writer of history. He is superior to the latter, however, in that he re-creates history a second time for us. Instead of telling us a dry story, he places us directly into the life of earlier times, giving us characters instead of characteristics and figures instead of descriptions. His greatest task is to come as close as possible to history as it actually happened." (The German Library, volume 83, p. 77). History as the basis for dramatic art has dominated German drama and still informs the plays of Heiner Müller. However, in his plays an essential paradigmatic change has taken place. He now deconstructs and questions the entire course of Western history. A few years later, a younger generation would discover other dimensions, turning to a theater of human sensibilities and the failure of communication. In the plays of Peter Handke, Botho Strauss, and others there was a noticeable break with political commitments and the preoccupation with the burden of history. Yet the fascination with, and the influence of, documentaries as well as the power of historic consciousness remain to our time. The three playwrights included in this volume are outstanding examples of this postwar era and this genre.

Rolf Hochhuth 1931–

After World War II, there were several attempts to find adequate dramatic forms to give testimony to the horrors of the Hitler era. Wolfgang Borchert had captured the despair of a lost generation in *The Outsider* (1947) and he tried to expose the deliberate amnesia that began to spread in the decade after the war. The radio plays *Dreams* (1953) by Günter Eich, admonishing the listeners not to forget what had happened in their name, had shocked and infuriated the public. Finally, Max Frisch asked for resistance to prejudice and indifference in *Andorra* (1958) and *The Fire Raisers* (1958). (See The German Library, volume 90, *Novels, Plays, Essays* by Max Frisch.) However, no other play created such an outcry as Rolf Hochhuth's *The Deputy* (1962). Erwin Piscator immediately recognized its political and moral significance. The publication of the book and the performance in Berlin took place simultaneously.

Rolf Hochhuth was born in 1931 in Eschwege, Germany, two years before Hitler came to power. His parents were solid burghers but remained skeptical about the rise and rule of the National Socialists. Hochhuth became an editor and finally a freelance writer. He published several stories, plays, essays, and a novel, *A Love in Germany* (1978), which was made into a film. He mentions Friedrich Schiller, Thomas Mann, Robert Musil, and Otto Flake as the inspirations for his development as a writer. Hochhuth received many awards for his works. He recently acquired the former Brecht Theater in Berlin for a foundation which, from 1998 on, performs *The Deputy* annually in memory of the Wertheim family of New York, who owned the property and who lost thirty-one family members in Auschwitz.

Hochhuth's first play, *The Deputy,* became an instant success that nonetheless polarized opinions. That it seemed to touch a raw nerve is demonstrated by the fact that it was staged simultaneously in Berlin, London, Basel, Paris, and New York. Its first performances in all cities had to be protected by police forces against large demonstrations in front of the theaters. On Broadway, *The Deputy* was on the program for about a year. The dramas that followed were not quite as sensational but were equally controversial. In the 1960s and 1970s, Hochhuth's plays became a staple of German theaters throughout the country. The best-known of his plays are: *The Soldiers* (1967), *Guerillas* (1970), *The Midwife* (1971), *Lysistrate and Nato* (1973), *Death of a Hunter* (1977), and *The Lawyers* (1979). The discussions and controversies that accompanied each publication and each performance were universal in scope, as his themes were always up-to-date and provocative. Above all, *The Deputy* dominated his other plays worldwide. The English translation reproduced here is by Richard and Clara Winston (1964). Since plays and notes run to over 300 pages, it has been abridged for this volume.

After extensive research, Hochhuth created a drama that deals with the persecution of the Jews and genocide in Auschwitz. The difficulty to come to poetic terms in the face of the horror of the persecution, transportation, and death of millions of people haunted many writers after the war. Hochhuth rejected the determinist nature of naturalistic depiction of the human condition by returning to both the aesthetic and philosophic conviction of Friedrich Schiller. Hochhuth adopted the classic dictum that rhythmic verse at crucial moments could impart the imaginary element necessary to transport historic events into human speech, and lend seemingly arbitrary facts a meaning and a moral force. Hochhuth also believes in the classic constellation of granting the individual the freedom of choice and independence although faced with irrational political powers and highly developed technical means to destroy the victims. In the play, the guilt and responsibility of the participants of the Hitler regime must be exposed, and the question is raised whether the failure of Pope Pius XII in the Vatican to intervene forcefully on behalf of the Jews was a personal, and by extension, an institutional abdication. The silence against violence and torture has to be investigated and, according to Hochhuth, should not be ignored or forgotten. The dramatist has the opportunity to transcend the historic inquiry by lending a voice to both the victim and the perpetrator. The historic figure of Pope Pius XII is bestowed with a cold and impartial mental state. He argues for the Catholic Church, which has nothing to fear, as Hitler will listen to reason and will show moderation in victory. The concordate between the Vatican and the Third Reich safeguards the Western World against the evil of Eastern communism. Father Riccardo Fontana, a fictitious character, and Kurt Gerstein, a historic figure who undertook the mission to join the SS voluntarily to fight the regime from within, urge the Pope to break his silence and openly protest in Berlin against the arrest and deportation of the Jews. The Pope, however, proclaims in general terms to end the suffering of humankind. He rejects all pleas to be more concrete in his demands in order to uphold the spirit of neutrality. The sanctity of the Curia against the Third Reich supports the attitude of great reserve. Father Riccardo is molded after the actual lives and resistance of Father Maximilian Kolbe and Prelate Bernhard Lichtenberg in Berlin, to whose memory the play is dedicated. Riccardo is haunted by the silence of the Pope and voluntarily joins a transport to Auschwitz. He declares: "God shall not destroy His church only because a Pope shrinks from His summons." As Christ's "real" deputy, Riccardo meets "the Auschwitz Angel of death," the highly intelligent, cynic doctor who selects the victims at the ramp to be sent to the gas chambers. The "charming devil" is no other but the actual, notorious doctor Mengele, who later escaped to South America.

In the final confrontation between Riccardo and the doctor, evil is triumphant when the doctor proclaims there is no individual, heroic death left. After centuries of murder and silence, Auschwitz proves that God is dead and the idea of life is over. The playwright, different from the historian, can show the monstrosities and the suffering behind facts and data. The reader should experience the revulsion at the perfidity and inhumanity exercised as manifestation of German superiority. Hochhuth divides his drama into five acts and leads the reader from Berlin to Rome to Auschwitz to show the involvement of many, and the resistance of a few. The psychological, private dispositions of his characters is of interest to the playwright only to show an ever-increasing revulsion.

Hochhuth deliberately focuses on the question of moral convictions in times of ideological obsessions. The entire scale of bourgeois attitudes is on display, from the naive to the horrendous, from the banal to the destructive. The involvement of the state, of industry, the army, research institutions, the law, and the church either directly collaborating with the perpetrators or remaining silent, destroys the illusion that each individual is solely responsible for the Holocaust. Nevertheless, individuals *are* called upon to rebel against so much injustice and indifference. The emotional impact of Hochhuth's drama is indisputably linked to the question of individual moral courage and rebellion.

Embedded in an inhuman political system, the individual is granted the freedom of an independent decision by Hochhuth—although the tragic end does not solve the dilemma. Hochhuth adheres to humane values as prerequisite for a dignified existence. Although a collectively accepted value system might be out of reach at the end of the twentieth century, it is still possible to show how to resist the perpetrators and act in solidarity with the victims.

Heinar Kipphardt 1922–82

In the 1960s, the theatrical aesthetics of Bertolt Brecht and new methods of documentation found a successful symbiosis in the plays of Heinar Kipphardt. His documentaries contributed to the public debate on the validity of the theater as an emancipatory institution. Like Brecht, Kipphardt was a man of the theater, and he was well aware of the problems of how to capture the attention of his audience. He maintains that it is not reality that is reproduced, but plays *about* reality (although historic events may form the framework of the plot).

Heinar Kipphardt was born in 1922 in Heidersdorf, Upper Silesia. From 1933 to 1938, his father was prisoner in the concentration camp Buchenwald. Kipphardt studied medicine, but also took courses in philosophy and the history of theater. During the war he was drafted, participated in the retreat from Russia, and eventually deserted his outfit. After the war, he finished his medical studies and became a psychiatrist in East Berlin. In 1950, he was appointed director of dramaturgy at the Deutsches Theater in the former German Democratic Republic (GDR). After political differences with the East German government, he left that country in 1959 and settled in what was then West Germany, first in Düsseldorf, then in Munich. Following publication of a controversial article, Kipphardt was forced out of his position as dramaturgist. He then worked as an editor and continued to publish poems, stories, a novel, and a string of successful plays.

Kipphardt's rational and critical understanding of contemporary conditions are reflected in all of his plays. His political conscience informed his dramatic imagination. He agreed with Brecht that the playwright has to avoid the "undignified intoxication" of emotional appeals and strive for a challenging confrontation with the audience. Already his early plays are free from what he believed to be supercilious accessories. His plays of the 1950s deal satirically with bureaucratic life in the GDR. His fame, however, rests on his plays of the 1960s, in which he concentrates on burning sociopolitical questions, frequently relying on available documentary material to dramatize issues: *Der Hund des Generals* (1962; *The General's Dog*), *In der Sache J. Robert Oppenheimer, Ein Szenischer Bericht* (1964; *In the Matter of J. Robert Oppenheimer*), *Joel Brand. Die Geschichte eines Geschäfts* (1965; *J.B.: The History of a Deal*), *Sedan-Feier* (1970; *The Sedan Memorial*), *Bruder Eichmann* (1980; *Brother Eichmann*).

These plays are remarkable examples of the theater of ideas. Kipphardt asked himself "whether our present-day theater perhaps does not do justice to our present-day world? If our theater is not able to deal with the key political questions of our time, then one will no longer be able to take it seriously." In an era in which slogans and ideologies cloud the essential core of an argument, the more scientific approach to contradictory topics leads the playwright to documentary techniques. The subject matter of *In the Matter of J. Robert Oppenheimer* lends itself to such a scientific attitude. The McCarthy era and the hearing on Oppenheimer's security clearance held before the Personal Security Board of the

Atomic Energy Commission in April and May of 1954 form the basis of the plot. Kipphardt sifted through three thousand pages of the hearing transcripts to distill and arrange the essence of the material. Slides, tapes, and film clips are incorporated in his play to support the factual side. Oppenheimer's monologues, however, as well as the final oral decisions on Oppenheimer's security status, are his own additions for dramatic effect.

The plot is not about Oppenheimer the man, but about the "case of Oppenheimer, to portray the contradictions and conflicts of the scientist in our age." (Kipphardt) What is being discussed are questions of loyalty, former sympathies for the communist party in the 1930s, guilt by association, treason, the power and limits of the government, freedom of thought, and the moral question of Hiroshima.

As in Brecht's *Galileo,* the central theme is that of loyalty, or rather the hierarchy of ideals and institutions that can lay claim to one's loyalty. There are three: that to ourselves, that to the state, and that to humankind. Just as the state stands above the individual, so humanity stands above the state. In a rather more complex form than that of Brecht's *Galileo,* we are confronted with the problem of treason, and it is noteworthy that here the decision does not mean the relatively simple choice between loyalty and disloyalty, but that any decision for one of the three sides automatically implies betrayal of one of the other two. In Kipphardt's play we no longer have the choice of whether or not we want to commit treason, but only of what we want to betray in favor of another loyalty.

This play is not the case history of an individual (as in *Galileo)* whose exemplary actions will change the course of history. Oppenheimer is only one among hundreds of physicists used in the secret machinery of the crash program of Operation Manhattan. His importance for the committee does not lie in his towering achievement as a scientist but in the fact that he, plagued by his own scruples, has become an unmovable cog in an otherwise well-oiled machine, and hence a security risk. It is neither the man nor the physicist Oppenheimer who is being investigated, but the function he fulfills (or does not fulfill) within the whole. Contrary to Galileo, Robert Oppenheimer is replaceable without jeopardizing the whole project: the building of the bomb. Hence Edward Teller's testimony on the witness stand: "Brilliant ideas can be organized. They are not tied up with particular individuals." The gap between this view and individual hero worship could not be wider.

Faced with this dilemma, Oppenheimer's response is to reject all responsibility for the end product of his scientific research: "It is not the fault of the physicists that today brilliant ideas always turn into bombs. As long as this is the case one can have a scientific enthusiasm for a thing and, at the same time, regard it with horror as a human being." This "as long as this is the case" implies two things: rejection of social responsibility as far as his person and his work are concerned, and at the same time tacit approval of conditions as well as an implied sense of moral bankruptcy.

However, during the course of the hearing Oppenheimer professes to believe in the integrity of the individual: "I think man cannot be taken to pieces like the mechanism of a fuse." But what if the many heterogeneous individuals come into conflict with conformity as necessitated by modern teamwork? Apparently there are only two possibilities. The seemingly easier one is to continue to play the conformist game outwardly and secretly to maintain the separation between "professional" work and "individual" opinion. The result will be either a double life, leading to neurosis or, in the extreme case, to schizophrenia: a slow betrayal of one sphere to the other. This latter possibility is put forth as a hypothetical explanation by the prosecution: "We have here a form of treason which is not known in our code of law. It is ideological treason, which has its origin in the deepest strata of the personality and renders a man's actions dishonest against his will." The claim of the state to loyalty thus extends to controlling the subconscious; in so doing it destroys the basis of all political freedom. For a man who wants to remain free, this is no solution.

There is the other alternative which Oppenheimer finally adopts. Since he can neither convince the state apparatus of his own doubts nor bow to conformity himself, the only way out is to retreat into private life and private research.

The result of the conflict of loyalties is resignation. Rejection of responsibility and reduction to privacy combine: in doing so the individual is no longer conceived as the cornerstone on which the state rests. Oppenheimer falls back on the position of the absurd hero. He consciously places himself outside of the general development and destroys his career in order to save his moral integrity, his dignity, his image as a human being. Like Galileo, he, too, withdraws, secretly pursuing science as if it were a vice. This means that the contemporary physicist who becomes aware of the problems of his discipline can no longer endure the conflict of loyalties. Oppenheimer's solution is the most horrible one: planned mediocrity. The Galileo-Faust, who strove to be a titan and who only failed because of his own weakness, has developed into a real titan, conscious of the impending apocalypse, who desperately wants to become an ordinary human being again and consequently resigns.

We are dismissed from the theater with more questions than answers. The comfortable liberal illusion that Oppenheimer is, at the end, exonerated, is just that: an illusion. We are still on trial. It is paradigmatic for the mid-century that scientists stand at the center of three powerful German plays: Brecht's *Galileo,* Friedrich Dürrenmatt's *The Physicists,* and Kipphardt's *In the Matter of J. Robert Oppenheimer.*

Heiner Müller 1929–95

Heiner Müller was born in Eppendorf, Saxony. His father, as a member and functionary of the Social Democratic Party during Weimar times, was sent to a concentration camp in 1933. In the former GDR, he became mayor of a small town, but left the country after a falling out with the Socialist Party to live in the former Federal Republic of Germany. Heiner Müller was drafted into the Wehrmacht shortly before the end of the war and finished school after 1945. In the GDR he held various positions in cultural institutions, notably as dramaturgist of the Berliner Ensemble in East Berlin.

As a GDR citizen, Müller gradually developed into a prolific playwright, poet, essayist, and commentator on the art of the theater as well as the problems of, and hope for, a universal discourse. His plays were not always welcome to the communist regime, and some of them were at times banned from the stage. Nevertheless he remained in the country, committed to the socialist ideals that are reflected in his provocative texts of the 1950s.

Müller remained in constant and fruitful discourse with the formidable Bertolt Brecht, but never tired of emphasizing that "to use Brecht without criticizing him, is to betray him." Brecht's theories on epic-dialectic theater remained personally influential, but in time other artistic and philosophical ideas became important as well. Müller entered into dialogues with Antonin Artuad, Samuel Beckett, Jean Genet, Alexander Majkowski, Jerzy Grotowski. Friedrich

Nietzsche, Walter Benjamin, Franz Kafka, Robert Wilson, and Richard Foreman. They all became instrumental in shaping his artistic and historic sensibilities.

In his early phase of writing, Heiner Müller still adhered to the hope of constructing a humane, liberating, civil society under the auspices of socialism. He wrote in the manner of Brecht's "Lehrstücke," but in his later pieces rather with greater emphasis on fear and terror than on reason and epic distance. He addresses the audience to overcome lingering fascist remnants and to codetermine a free and solidary existence as in *Die Schlacht* (1951; *The Battle)*, *Traktor* (1955; *Tractor), Die Lohndrücker* (1956; *The Scab)*, Die Korrektur (1957; *The Correction), Die Umsiedlerin oder das Leben auf dem Lande* (1956–61; *The Resettled Woman; or, Life in the Country)*, and *Der Bau* (1963/64; *The Construction Site)*.

In the ever-faster-moving political and economic world, Heiner Müller realized that the era of class struggle and revolutionary change had run its course and no longer inspired dramatic projects. Brecht's Hegelian and Marxist belief in the linear-progressive development of history undergoes a radical change. A close affinity to Walter Benjamin's position begins to dominate Müller's thinking. A preoccupation with European history, as well as the failure of many revolutionary attempts, haunts the playwright. Müller shares Walter Benjamin's conviction, that a new beginning can only be achieved through the destruction and discontinuation of the past. History as we know it is nothing but a heap of ruins. Without following Benjamin's ultimate vision of a paradise regained, Müller agrees that the future can only be made possible through a rupture with the past. In his plays, the failures of history and revolutions can best be made visible through metaphors of terror, awe, and destruction: "In order to get rid of the nightmare of history you have to acknowledge, first of all, the existence of history. You have to know history. It would otherwise reemerge in its old-fashioned form, a nightmare, Hamlet's ghost. You first have to analyze it, then you can denounce it, get rid of it." (H.M., *Gesammelte Irrtümer*, Frankfurt 1986, p. 78). Plays now become laboratories to deconstruct history, accompanied by ingenious fragmentary collages, and thus constitute a break with traditional and Brechtian models. Both in treatment and structure of historic vistas as well as breakdowns of human aspirations, Müller's plays of the 1970s have much in common: *Mauser* (1970; *Mauser), Zement* (1972;

Cement), *Germania Tod in Berlin* (1971; *Germania Death in Berlin*), *Das Verkommene Ufer/Medea-Material/Landschaft mit Argonauten* (1982/83; *Despoiled Shore/Medea Material/Landscape with Argonauts*), *Leben Gundlings Friedrich von Preussen Lessings Schlaf Traum Schrei* (1976; *Gundling's Life Frederick of Prussia Lessing's Sleep Dream Scream*), *Hamletmaschine* (1977; *Hamletmachine*), and *Der Auftrag* (1979; *The Task*).

Müller traveled widely in the East and West. In 1975/76 he visited the United States for the first time. Extensive stays were to follow. His plays began to be performed worldwide. More followed, for instance: *Bildbeschreibung* (1984/85; *Description of a Picture*), *Wolokolamsker Chaussee* (1985; *Volokolamsk Highway*), *Mommsens Block* (1993), and *Germania 3* (1994/95).

After the fall of the Berlin Wall, Müller had already become the most acclaimed German playwright after Brecht. In 1995, he was appointed artistic director of the Berliner Ensemble, where he had once started his theatrical career under Brecht. Müller had become Brecht's undisputed successor.

Heiner Müller died of cancer on December 30, 1995.

In his autobiography, Müller confesses: "For me the most important play is *Hamlet*. Probably because it was the first play by Shakespeare that I tried to read, and because it has more to do with myself and Germany." In *Hamletmachine,* his obsession with the horror of history and Shakespeare's figure of Hamlet form a tableau of the disintegration of Western history. Hamlet becomes the incarnation of the brooding intellectual and participant in the constantly reoccurring power play that inevitably leads to the victimization of the Other—Ophelia. Hamlet's attempt to free himself from the historic burden that is choking him with nausea is doomed to fail. Ophelia, however, strikes out in revolt. She breaks her shackles and takes to the street, only to discover herself surrounded by the debris history has left behind. She truly lives in what Joseph Conrad calls the heart of darkness. Gradually smothered, she defiantly rejects all roles expected from women throughout history. In the end, she proclaims "hate and contempt, rebellion and death." The play of only a few pages has five short scenic fragments and totally dispenses with dialogue. Innumerable references to public names and places (such as Rosa Luxemburg, Stalin, Lenin, Marx, Mao, Noske, Susan Atkins of the Manson family) and to alienated literary quotations (by T. S. Eliot, Shakespeare, Brecht, Schiller,

Dostoevsky, Büchner, Conrad, the Bible, and Müller himself), complicate the text and require decoding. As a parable, *Hamletmachine* includes the self-analysis of the artist-intellectual and his own historic moment. Both history and Hamlet had to be analyzed. Then "you can denounce it, get rid of it," for: "the first shape of hope is fear, the first appearance of the new arouses a feeling of horror." (H.M., "Reflections on Postmodernism," see The German Library volume 83, p. 348).

Heiner Müller always insisted that "the subject matter of art is the unbearableness of existence." *Hamletmachine* is the paramount example of his belief.

M. H.-S.

ROLF HOCHHUTH

The Deputy

To the memory of

Father Maximilian Kolbe
Inmate No. 16670 in Auschwitz

Provost Bernhard Lichtenberg
of St. Hedwig's Cathedral, Berlin

Characters

POPE PIUS XII

THE CARDINAL
FATHER RICCARDO Fontana, S.J.
COUNT FONTANA, his father, Council to the Holy See
The Apostolic Nuntius in Berlin
The Abbot, Father General of a religious order

KURT GERSTEIN, Obersturmführer SS

THE DOCTOR

DR. FRITSCHE, Sturmbannführer
BARON RUTTA, Reichs Armament Cartel
MÜLLER SAALE, of the Krupp works in Essen

LUCCANI SR., a converted Jew
JULIA LUCCANI
JULIA LUCCANI'S CHILDREN (a boy of nine, a girl of five)

HELGA
CARLOTTA
JAKOBSON

A servant in COUNT FONTANA's house; Swiss Guards in the Papal Palace; a Father in the Papal Legation; a scribe; an old monk; a photographer; a Jewish capo; officer of the day in Auschwitz.

Aside from the Pope, the Nuncio, and Gerstein, all characters and names are fictitious.

Act 1: The Mission

Beware of the man whose God is in Heaven.
BERNARD SHAW

SCENE 1

Berlin, a late afternoon in August 1942. The reception room of the Papal Legation on Rauchstrasse. A few pieces of Empire furniture. The only thing tempering the austerity of the room is a large copy of Rubens' Descent from the Cross. *In these surroundings the picture seems bright, even agreeable.*

Two French doors; one, rear left, leads to the Nuncio's study; the other, at right, to waiting rooms and the stairwell.

THE NUNCIO, HIS EXCELLENCY CESARE ORSENIGO, *is sixty-nine years old. Newspaper photos show him as a man of medium height, still extremely vigorous. There are no empty spaces in his lean face; it is completely dominated by a mouth and nose which, like his chin, are abnormally large. His expression is candid and tolerant. The face stamped not so much by intellect as by will and enormous self-discipline. Baron Ernst von Weizsäcker, State Secretary in the Foreign Office until the spring of 1943 and thereafter Hitler's Ambassador to the Holy See, describes the Nuncio as a realistic Milanese who preferred to avoid "elevating the irreconcilable differences between the Curia and the Third Reich into matters of principle" He also attests that when Orsenigo presented his complaints—as he did, for instance, about the treatment of Polish priests in Hitler's concentration camps—he managed to do so "in a calm spirit and with a friendly manner."*

Let us leave that aside. The Nuncio resided in Berlin throughout the Hitler era. By November 8, 1938 at the latest he must have witnessed with his own eyes the acts of terror committed against the Jewish citizens of Germany. It is hard to say how a man with so likable a face could in good conscience, reconcile himself to the continuance of the Concordat between the Curia and the Government of the Third Reich, even when Catholic Jews were deported. It would seem that anyone who holds a responsible post for any length of time under an autocrat—whether it be Hitler or Pius XII—surrenders his own personality. There is no way for him to express his personal feelings; in his official conduct he is reduced to the level of a flunky. Perhaps the use of equivocal diplomatic jargon makes this easier.

In bringing historical persons to life on the stage, we need no longer seek an accurate likeness. Available photographs of Adolf Hitler and Hermann Göring, no matter how carefully we may scrutinize them, even after the event, fail to provide the slightest clue to the acts of which these two of the Nuncio's confabulators were capable. It seems to be established, therefore, that photographs are totally useless for the interpretation of character. The essential thing, then, is that the Nuncio be played by an actor of mature years, and that he wear the standard attire of a titular Archbishop: pectoral, black soutane, purple cap, collar and cape.

RICCARDO FONTANA's solidarity with the victims of persecution, and his voluntary martyrdom for the Church, are freely drawn after the acts and aims of Provost Bernhard Lichtenberg of Berlin Cathedral, who came forth and prayed publicly for the Jews, was sentenced to jail, and asked Hitler's henchmen to let him share the fate of the Jews in the East. His petition was granted. But Lichtenberg—who, by the way, was eager to know what the Pope thought of his decision—was not taken to a ghetto in the East. Instead he was sent to Dachau. He died on the way, in 1943, presumably from natural causes. The Nazis evidently were enough in awe of Lichtenberg's reputation to deem it wise to release his body, and to allow several thousand Berliners to attend his funeral.

The Jewish community of Paris has had the name of SS Obersturmführer (Lieutenant) KURT GERSTEIN inscribed on the memorial for the victims of Fascism. Gerstein, as the English historian Gerald Reitlinger says, undertook perhaps the most extraordinary mission of the Second World War. So uncanny, divided and mysterious a personality seems more like a fictional creation than an historical personage. This is not the place to sketch his strange biography, a resumé of which he handed to the Allies in 1945; all trace of him was lost while he was in a Paris prison. Nor can we discuss the consistently favorable statements concerning him which have been provided by reputable members of the Protestant and Catholic clergy, and by Baron von Otter, Secretary of the Swedish Embassy. Gerstein, as a photograph dating back as far as 1931 shows, seems to have been a marked man from the first, so "modern" a Christian that we can scarcely understand him without considerable background in Kierkegaard. In 1942, when he called at the Papal Legation and was ejected, he was thirty-seven years old.

He wears the field gray uniform of an officer of the Waffen-SS, the SS Armed Forces.

The FATHER *who serves the tea wears a habit.*

The NUNCIO *has a map of Berlin in his hands. He speaks to* RICCARDO.

NUNCIO: You see? Over here—St. Hedwig's Church.
    Ten years ago we had no more than forty-four
    churches in Berlin—omitting, naturally,
    the chapels in the monasteries.
    The Jews had just as many synagogues.
    The number of our churches has increased,
    in spite of everything;
    but not a single synagogue is left.
RICCARDO *(casually)*: Could not Your Excellency intervene?
NUNCIO *(raises his hand in a gesture of abnegation; his calm is imperturbable)*:
    It is not my place, as Nuncio, to speak
    of *that*. When, for example, I try to remonstrate
    about conditions in Poland,
    confining my protests to the mistreatment
    of priests, Herr von Weizsäcker politely
    shows me to the door. Outside of my domain,
    he says. First we must recognize the new frontiers.
    Concerning Jews, he says, they'd fall within my scope
    only if they were baptized.
    But Herr Hitler is careful
    not to deport the baptized Jews.
    Ah, the Father himself
    is bringing us our tea, how nice, thank you.
    Might there be a bit of cake to go with it?

A FATHER *has entered, and arranges the tea table. He speaks a Bavarian dialect.*

FATHER: In a second, Your Excellency.
    I've brought you a kettle of water
    in case you should find it too strong again.

NUNCIO *(folding the map, with smiling pedantry):*
    Thank you, that's very thoughtful . . .
    There, the map's for you.
    I always like to give my aides
    who don't know Berlin a map of the city
    before anything else.
    So that you'll not get lost here.

RICCARDO *(bows, pockets the map; the* FATHER *goes out):*
    Thank you, Your Excellency, very kind of you.

NUNCIO *(at the tea table, in a more personal tone):*
    You weren't a bit nervous about coming to Berlin?
    In Rome you were safe from bombs.
    We have a raid every night.

RICCARDO: For someone of my age, Your Excellency,
    a priest's life is much too safe.
    My cousin was killed fighting in Africa.
    I'm happy to have gotten out of Rome.

NUNCIO *(amused):* How young you are! Twenty-seven
    and Minutante already.
    You will go far, young friend.
    It was considered remarkable that His Holiness
    became a Minutante at twenty-six.

RICCARDO: Your Excellency must consider
    that I've chosen the right parent.

NUNCIO *(cordially):* You are too modest.
    If you were nothing but your father's son,
    the Cardinal would never
    have called you to the Secretariat of State.
    (Confidentially.) Is our Chief still
    so ill disposed to me?

RICCARDO *(embarrassed):*
    But, Your Excellency, no one is ill disp . . .

NUNCIO *(placing a hand on his arm, then rising, holding the teacup):*
    Come now, you too are well aware
    that I have long been persona non grata in Rome . . .

RICCARDO *(hesitantly, evasively):* Possibly at the Vatican
  it seems easier to represent the Holy See
  than here in Berlin. . . .
NUNCIO *(vehemently justifying himself; he paces the room):*
  The Pope should decide what he prefers:
  peace with Hitler at any price, or else
  let me be authorized to take a stand
  the way my brother Nuncio in Slovakia
  did two weeks ago when he spoke up
  against the wholesale killing of Jews from Bratislava
  in the Lublin district.
  He made a strong protest . . .
  My dear friend, what does Rome expect?
  if I were not afraid my post would fall
  into the hands of some nonentity!
RICCARDO: Does that mean Your Excellency favors
  abrogating the Concordat with Hitler?
NUNCIO: Oh no, on the contrary. His late Holiness Pius XI
  might well have done that.
  But since the death of the old Pope
  Herr Hitler has put a stop to certain measures
  some of his more stupid underlings
  wanted to take against us. He himself
  is neutral in his official policy toward the Church,
  impeccable, like Marshal Göring.
  In Poland, though, he *is* trying to blackmail us.
  Herr Goebbels, his Propaganda Minister,
  can be talked to. You might almost call him
  obliging. It's strange they haven't dared
  touch Bishop Galen, even though he publicly
  denounced, right from his pulpit,
  the murder of the mentally ill.
  Hitler actually gave in on that!
RICCARDO *(enthusiastically):*
  Surely the Church can issue such demands,
  Your Excellency! Especially now when bishops
  in half of Europe are drumming up support
  for Hitler's crusade against Moscow. On the train
  I was reading what an army bishop
  at the Eastern Front had said to . . .

NUNCIO *(energetically, vexed):* You see, Father, that is precisely
    what I oppose. We should *not*
    be drumming up support for Hitler
    as long as this wholesale killing
    goes on behind his front lines. . . .
    London speaks
    of seven hundred thousand Jews in Poland alone!
    Of course, we've seen that sort of thing before.
    Crusades begin with killing of the Jews.
    But in such numbers—horrible.
    I hardly think they are exaggerated.
    You know how in Poland they are killing even the priests.
    Our attitude should be one of great reserve.
    For instance . . . just recently, did the bishop
    of Bohemia and Moravia *have* to plead with Herr Hitler
    about that man Heydrich,
    the Police Chief of Berlin and Prague . . .
RICCARDO: The one who was shot, assassinated?
NUNCIO: Yes, right in the street. They took reprisals
    against a whole village, including the women and children.
    Was it *necessary* for the Moravian bishop
    to plead with Hitler hat in hand
    if they might ring the bells for the deceased
    and read a requiem for him?
    (With great indignation.)
    A requiem for Heydrich is in bad taste.
    That's really going too far. . . .
    (The FATHER *brings cakes.)*
    So—we have something to nibble on.
    Thank you, my friend, thank you.

The FATHER *leaves the door open. The fanfare preceding a special
communiqué can be heard: the heroic theme, with trumpets and
drum rolls from Liszt's* Preludes.

FATHER: Here you are, Your Excellency—some nice cake.
    And there's a special bulletin coming on. . . .
NUNCIO: Please, have some, Father Riccardo . . . There!
    Well, let us listen to the news
    (He smiles, and says in explanation to RICCARDO)
    The ritual introduction. The ideas

of the Hitlerites present no problems for us,
but the Nazi rituals are strong competition,
superbly geared to mass psychology.

The FATHER *steps back toward the door, but remains in the room.
The music dies and is replaced by the announcer's voice:*

"Attention! Attention! This is the radio of Greater Germany.
We bring you a special comuniqué from the Führer's headquarters, April 25, 1942: The High Command of the Armed
Forces announces that at noon today German mountain
troops, overcoming bitter Soviet resistance, captured the peak
of the Elbrus at an altitude of eighteen thousand five hundred
feet and hoisted the war flag of the Reich. This puts the Cau-
casus firmly into German hands.

The heroic theme once more, then the melody of the song: From
Finland to the Black Sea.

FATHER *(proudly):*
    More than eighteen thousand, that's higher than the Mont
        Blanc!
    My nephew's with the mountain troops in the East.
    He was in the fighting at Narvik—was wounded, too.
NUNCIO *(with polite disinterest):*
    Ah, your nephew. God protect him.
FATHER: Thank you kindly, Your Excellency. Yes, let's hope so.

Exits, closing the door; the music fades, ceases.

RICCARDO: Does Your Excellency think there are grounds to fear
    Herr Hitler will respect the Church
    only for the duration of the war?
NUNCIO: It did seem so a little while ago, my dear Father,
    for victors always act immorally.
    But ever since Herr Hitler, much against his will,
    was pushed by Japan, and Mr. Roosevelt, too,
    into declaring war on the U.S.A.—
    ever since that folly (or was it dira necessitas?),
    the Church of Christ at any rate
    no longer need to stand in fear of him.
    He will not force England *and* America

to their knees.
Not even if he moves into the Kremlin.

RICCARDO *(incredulously):*
> Once he has beaten Russia, Your Excellency,
> he will be economically invulnerable.
> Who would be left to overthrow him then?
> His tanks have pushed their way into Egypt
> and almost to Stalingrad,
> and in the Atlantic his U-boats . . .

NUNCIO *(interrupts again, his tone kindly, ironic, superior):*
> Gently, young friend, not quite so fast.
> In von Ranke's book on the Popes—

He goes to a bookcase, selects a volume, leafs through it.

> one of the many excellent books which we
> place on the Index—
> I recently came across a statement
> I found immensely reassuring.
> At times, says Ranke, when *any* principle, no matter what,
> seeks to impose its rule upon the Western World,
> a firm resistance counters it infallibly.
> That opposition stems from
> the deepest sources of our life; it is the very
> spirit of old Europe. Philip the Second
> found his master in England. Napoleon
> in England *and* the Czar. May not the same
> happen to Hitler?
> Baron von Weizsäcker tells me in confidence
> that Russia is far from beaten yet.
> And then the U.S.A.! No matter how
> he comes out of it, it will be a Pyrrhic victory.

RICCARDO: You think then, Your Excellency, that Herr Hitler
> will *have to* listen to reason?

NUNCIO: Oh yes! He will even prefer to.
> We saw that at Dunkirk, after all.
> He let the British make their getaway. His policy
> was obviously moderation in victory.
> I grant you, Mr. Churchill gave him no thanks for it . . .
> Please do have some more cake . . .
> With the Spaniards and the French,

the Balkan nations and the Italians,
the Belgians and above all his own Catholics
here in Germany, all of them
willingly or not supporting his crusade
against Moscow—with half of Europe Catholic,
even Hitler cannot risk a schism.
If he should brand us enemies of state,
the Rome-Tokyo-Berlin Axis would fall apart.
It's fortunate that at this very moment
Japan is making every effort
to sign a Concordat with us.
The efforts of the White House to prevent it
only serve to prove
how eagerly both sides are courting us.
On Sunday in St. Hedwig's,
during the bishop's ordination ceremonies,
I saw a lieutenant of the SS. He went to confession,
took Communion—oh no,
where the Church is concerned, Herr Hitler
remains a realist.
He wants the nations helping him in Russia
to go on backing him when he is forced
to negotiate with England and the U.S.A.
Consider how in the United States
day by day the Catholics' power grows—
Herr Hitler has to reckon with that, too.
He will discover what his friends, Franco
and Mussolini, learned long ago:
Fascism is invincible only *with* us,
when it stands with the Church and not against it.
Molotov saw that ten years ago;
in 1934 Molotov admitted
that if the Church in Germany
should strike up an accord with the Hitlerites—
and at the time there were some signs of that;
a promising beginning had been made—
then Communism in Europe would be finished . . .
What's that, what's the commotion?
What's going on out there?

The Nuncio *rises, remains standing and listening a moment, then goes toward the door to the waiting room, murmuring to himself. There is an excited altercation backstage; people begin to shout. The* Father *is heard, his dialect thickening as his voice grows louder. Amid fragmentary phrases, only half intelligible, sounds the insistent, pleading voice of a man who is obviously holding himself in check with difficulty in the effort to remain polite.*

Both *(backstage):* You're in uniform!
> But—you *must* announce me!
> The Legation is extraterritorial—be off with you
> or I'll send for the police.
> Please, give me five minutes with His Excellency.
> The Nuncio has a visitor from Rome.
> He *must* hear me.
> Anything the likes of you may want to say
> is no affair of ours.

Riccardo, *intrigued, has moved back against the wall, while the* Nuncio *opens the door to the waiting room. The SS officer,* Kurt Gerstein, *bursts in, cap in hand. The* Father *tries to block his way and then to push him out again.*

Gerstein and Father *(simultaneously):*
> Your Excellency, isn't this the limit?
> I must speak with Your Excellency, just for
> two minutes—please—I beg you!
> Shall I call the police?
> Pushing his way in like this . . . who ever heard . . . ?

Nuncio: What's going on? Whatever are you thinking of?

Gerstein: Gerstein is my name, Your Excellency—please
> hear me out. I have a message
> for the Vatican that . . .

Nuncio: Sir, I am astounded
> that you invade this building in this manner . . .
> I suppose your headquarters
> are on Prinz Albrecht Strasse . . .

The Father *has hurried across the room to a telephone. He lifts the receiver.* Gerstein *dashes after him, saying:*

Gerstein: Your Excellency, please, no phone calls.
> If headquarters were to hear of this visit . . .

NUNCIO *(gesturing to the* FATHER *to put down the telephone):*
> You call this scene a visit?

FATHER *(quickly):* Go now, just get out of here.

GERSTEIN *(just as quickly):*
> Your Excellency, a message for the Vatican.
> It will not bear a single day's delay,
> not one single hour. I have just come from Poland—
> from Belzec and Treblinka, northeast of Warsaw.
> Your Excellency, daily,
> every single day in those places,
> ten thousand Jews, *more*
> *than ten thousand,*
> are being murdered, put to death with gas . . .

NUNCIO: For God's sake, hold your tongue!
> Tell that to Herr Hitler, not to me.
> Leave this place.
> In the German Government's view
> I am not authorized
> to say a word about these . . .
> these conditions in Poland.

GERSTEIN *(a shout):* Your Excellency!

NUNCIO: Who are you, anyhow! I am not authorized,
> I tell you, to have any dealings
> with members of the German Armed Forces . . .
> Are you Catholic? In any case I request you
> to leave at once . . . Go, go.

His Excellency is determined not to hear confirmation of such monstrous crimes. For he is basically a man of deep humanity, and official acknowledgment of this message would make it difficult for him to continue to deal with Weizsäcker as he has done in the past, "indifferently, without much distinction, in a calm spirit and friendly manner."

FATHER *(has gone to the door, holds it open and says very mildly):*
> Well now, will you be off at last.

GERSTEIN *(loses his temper, shuts the door violently and strides up to the* NUNCIO. *He speaks jerkily, under great stress):*
> Your Excellency, every hour I see trains pull in
> bringing fresh loads from all of Europe to those death
> factories. . . .

No, I am not Catholic. But Pastor Buchholz
who cares for the condemned in Plötzensee
is my friend. Another reference I can give
is Superintendent Otto Dibelius and Church Councilman
Hermann Ehlers. Before he was arrested,
Pastor Niemöller of Dahlem . . .

NUNCIO *(politely but very firmly):* All very well, but I regret
I must now terminate this . . .
I'm very sorry, but you'll have to go.

GERSTEIN: Speak to von Otter
of the Swedish Embassy, Your Excellency.
At this point, only the Vatican can intervene.
You must help, sir!

NUNCIO *(indignant, since he does not know what to do):*
Why do you come to me? You yourself
are wearing the uniform of the murderers.
I tell you, I have no authority to interfere.

GERSTEIN *(shouting):* Authority! Here in Berlin you represent
the—the Deputy of Christ,
and you can close your eyes to the worst horror
that man has ever inflected upon man.
You hold your peace while every hour . . .

NUNCIO: Control yourself . . . keep your voice down . . .
we don't shout here.
I am terminating this conversation now . . .

GERSTEIN *(pleading):* No, please—I beg your pardon.
I know very well, Your Excellency—you can't do anything.
But the Holy Father must take action,
must speak for the world's conscience . . .

The NUNCIO *withdraws; he does not go all the way through the door to his study only because* RICCARDO *resists following him.* RICCARDO *stands listening in fascination to* GERSTEIN.

GERSTEIN: Your Excellency, please, listen to me;
(As if in a trance.) I can't bear it any more—I've seen it—
I see it all the time—it haunts
me right to this room.
Listen . . . the . . . I must
tell you about it . . .

Covering his eyes, GERSTEIN *drops into a chair. He rises to his feet at once, not looking at any of the others in the room; his gaze is turned inward and his eyes have a wild, restlessly flickering expression.* [*Thus Frau Bälz described him in her report to the Institute for Contemporary History. His nocturnal conversation with Frau Bälz took place at about the same time as his ineffectual call on the* NUNCIO. *Baron von Otter, the Secretary of the Swedish Embassy, writes that* GERSTEIN *told his tale to him in the aisle of the train "weeping and in a broken voice."*]

The following passage is spoken in a great variety of tones. At times GERSTEIN'S *sentences taper off into inarticulate murmurs; then again he speaks loudly, distraughtly, or in a series of brief outcries, like someone crying out in his sleep. After the first few sentences the* NUNCIO *takes several steps toward him. The* FATHER *closes the door, but stays in the room, while* RICCARDO *keeps his eyes on the* NUNCIO *so probingly that his look verges on the insulting.*

GERSTEIN *(abruptly):*
    So far they've been running the gas chambers
    on carbon monoxide, common exhaust gas.
    But many times the motors will not start.
    In Belzec recently I had to watch—
    this was on August 20—
    while the victims waited two hours and forty-nine minutes
    until the gas came on.
    Seven hundred and fifty persons
    in each of four chambers—
    each room with a volume of sixty cubic yards—
    three thousand human beings.
    Some pray, some weep, some shriek.
    The majority keep silent.
    The gassing operation takes twenty-five minutes.
    Now they want to speed it up,
    and so they've brought me in for consultation.
    I am an engineer and medical man.
    (Screams.) I will not do it, I will not do it. . . .
    Like marble columns the naked corpses stand.
    You can tell the families, even after death
    convulsed in locked embrace—with hooks

they're pulled apart. Jews have to do that job.
Ukrainians lash them on with whips.

He can no longer concentrate, loses himself in details, his eyes vacant.

There was the manager of Berlin's biggest store . . .
There was a violinist, too, decorated in World War I . . .
Fought at the front for Germany.
And bodies of dead children. A young girl
ahead of the procession, naked like the rest.
Mothers, all stripped, babies at their breasts.
Most of them know the worst—the smell of gas . . .

NUNCIO *(starting to leave):* Enough—I cannot listen any more.
You Germans, why! Why . . .
My dear man, my heart is with the victims.

GERSTEIN: Your Excellency, the Vatican
has made a pact with Hitler!
Yet you can see it in the streets, here in Berlin,
in Oslo, Paris, Kiev—for more than a year
you have seen, *every* priest has seen
how they're rounding up the Jews. The Allied radio
reports that thousands upon thousands
are being exterminated.
When, Your Excellency, when,
will you tear up the Concordat?

RICCARDO *(overwhelmed):*
Your Excellency, all this agrees completely
with the reports my Order has received,
but no one could quite credit them.

NUNCIO *(with genuine concern, deeply moved but helpless):*
My dear Father, please keep out of this . . .
Why doesn't this man go to Herr Hitler!

GERSTEIN *gives a terrible laugh.*

RICCARDO *(pleading):* But he is not an agent provocateur,
Your Excellency . . . Count Ledochowsky has received
the same sort of reports from Poland . . .

NUNCIO *(tried beyond his patience, losing composure):*
Why does he come to *me?* The Curia
is not here to aggravate strife.

God has charged it with the mission
to work for peace . . .
GERSTEIN: Peace with murderers too? Your Excellency!

He points to the painting of the Crucified Christ and exclaims:

Cursed are the peacemakers!
He felt He was authorized, Your Excellency—
but His Deputy does not?
NUNCIO *(deeply moved and paternal):*
Herr Ger—stensteiner, compose yourself!
I share your sorrow for the victims.
GERSTEIN *(screaming):* Every *hour*, Your Excellency, *every* hour
thousands more killed—those are factories
for killing. Factories, won't you understand?
NUNCIO: Please, sir—whatever my own feelings in this matter,
I cannot simply take account of them.
I intervened, in private, as far back as
nineteen thirty-nine. But I am charged
by my position not to involve myself
in any cause of conflict between Rome
and your authorities. I should not even have
this talk with you—please,
you must go. Go now, please.
God bless you, God help you.
I shall pray for the victims.

He beckons to RICCARDO *to follow him, walks to the backstage door and opens it.*

Father, please come—I must insist.
RICCARDO: Your name is Gerstein—I will find you.

GERSTEIN *pays no attention to these words; he sees only that he has accomplished nothing. The* NUNCIO *has returned to* RICCARDO, *puts his hand on his shoulder and propels him almost forcibly through the door to the study. Before the* NUNCIO *can close the door,* GERSTEIN *follows him once more, passionate, beside himself.*

GERSTEIN: Your Excellency, listen, you must hear
the dying words of an old Jewish woman—
as she was driven on by whips into the gas
she called down on the murderers' heads

the blood they're spilling there. That blood guilt,
Excellency, falls upon us all
if we keep silent!

NUNCIO *(turning once more, softly):* Compose yourself. Pray!

Exit. The FATHER *closes the door behind him and speaks mildly:*

FATHER: Have some sense, man, how can you
come at His Excellency like this?
Can he help it? Now please, take yourself off.
There isn't anything one of us can do.

GERSTEIN *(has realized that he has lost. One more pointless
attempt; he reaches into his coat pocket, takes out a batch of
papers, and tries to interest the* FATHER *in them):*
Here is more proof—look at them!
Orders from the camp commandants
of Belzec and Treblinka
for the delivery of hydrocyanide.
They want me to supply the prussic acid—
I'm with the SS Public Health Department—look at these—

*He is alone in the room. He turns in a circle, the papers in his hand.
The* FATHER, *who has gone out and now returns with a tray to
clear away the tea things, says in a voice which mingled threat and
helpfulness:*

FATHER: Don't you realize
they have policemen watching the Legation?
If they should catch you on the premises,
in uniform . . . Now run along, please.
Mary and Joseph, what a tale!
It's true they're Jews, but still. . . .

> GERSTEIN *leaves before the sentence is finished.*

CURTAIN

> Because they have feet, you do not see
> they are automatons.
> OTTO FLAKE

> The glory of Creation, man, the swine.
> GOTTFRIED BENN

scene 2

The following morning. GERSTEIN's *apartment in Berlin W35.*
GERSTEIN, *in an old SS uniform, stands on a stepladder, a trowel in
hand, mending a long crack in the wall. He scoops the plaster from
a used marmalade tub. He is smoking as he works. Newspapers are
spread out at the foot of the ladder.*

*The room bears many marks of the severe air raid the night be-
fore. A fallen lamp is still lying on the floor. A picture, badly torn,
is leaning with its face to the wall. Cardboard has been tacked over
the window at the back of the stage, which looks out on the street,
but is open at the moment, revealing a ruin across the street, evidently left by a raid some time ago. The room's other window, at
the right of the door, is undamaged, as are its curtains. A large
carpet lies rolled up diagonally across the room. The simple furnishings of a man's room have been pushed together in one place
so that the splinters of glass, dirt, bits of plaster and tatters of wall-
paper can be swept up. The sweeping is done by a man of about
thirty, in civilian dress, who looks older than he is. He is a Jew
named* JACOBSON *whom* GERSTEIN *is hiding. He speaks cautiously,
timidly; his movements are somewhat awkward. It is evident from
his manner that he misses freedom; he also looks as if he has not
been in the fresh air for a long time. Both men work in silence.*
JACOBSON, *too, smokes a cigarette. The noise of a big city can be
heard, although not very intrusively; after a while, from far away,
come the fanfares of an approaching parade of Hitler Youth.*

GERSTEIN: Can we close the window now?
JACOBSON: The air is still so dusty; a minute more.

*He goes into the next room and brings back two pails filled with
trash, and a dust pan.*

> There, now, the place is fairly clean again.
> Herr Gerstein, why don't you let *me*
> plaster the wall, there's nothing else to keep me busy.
> With the window covered over
> nobody can see me on the ladder.

GERSTEIN: All right—if you would like to, by all means.
> I'll take the pails down to the yard.

*He steps down from the ladder and closes the window, hands the
trowel to* JACOBSON, *who climbs the ladder and sets to work.*

I must say, Jacobson, I felt concern for you last night,
a raid as bad as that, and you can't
even go down to the cellar.

JACOBSON *(smiling):* Lucky my parents
can still go to the cellar in their house.
Would you drive by a little later
and see whether their house came through the raid?

GERSTEIN *(his back to* JACOBSON): Gladly, Herr Jacobson.

JACOBSON: Thanks. It wasn't any fun, I must admit,
when window glass began to fly last night.
But I'd sooner catch it here than—
than in Auschwitz.
Forgive me, please, I know that's very selfish.
But how much longer can I stay with you?

GERSTEIN *hands him another cigarette. They cannot go on talking
because of the blare of the band. But now, as the column of march-
ers passes directly by the house, it begins singing. In spite of the
closed windows, the song penetrates into the room.*

> *Es zittern die morschen Knochen*
> *der Welt vor dem grossen Krieg.*
> *Wir haben die Ketten zerbrochen,*
> *fü uns war's ein grosser Sieg.*
> *Wir werden weiter marschieren,*
> *wenn alles in Scherben fällt,*
> *denn heute gehört uns Deutschland*
> *und morgen die ganze Welt.*

GERSTEIN *(glancing briefly into the street, with intense disgust):*
They have to have their music all the time. Even in Auschwitz
they've organized a band of Jewish women
who must play Viennese waltzes
while victims for the gas are picked.

> *Both fall silent. After a while* GERSTEIN *says reassuringly:*

I'll have a passport for you
before the house is bombed to smithereens.
They won't come looking for you here, unless
they get suspicious about me, my own
past record of imprisonment

in a concentration camp.
(Smiling.) Too bad you're just a shade too dark
to pass for a typical Swede.
I haven't yet been able to make contact
with any Spaniards or Italians.

JACOBSON *(as he plasters the wall):* Next time you see the Swede,
the one here at the Embassy,
you'd better have a passport issued
for yourself. Go off to Sweden.
Only your wife would know you've gotten out.
Officially, you'll just go down as missing.

GERSTEIN *(pauses in his sweeping):*
Go into exile just like that? My God,
I see men dying in the chambers every hour.
As long as there is still the slightest hope
that I can save a single one of you
I have to face the chance that later on
I may seem the spit and image of the murderers.

JACOBSON: Your visit to the Nuncio was the last
risk you should take. It's time for you to go
to England by way of Sweden. Here, by now,
it's very likely they found out about you.

GERSTEIN *(with a sphinxlike smile):*
Found out about me? Not a chance.
No one has found out about me yet.
It may be that they have their eye on me—
that worries me, sometimes, especially
for my family's sake and yours.

JACOBSON: You'd better telephone your wife
before the daily communiqué reports
that Berlin's had another raid.
No need to let her know about the wrecked apartment.
She's got enough to worry her.

GERSTEIN: I'll have the call to Tübingen placed
at the office; they'll put it through without delay.
I hope I'll have a chance to drive back home
over the weekend . . . Have you enough to eat?

JACOBSON: Yes, quite enough, thank you.

GERSTEIN: You really must tell me if you're hungry.
You're not depriving me at all, you know.
I get enough to eat at headquarters.

JACOBSON: Thank you again, Herr Gerstein.
　　But I would appreciate a few more books . . .
　　Let me give you some money . . .

He takes out his wallet.

And maybe you could try once more
to find a Russian grammar for me . . .
GERSTEIN: Oh yes. Hold on to your money
　　until I know what the books will cost.
　　As for the grammar, I'm sure I can locate one secondhand.
　　Well—let's go on.

JACOBSON *picks up the trowel,* GERSTEIN *the pail, intending to carry it down. Just as* GERSTEIN *is about to leave the room, the doorbell rings. Both show their nervousness. Without a word,* JACOBSON *jumps down from the ladder and flees into the adjoining room.* GERSTEIN *closes the door behind him. The bell rings again.* GERSTEIN *goes out. He can be heard opening the hall door and saying:*

Heil Hitler—oh, it's *you,* Doctor.
DOCTOR: How are you, Gerstein. Have you heard? It's frightful. . . .
GERSTEIN: What's happened?

During this exchange he has admitted the DOCTOR *and closed the door behind him. Rapid footsteps in the hall. The* DOCTOR, *in a smart long black cape with silver clasps and chain, has preceded* GERSTEIN *into the room and now says breathlessly:*

DOCTOR: I suppose the bombs knocked out your radio.
　　Then you don't know . . .
GERSTEIN: Speak up, Doctor, I have no idea.
DOCTOR: Assassination of Hitler?—Göring and Himmler
　　were also on board—a plane crash.
GERSTEIN: *(stunned by this turn of affairs, shaken):*
　　Good God—all three of them?
　　That can't be true, Doctor!
　　No one was saved?
DOCTOR *(diabolically grinning):* Saved? Why yes! Guess who.
GERSTEIN: Who . . . ?
DOCTOR: GERMANY!

His infernal laughter clatters like sheets of metal roofing being loaded on a truck. GERSTEIN *has sat down, partly because he is frightened at this sudden descent by the* DOCTOR, *partly because he is unnerved by his disappointment*

GERSTEIN *(slowly):* Not very funny, Doctor, I fail to see the joke.

DOCTOR: Maybe you think it funny your apartment
  has undergone such stylish renovations?
  My girl friend's house is wiped out down to the cellar.

GERSTEIN *(carrying a second chair over from the table):*
  Sit down, Doctor. Nice of you to drop by.

DOCTOR *(both arms still hidden under the cape):*
  No, thanks, I'm rushed. I won't sit down.
  I tried to call you but your telephone,
  it seems, has also been knocked out.
  I'm driving down to Tübingen tomorrow morning,
  so I can offer you a ride to see your family.
  Also we'll have a chance for a good talk.
  You're the only one worth talking to.

GERSTEIN *(smiling to conceal his fear):*
  I'm complimented—but how do you mean,
  the only one?

DOCTOR: Just that. The rest of our colleagues are,
  without exception cold-blooded, heavy-footed
  German blockheads. What brains
  they have is all used on technology . . .
  I plan to leave at seven—does that suit you?

GERSTEIN: Fine. I'll be waiting by the front door,
  if it's still standing, the front door, I mean.
  What's taking you to Tübingen? Don't tell me
  you're going to be a professor after all?

DOCTOR *(has been seated, but is again on his feet):*
  Not so fast. I still have to get my degree.

GERSTEIN: Will you be allowed
  to use the experiments you've done in Auschwitz?
  I ask because of the matter of secrecy.

DOCTOR *(lost in thought; he has been looking at the ripped
  painting):* Oh, that—no, I don't plan to go to Tübingen
  as a *medical* man. No, no, to teach philosophy.
  Medicine is only my profession, not my chief interest.

Aside from that: the human experiments on prisoners
aren't so secret as all that. We did some right here in Berlin
only last May—everybody who counted
was present, including the Army and Air Force.
Even Professor Sauerbruch put in his two cents.
Incidentally, instead of flowers, might I
leave this with you for a while?

*He abruptly draws his left hand from under his cape. He is holding
a glass jar shaped like a melon mold, which he has been clasping
under his arm. He shows its contents, a mass of grayish-white or-
ganic matter, the brains of two Jewish children, to the horrified*
GERSTEIN, *who does not conceal his repugnance. Casually:*

Brain tissue from a pair of Jewish twins,
two kids from Calais, preserved in formaldehyde.
Rather interesting comparative sections.
I brought the specimen with me for a girl
who's taking her first course in histology.
But her house has been bombed out and I've no idea
where my little student has moved to.
I gave her a skull a while back.
I suppose that's buried in the rubble now.

GERSTEIN: Nice little gift . . . Twins' brains . . .

DOCTOR: As soon as I find out if she is still alive
she can come here to pick it up, all right?

GERSTEIN *(hesitantly takes the glass jar, again hesitates as he is
about to set it down on the table and finally deposits it on a
chair):* Easier had in Auschwitz than flowers, eh?

DOCTOR *(seemingly only concerned with teasing* GERSTEIN*):*
For you, as Christ's disciple, this must be upsetting.

GERSTEIN *(anguished):* I know what you are doing . . . horrible.

DOCTOR: Tell me this, it interests me.
How can these two things be reconciled
in our day and age:
To have a good mind—and still remain a Christian?

GERSTEIN *(he expresses himself slowly, with deep awareness of the
need for caution):*
You may recall how Bismarck answered that,
who also, in his youth, was wild and Byronesque
and later had to make the same detour

common to so many intellectuals:
the way to God through nothingness.
He said—and for my part I know no better answer;
I think it is the ultimate wisdom for us—
he said: I have, *with full awareness,* stopped
at a specific stage of my development.
DOCTOR: And you suppose that helped him
plot three wars without compunction?
Come, now—
he knew he was pretending to himself.
All those old fellows knew quite well
their systems had a factor of illusion, even Hegel.
And so do you—today—you know it too:
the man who says what he thinks is finished
and the man who thinks what he says is an idiot.
GERSTEIN *(laughing):* Then so am I. I thought
what I just said to you, and always say what I think.
DOCTOR *(close to him, diabolically):*
Sometimes, Gerstein, sometimes . . . you're a sly dog!
You don't fool me.
Whom are you swindling anyway—
the church and yourself,
or us—the SS?
GERSTEIN *(senses that he won't be able to stand up to this
interrogation; therefore he makes a great show of putting all
his cards on the table and revealing himself as an unworldly
idealist):* What do you mean, swindling! I do say what I think.
Forget about the Christian, Doctor—of course
I'm a Christian—and with Himmler's blessing, if you want to
know.
But—is it necessary for a man to be a Christian
to—to have his doubts? *(Deliberately wandering.)*
You know, day before yesterday the news came
that my cousin had been slaughtered by partisans.
When we first marched into Russia
there weren't any partisans.
A man who's truly loyal to the Führer . . .
DOCTOR *(attempting to trip him up):*
As you are—as loyal as you are, Gerstein!
GERSTEIN *(hardly daunted):*
What's that? . . . Yes, but who am I to tell him:

race policy excludes a policy of conquest.
That much I learned in high school.
It's either one way or the other; you never could have both.
Alexander the Great married his Macedonians off
to daughters of the conquered peoples.
But we exterminate the conquered.
Do *you* believe this bodes well for the future?

DOCTOR *(laughing, his hand already on the door knob):*
Believe! Who still believes in belief?
Or in the future for that matter!
Why look at me that way? I know,
to you I am the principle of evil in the flesh.

GERSTEIN *(laughing, tries to sidestep the trap):*
The principle of evil! Whose phrase is that?

DOCTOR *(amused, quotes):* Otto Weininger's.
"The principle of evil is despair
at giving life some meaning."

GERSTEIN *(laughing):* I shall have to report that to Eichmann.
You read Viennese Jews.

DOCTOR *(not without vanity):*
Oh well, I *roast* them too.
On Tuesday I piped the sister of Sigmund Freud
up the chimney.

He gives his characteristic laugh. Already outside, he calls back:

Seven in the morning, then. Looking forward to our trip . . .

GERSTEIN *(outside):*
It will be nice to have a chance
to spend some time together. See you, Doctor.

Slowly returns to the room. Leans for a moment, exhaling heavily, against the door, then starts to go in to JACOBSON *in the other room, sees the glass jar, picks it up, does not know what to do with it, and repeats:*

Instead of flowers. . . .

The doorbell rings again. GERSTEIN *starts violently; for the moment unable to move he says:*

What does he want *now.*

He makes a motion to open the door, cannot complete it, and only forces himself to it when the bell rings for the third time. He is heard saying outside:

Heil Hitler—what can I do for you?
RICCARDO: Good morning, Herr Gerstein . . .

GERSTEIN *has evidently admitted him. The closing of the door is heard, then footsteps in the hall.* RICCARDO *precedes* GERSTEIN *into the room and says with some embarrassment, since* GERSTEIN *is extremely reserved in manner toward him:*

Oh, the raid certainly hit you hard.
GERSTEIN *(coldly):*
What brings you here? Who are you?
RICCARDO *(even more constrained):*
We met yesterday at the Papal Legation,
Herr Gerstein.
GERSTEIN *(interrupts him with sharp reproof):*
Where? Where did you say!
I don't know you, I've never seen you.
What do you want?
RICCARDO *(with animation):*
I told you yesterday, at the Nuncio's,
that I would look you up.
I wished I could have gone right out with you.
My name is Father Fontana, I am attached
to the Secretariat of State of the Holy See.
GERSTEIN *(still cautious, without looking straight at* RICCARDO*):*
What do you have to say to me?
RICCARDO: That the Vatican will help you.
You and Hitler's victims.
Believe me, I was ashamed
to watch the conduct of the Nuncio.
But I suppose his situation forced him
to speak in such a neutral tone.
GERSTEIN *(impersonally):*
How can I possibly go on believing that
the Vatican will summon up concern
for the suffering of the Jews.

A good two months have passed
since the reports from London, and the Pope
has not yet intervened. *(Abruptly.)*
Whom did you just meet on the stairs?
Did you see an army officer in a cape?

RICCARDO: Oh yes, I noticed him. But in front of the house.
He was getting into his car.

GERSTEIN *(agitated):*
Good. I'm glad he did not see you on the stairs.
Do you know *who* it was you met?

RICCARDO: I had the feeling he looked back at me.

GERSTEIN *(forcing himself to remain calm):*
Oh well, this is a large apartment house.
You might have come to any one of twenty families.
Let's come right to the point, Father Fontana.
Undoubtedly the Polish government in exile
already notified the Pope himself as well.
The Father General of the Jesuits in Rome
has now for many years received exhaustive and precise
reports from Polish agents—as I said, *for many years.*

RICCARDO *(embarrassed):*
Before the day is out a courier will be taking
a letter to my father. My father
is a layman at the Holy See, most highly placed.
I give my *guarantee,* Herr Gerstein,
His Holiness will make a protest.
I have the honor to know the Pope well,
personally.

GERSTEIN *(close to cynicism):* Be careful with your guarantees!
They may come back to haunt you.
Why didn't he do something for old Lichtenberg,
Cathedral Provost of St. Hedwig's?
The scum threw him in jail merely because
he included the Jews in his prayers.
Your priests pray for the Führer too, you know—
how can the Pope look idly on
when priests are thrown in jail because they pray for Jews?
Since 1938 he's done no more
than that—merely looked on.
Lichtenberg, whose sentence is completed,

petitioned the Gestapo for permission
to let him share the fate the Jews
of Eastern Europe must endure—are you aware of that?
RICCARDO: I've heard of Lichtenberg,
    Herr Gerstein. I ask you, please, to understand
    that all these painful problems are still new to me.
    Believe me, though,
    the Pope will help. The commandment
    "Love Thy neighbor" . . .
GERSTEIN *(now cordial; he grasps* RICCARDO's *shoulder)*:
    I've come to be so terribly despairing
    of hope, as far as all the churches are concerned.
    As for myself, I am a member of the Confessing Church;
    I am a friend of Pastor Niemöller
    who's been in concentration camp
    for nearly five years by now . . . He used to call me
    an inveterate saboteur,
    and I suppose he understands
    the reasons why I sneaked my way into the SS . . .
    You cannot fight the Nazis
    with pamphlets, as I used to do.
RICCARDO: You *voluntarily* put on this uniform?
GERSTEIN: Yes—I had to—but, please, do have a seat,
    if you can find one in this mess . . .
    Here.

*He brings two chairs from the cluster around the table, dusts them
off; they sit down. But after a moment* GERSTEIN *gets up again,
restless as a wolf in a cage.*

    Yes, last year they finally found out
    that I'd been locked up twice before
    because of Christian leaflets I distributed.
    I drew a prison sentence first, and then the camp.
    Of course, I had not told them when I entered
    the SS. They made a lot of trouble,
    but then, on orders from the highest quarters
    nothing was done to me. I was forgiven.
    You see, in 1940 I suppressed
    a typhus epidemic in the barracks and prison camps—
    engineering and medicine are my specialities.

That saved my life. They think I'm mad.
In the eyes of those gangsters I am a cross
between technical genius and unwordly idealist.
Unwordly because I'm Christian!
They laugh at that and let me go
to church without much fuss.
They also know that many of my friends
are highly placed among the Protestants.
All the same! *(Suddenly extremely uneasy, jerkily.)*

RICCARDO: Father Fontana.

GERSTEIN: Fontana—why have you come to see me, Father?
We must prepare an explanation
if one of my associates—these splendid men,
each one a murderer with academic honors—
should happen by just now.
(He considers, then grasps RICCARDO's *arm.)*
Listen—how come you speak such perfect German?

RICCARDO: As a child I lived in Königsberg a while.
My mother, dead now, was a German and a Protestant.

GERSTEIN *(coldly, almost rude, but reassured):*
I have it: we'll say
you're an SS spy,
Foreign Intelligence Department 2, Italy.

RICCARDO *(swallows, offended; then speaks with cool aloofness):*
Well—that seems far-fetched, to say the least.
I am a Jesuit priest—do you believe
they would credit such a story?

GERSTEIN *(impassively, perhaps glad to have an occasion for saying
this for once):*
More plausible than any other story, Father.
You would not be the first priest, after all,
to serve these hangmen as a spy.
There's a spy right in the Vatican itself.
The right-hand man of Heydrich told me once
he was recruited into the Gestapo
by a Jesuit—yes, a Jesuit priest,
when he was at the university in Bonn.
Himmler is a great admirer of your organization;
he fashioned the Order of the SS
according to the rules of St. Loyola.

Pedantically, as he does everything,
he read his way through a whole Jesuit library.
RICCARDO *(offended)*: And is there no way of finding out just who
the SS agent is in the Vatican?
GERSTEIN: Impossible, since I don't belong to the Gestapo.
In any case, they use no names, just numbers.
(Abruptly, once more very uneasy.)
No, there wouldn't be any point to it
if *he* comes back, the man you just ran into.
RICCARDO: The officer in the black cape?
GERSTEIN: Yes—I won't even try a bluff.
It wouldn't work with him.
RICCARDO: Who was that man?
GERSTEIN *(frazzled with nervousness)*:
Man? Not a man at all, not human.
You've just met the Auschwitz angel of death.
He comes here just to sound me out
and hopes to hand me over to the hangman.
But let's not talk of that. Please, I must ask you,
if the doorbell rings,
hide quickly in the other room.
And don't say anything. There's someone else in there.
(Only outwardly composed.)
Now we have taken care of that . . . Why
do you look at me that way? You're horrified
at all the tricks that I have up my sleeve?
But if a man plays poker with assassins
he has to wear a poker face like theirs.
RICCARDO: But why, Herr Gerstein,
do you choose to play with them at all?
GERSTEIN: You cannot drive unless you're at the wheel.
Dictatorships can be demolished only from within.
But let us come straight to the point: my visit
to the Nuncio and your bishop's secretary
was high treason . . . *(Smiling.)*
You're shocked.
RICCARDO *(uncomprehendingly, with reserve)*:
I don't presume to judge you.
No doubt you underwent some terrible ordeal
before embarking on this treasonable course.
You swore an oath to Hitler, did you not?

GERSTEIN: I must disillusion you, Father.
   There was no terrible ordeal,
   no pangs of conscience, none at all.
   Hitler himself has written: the rights of men
   invalidate the rights of states. *Therefore:*
   oath or not, a man who sets up factories
   which serve no other purpose but
   to kill his fellowman with gas—
   this man must be betrayed,
   must be destroyed, no matter what the cost!
   His murderer would only be his judge.
RICCARDO: But if we overlook what Hitler
   is doing to the Jews and to the Russian prisoners . . .
GERSTEIN *(outraged)*: Overlook it! How could you as a priest . . .
RICCARDO: I beg your pardon—I did not mean it that way.
   But, Herr Gerstein, what troubles me
   as much as does the awful fate of all these victims
   is this: How can it be that this is done
   by the *one* man who, without doubt,
   is now the last of Europe's men, with Europe at his side,
   to follow in Napoleon's path?
   Who can deny this man who fought at Kiev
   the greatest battle in world history—
   six hundred thousand prisoners of war—
   who overran France in six weeks—
   who can deny him greatness?
GERSTEIN: Father, you speak like the historians of the future.
   Perhaps they also will dispose
   of Hitler's victims in two sentences.
   I cannot tell you *how* that horrifies me,
   how it disgusts me . . .
RICCARDO: Of course, my father looks on Hitler's victories
   also with grave misgivings;
   but recently we entertained at home
   the Spanish Foreign Minister
   (who had just come from Hitler.)
   All evening long he told us of
   his meeting in the German Chancellery.
   Our friend is using every trick he knows
   to keep his country out of conflict—he's a patriot.

In short, he has no love for Hitler.
But *how* he talked about him!
I was impressed. A man, he said, who with
the invincibility of the chosen
follows his destiny, a Messiah—
and if he were to fail, he said, he
would pull all of Europe down with him.
He's come a long way, a legend in his lifetime . . .

GERSTEIN *(can no longer listen):*
For God's sake, Father, do not talk that way!
Believe me, no legend will attach to that man's name.
(Very uncertainly.) Be on your guard against attributing
the qualities of diabolic genius to
a man who's nothing but a master criminal,
only because—because his
foolish and irresolute contemporaries,
cabinet ministers, parliamentarians, generals, priests,
surrendered all of Europe for a time
to such a scoundrel.
(Gradually becoming more firm and forceful.)
Let's not get off on this. Remember,
every hour costs a thousand—please,
just think of what this means—
every hour costs a thousand victims,
whole families pushed into the ovens,
after a ghastly death.
Act. If you cannot sway the Nuncio,
go to Rome.

RICCARDO: Of course . . . Only, please understand:
How shall I identify my source?
Who my informant is?

GERSTEIN: I understand: in the eyes of Rome a traitor is too
questionable to . . .

RICCARDO: I beg your pardon—no, I meant . . .

GERSTEIN: I don't mind—I'm altogether insensitive
on that score, God knows!
The traitors, they alone, today
are saving Germany's honor.
For Hitler is not Germany,
he's Germany's destroyer—the verdict

of history will acquit *us*.
I will not survive the work that I must do.
A Christian in these days *cannot*
survive if he is truly Christian.
I don't mean Sunday Christians—
beware the steady churchgoers—
I am thinking of the Christians Kierkegaard
had in mind: the spies of God. I am
a spy in the SS.
And spies are executed—
I am aware of that.

RICCARDO: No, you must think of your safety.
I shall not speak of you by name.

GERSTEIN: No need to shield me. But aside from that,
it would be better anyhow for you
to quote reports from London and from Poland.
No need for you to tell Rome anything that's *new*.
Only arouse a sense of outrage.
Those who keep silent are accessories to murder,
and they imperil their immortal souls.

RICCARDO: You can rely on me.
I'll go now, to endanger you no further.

GERSTEIN: No, please stay.
I have a question for you . . .

RICCARDO *(with animation):* So do I, Herr Gerstein, so do I.
One question that leaves me no peace.

GERSTEIN: Yes?

RICCARDO: Why the German people,
the nation of Goethe, Mozart, Menzel—
how the Germans could become so barbarous.

GERSTEIN: We Germans are no worse
than other Europeans. First of all
the great majority have no specific knowledge
about the killings, though, of course,
a lot of soldiers in the East have watched
the massacres, and the whole nation looks on
while Jews are shipped out of the cities
like cattle. But anyone willing to help—what can he do?
Are we to castigate a man
who does not want to die for others?

Not long ago the Jews employed in Berlin factories
were to be sent to Auschwitz. The police
did not descent at once, but first informed
the factories. And the result was that
four thousand Jews managed to disappear.
They were hidden by Berliners, fed by them—
four thousand—and every Berliner
involved is risking his own life!
The lives of his whole family as well.
You see, not every German has forgotten
the debt he owes to Germany's name.
And there are scoundrels everywhere. In Holland
the Dutch police are working hard
to round up every Jew; in France they don't cooperate
with so much zeal, but still they do their part.
In Hungary too, but worst of all in the Ukraine . . .
The Ukrainians shoot their Jews themselves.
Some time ago, when seventeen thousand Jews
were shot in Maidanek, a lot of Poles
got drunk to celebrate this festive day. Only
on rare occasions can a Jew in Poland find a place to hide
outside the towns. His kindly neighbors
turn him over to the German murderers
for a small bounty. *We* have no right to speak,
Father. The Germans
bear the greatest guilt. Their leader
has conceived the program. As for the *people*—
the other peoples hardly are much better.

RICCARDO: What you tell me is shattering,
    Herr Gerstein—and nevertheless,
    as an Italian and as a priest
    I have to disagree. At home in Rome
    (with pride, slightly declamatory)
    such things would be impossible. From the Holy Father
    down to the chestnut peddler in the piazza,
    the entire nation would rise up
    against such cruelties, if Jewish fellow citizens
    were arrested. Or at any rate, arrested
    by policemen of a foreign government.

GERSTEIN: It's touching, Father, it is enviable,
    to be so sure of one's own countrymen.

I believe you! *(Now cynically.)* All the more bitter, then,
if in its attitude the Church should be
equivocal. Not long ago Dr. Edith Stein,
Europe's most celebrated nun, I believe,
was gassed in Auschwitz. A convert
for many, many years, a famous
Catholic writer. I ask you:
How could the Gestapo have discovered
that this one nun had Jewish blood?
They came and got her, right out of her Dutch convent.
I simply cannot understand why in a convent
of her own order a nun can't be concealed.
Poor woman!
I suppose she could not understand it herself.

RICCARDO: The raid must have come too suddenly.

GERSTEIN *(sarcastically):*
It's clear, then, how much protection
the Church will offer the converted Jew.
A dozen members of various orders
were actually *handed over* from Dutch religious houses.

RICCARDO: But only under duress.
The bishops protested, Dutch labor groups protested,
But that just made the situation worse.

GERSTEIN *(angered, violently):*
Worse? There was no consistent policy.
Rome left the bishops in the lurch!
It's not the Dutch I blame.
But how can Rome be silent
when monks and nuns are carted off?
With the result that no one even knew
of these outrages.

Silence.

There is another question preying on my mind,
it's one I'd like to place before a priest.
The facts are these: by the end
of the coming month I am ordered to store
more than two tons of poison gas—
Cyclon B, the very gas with which the Jews
are being killed—in a warehouse in Berlin.

I don't know what they mean to do with it;
I rather feel they don't know yet themselves.
It's just to have the poison gas available.
Maybe they mean to kill some foreign workers
or prisoners, as the occasion offers.

Pause. RICCARDO *is speechless.*

This, Father, is the question I must face:
should I instruct the firms to send the bills
to this address, and in my name?
RICCARDO: Of course not. What would be the point of that?
GERSTEIN: Because only that way am I in a position
    to keep my eye on the poison after delivery.
    Then, some time in the near future, I might—
    might get rid of it, by using it for
    disinfection, say, in various places.
    I can also say that part of it
    has decomposed.
    I have already worked things so that
    this poison gas will *not* be stored here in Berlin—
    I gave the air raids as a reason.
RICCARDO: Bills for such materials in your name!
    Is there no other way?
GERSTEIN: Of course, I could easily get out to Sweden.
    I have some business in Helsinki soon.
    Only—who would get my job,
    and what could a fanatic do with it?
RICCARDO: It's difficult, yes, Herr Gerstein.
    What does your conscience say?
GERSTEIN: Conscience? Who could trust that!
    Conscience or God:
    men never have wreaked such havoc
    as when invoking God—or an idea.
    Conscience is a treacherous guide. I am convinced
    that Hitler acts according to his conscience.
    No, I need an answer from outside myself.
    We Protestants depend too much
    upon ourselves. One cannot always bear it.
    Don't we, indeed, have every ground to doubt . . . ?

But answer me with the objectivity
only a priest can have: what must I do?
RICCARDO *(after a pause):*
To lend your name to something monstrous . . .
GERSTEIN *(alarmed and therefore indignant):*
My name! What is a name?
Is it my *name* that matters? Only the lukewarm,
who are scarcely better than the murderers,
only they find it easy to survive
in times like these with a good name and
a reputation as immaculate as—
forgive me, Father—
the Pope's white vestments.
RICCARDO *(trying to conceal the fact that he is offended):*
You asked me my opinion, Herr Gerstein.
You have another choice: to flee to England.
(He gathers animation.)
Broadcast from London. You, Sturmführer Gerstein
of the SS Public Health Department, speaking
ex officio and offering as your affidavit,
figures, dates, bills for poison,
reporting all the details
of what is happening here.
(Enthusiastically, naively.)
Make a full confession,
what you have done, what you have managed to prevent . . .
and what you could not prevent.
GERSTEIN *(passionately):*
Good Lord, are you aware of what you are asking.
I'm willing to do anything—but this I cannot do.
One speech by me on Radio London
and my entire family in Germany would be wiped out.
RICCARDO: Oh, I'm sorry, I didn't realize!
GERSTEIN *(more calmly):* They would not only kill my wife,
my children—they would also
torture my brothers to death in a camp.
RICCARDO: Forgive me . . .
GERSTEIN *(his tone colder):* Nor is there any need for it,
no need at all!
Reports on Radio London long ago told all

about what's going on in Poland. People already know!
They must at least suspect, if they have sense.
And Thomas Mann as well has recently repeated all the
    figures.
Did he not also broadcast news
about the gassing of the Jews from Paris and from Holland?
All I could do is tell it all again, along with details
no one would believe.
And who am I? Nobody heard of *me*.
I'd only be a questionable renegade, and nothing more.
Why is there not a single word
heard from the only man in Europe
still free today from any taint of propaganda:
the Pope.
(Laughing hysterically.) Oh God—my God! Here I contend
with Him as I did in my student days. Did He,
I wonder, not become a Christian
only to ease His conscience with the thought that—
just like His Deputy today—
Jews do not fall within His competence.

RICCARDO *(kindly, but firm)*:
    No more, Herr Gerstein—you don't want
    to give up God as well, not now.

GERSTEIN: He must forgive me for it, since He
    taught me that object lesson in Poland and . . .
    since the Nuncio in Berlin
    has thrown me out.

RICCARDO *(solemnly, very sure of himself)*:
    The Vatican will act—God knows,
    it will be done, I promise you.

GERSTEIN *(unmoved)*: How can I still believe you now?

RICCARDO *(indignant)*:
    Herr Gerstein, please—what did I do to merit that?

GERSTEIN: I beg your pardon—I thought of you
    only as representing your superiors.
    It's not your personal sincerity I doubt.
    My candor should assure you that . . .
    (Without transition.)
    Would you, right now, put in my hands
    your cassock and your passport?

RICCARDO *(shocked):*
> What do you want with them—my passport,
> my cassock?

GERSTEIN *(mysteriously):* A proof of your good will.

RICCARDO *(with mounting distaste, indignantly):*
> Proof—no, Herr Gerstein.
> I vowed when I was consecrated
> never again to lay aside the cassock.
> What are you asking of me?

GERSTEIN: It's not that I mistrust you—the truth,
> then. Your passport and your clothing
> can help a Jew to cross the Brenner Pass.
> You, as a diplomat, should have no trouble
> getting a new passport from Rome.

RICCARDO *(reluctantly, hesitantly):*
> Oh, I see. Need it be right away?

GERSTEIN *(has opened the door to the adjoining room):*
> Herr Jacobson?

JACOBSON: Yes, Herr Gerstein?

He appears quickly, instinctively starts back, composes himself, and enters the room.

> Good day.

RICCARDO: Good day.

GERSTEIN *(adroitly, rapidly):*
> Father Fontana—Herr Jacobson.
> Gentlemen, let's not deceive ourselves.
> Black hair and similarity of age
> are poor prerequisites for an exchange of passports.
> But, on the other hand, Herr Jacobson—I hardly think
> I'll have another chance to offer you
> a cassock and a diplomatic passport from
> the Holy See. Are you prepared
> to try to cross the Brenner Pass with them?

JACOBSON *(no longer as quick to apprehend as he has been in the past):* What's that—do I hear right—is there a chance . . .
> *(Now addresses* RICCARDO *cordially.)*
> You are offering me escape?

RICCARDO *(struggling not to show his reluctance):*
> Oh yes, of course—indeed. When would you want . . .

GERSTEIN *(quickly):* I propose tonight—if there's
a sleeping car available, Herr Jacobson.
I'll buy a ticket when I drive the Father
back to the vicinity of the Papal Legation.
Without a passport and in Herr Jacobson's attire
it will be better for you not to walk
through town. *(Smiling.)* I wonder, Jacobson, if you could
do without your glasses altogether.
Or maybe only when the border check comes up?
I hope the collar fits.
Can we change right away—Herr Jacobson,
good Lord, man, what's the matter?
You're finally through with living like a prisoner!

JACOBSON *has dropped into a chair; he is done in. He takes out a
handkerchief, smiles, cleans his glasses with an embarrassed air.*

JACOBSON *(with frequent pauses):*
Forgive me, it was only the surprise.
Just now, back in the room there,
when I heard your voices—and also,
last night's air raid . . . the excitement,
I kept thinking if the place caught fire
and people came to put it out
and found me here with you—an officer of the SS—
you would be—they'd tear you to pieces . . .
GERSTEIN: That's all over now, Herr Jacobson.
JACOBSON: Yes—over. How easy it is to say.
Five minutes ago the thought passed through my mind
that next time there's an air raid
I'd better leave
in order not to put you . . . in . . .
GERSTEIN *(to* RICCARDO):
You see—a nasty case of cabin fever—it's high time . . .
JACOBSON: How can I ever thank you—and you . . .
(To RICCARDO.) Now you are the one I am endangering.
Do you know that?
RICCARDO *(has come round completely; warmly):*
I thank God for the opportunity to help.
It's little enough. I live at the Papal Legation.

> Not even Hitler personally could harm me there.
> Be sure to send a card from Rome, won't you?

GERSTEIN *(friendly but anxious, looks at the clock):*
> You must brief Jacobson about your father,
> your own and his position in the Vatican . . .
> You have to know enough to answer
> any questions from the German border guards.
> The rest remains a gamble. Change your clothes.

He gestures toward the door to the adjoining room.

JACOBSON *(has composed himself):*
> Sleeping car—really—is that essential?

GERSTEIN *(smiling, impatient):*
> If possible, yes—you're a diplomat, remember?

RICCARDO: There is only one inspection at the border
> and that's done very courteously, I think.

JACOBSON: Oh, fine. But if I go by sleeping car, of course,
> I cannot leave before tomorrow night, Herr Gerstein.
> When it gets dark tonight I'm going home
> to see my parents and to say goodbye.
> *(Almost happily, not noticing* GERSTEIN's *embarrassment;
>   resolutely.)*
> And once in Rome I'll leave no stone unturned
> to have the two placed under the protection
> of some neutral power.
> An emigration visa—perhaps that can be . . .

GERSTEIN *(quite convincingly):*
> Don't put your parents into danger—
> depart tonight, at any cost.
> I'll drive you to the station in the car.
> *(Rather uncertainly.)* No visits home.

JACOBSON *(disturbed, mistrustful):*
> You mean I am not to say goodbye?
> Herr Gerstein, it's not like you to be so nervous . . .
> *(Sees through him, horrified.)*
> Or—tell me—have they—please, the truth!
> Have they already shipped my parents off?
> Please—now you must . . .

GERSTEIN *(softly):* Yes. I couldn't deliver your letter
> on Tuesday.

He takes a letter from his jacket, relieved that he can report something factual. He speaks rapidly, but jerkily.

But I could not tell you either. The door is sealed.
I almost didn't notice, almost dropped
the letter in their box.
If I had left it there, they would be looking for you now.
The people who now run the store
saw me go off. They wanted to give me
a message—the woman beckoned to me
through the store window . . .

JACOBSON *(fighting back his tears):*
Frau Schulze—yes, she was always decent.
Without her help my parents would have starved to death by
now.
Did she—have a chance to speak to them?

GERSTEIN *(at first cannot answer; then):*
I left. I suddenly felt scared.
I looked away—I had to force myself to walk, and not to run.
(He grasps JACOBSON'S *arm, emotionally ravaged.)*
I'm sorry—I—I—I thought
I'd go see the woman in the store
some time during the next few days . . . and ask what . . .
I'll go there afterwards, at once.

JACOBSON *turns the letter in his hand back and forth.* RICCARDO
speaks to break the silence.

RICCARDO: Should I try to ascertain where
they were taken? The Nuncio surely could find out.

JACOBSON: Don't bother. They're sure to get to Auschwitz now.
Tuesday . . . three days . . . Do you think, Herr Gerstein,
it was on Tuesday? Or could it have been earlier?
How long do those transport take?—Ah, questions!
(To RICCARDO, *making an extreme effort to control his
voice.)*
No point in asking questions. The old—
it's true, isn't it, Gerstein—are—gassed immediately.

GERSTEIN: N-not always, no. Some are—
your father, as a badly wounded veteran
of the first war, would surely have been sent
to Theresienstadt.

JACOBSON *(changed, composed):*
> Germany, your gratitude! Gerstein,
> you saved my life. But there's no need
> for you to lie to me. I—don't you understand—
> I don't want consolation now.
> I've known that it would have to happen—
> known it long. *(Violently, tormented, but firmly.)*
> It will not kill me—I won't do the murderers
> that favor. I will . . . now . . .
> now I must . . . get out of here . . . get away.

He crushes the letter in his hand; then he tears it twice. His movements are tightly spasmodically resolute. He is wholly transformed, unnaturally composed, and now speaks with something of the harshness of the Old Testament, while his pallid, kindly librarian's face takes on a streak of cruelty.

> Gerstein, reconsider
> whether you want to help me cross the Brenner.
> For now—after this news—
> I am no longer German. Now,
> whether or not you understand,
> each German—every one—becomes my enemy.
> This is no longer flight—I want to leave
> in order to come back, as an avenger. An avenger.
> Once I reach Italy I'm practically in England.
> *(Wildly, alarmingly.)*
> No one shall say we Jews let ourselves
> be driven to the slaughterhouse like cattle.
> I shall come back—as murderer,
> as bomber pilot. Killing for killing.
> Phosphorus bombs for gas, fire for fire.
> Gerstein, I warn you. This is my thanks to you
> for hiding me. I tell you honestly,
> the man you're helping to escape is now your enemy.
> Drive me out on the street as I stand here.
> For I shall never—never forgive the Germans,
> all Germans, for this murder of my parents—
> good Germans themselves.

He has dropped the scraps of the letter into one of the trash pails.
GERSTEIN *goes over to it without a word and takes the scraps out*

again. With his lighter he ignites the pieces one after the other and lets them fall flaming into the pail.

RICCARDO *(to* JACOBSON; *he sounds theoretical but sincere):*
    Do not harden your heart—you simplify.
    (He points to GERSTEIN.)
    How many Germans help your brothers!
    Is it their children that you want to bomb?
    Hatred can never be the final word.
JACOBSON *(aloofly, objectively):*
    Hate strengthens. I must now stand firm.
GERSTEIN *(morosely, hoarsely, without looking at* JACOBSON):
    Each to his post. Neither of us
    is going to survive this war.
    Change your clothes—it's getting late.

He takes the two pails and carries them out to the hall. As he returns, JACOBSON *is holding out to* RICCARDO *his passport [a large boldface J is visible on the inner pages] and the yellow star, a scrap of cloth as big as a man's palm.*

JACOBSON *(smiling):* You are making a poor trade, Father.
    You give me your cassock, and I—
    here—this—this is all I have to offer:
    only the stigma of the outlaw.

All three fall silent. RICCARDO *takes the yellow star and examines it. He looks at the star, then looks up at* GERSTEIN *and* JACOBSON. *Shakes his head. Holding the star against his cassock over his heart for a moment, he asks, as the curtain swiftly falls—*

RICCARDO: Here?

CURTAIN

Act 2: The Bells of St. Peter's

Rome, February 2, 1943. Palazzo Fontana on the Monte Gianicolo. Grand salon. Under a conventional painting of the Madonna stands a narrow Renaissance prayer bench. To the left and right family portraits. Women of various eras, soldiers, a cardinal. In the foreground, surrounded by flowers, a large photograph of a middle-aged woman: RICCARDO'*s recently deceased mother.*

The backstage wall of the room is almost entirely taken up by tall windows, and by the veranda door; through these we see a steeply sloping garden with stone pines and cypresses. Above the wall of this garden, chalky gray, very large and sharply silhouetted against the cold blue sky, is the nearby dome of St. Peter's.

The veranda door stands open. The bells of St. Peter's are clanging loudly.

COUNT FONTANA, *sixty years old, rimless glasses, heavy mustache, belongs—along with a tiny, select group of European aristocrats, such as, for instance, Herr von Papen, Hitler's Vice-Chancellor—to the Apostolic Privy Chamberlains di* spada e cappa. *His is the high honor of being permitted to stand, on ceremonial occasions, in Spanish court dress directly beside His Holiness.*

But FONTANA, *as one of the highest-ranking laymen in the service of the Holy See, regards the costume as something of an affliction, for he has nothing in common with the many picturesque trappings and museum pieces which contribute so much to the general atmosphere of the Vatican.* FONTANA *is a "manager." He is overworked, intelligent, cultivated, capable of kindliness and suffering, even graced with some fair understanding of the social necessities of the twentieth century. His discomfort at being photographed now in the rich and somber court dress of Henry II is quite genuine. He is a sober, self-assured financier who knows very well that he has performed unique services for the Curia and for that very reason does not like being uniformed like the other chamberlains, who for the most part are entitled to wear their buckle shoes, silk stockings, knee breeches, ruffs, slashed sleeves, lace cuffs, cardinal's hats, swords and medallion chains only because they are descended from families formerly important in Rome. The Fontanas still have fresh, vigorous blood. Like the Pacellis, they were first ennobled in the middle of the nineteenth century, still do serious work, and hence are not taken quite seriously in their circles.*

Nevertheless, His Holiness Pius XI had early nominated the "exemplary Catholic employer" Fontana a Knight of the Order of the Holy Sepulchre, and at the Pope's request His Majesty, Victor Emmanuel III, in 1939 made Fontana a count, with the title to pass to his descendants.

As the curtain parts, an old-fashioned PHOTOGRAPHER *with mustache and velvet jacket, crouched behind the black cloth, is directing his cumbersome photographic apparatus at the open veranda door. Then he himself steps to the threshold of the veranda, where his subject is to pose, and looks directly into the lens in a posture of "importance." As he stands there, trying to look like Garibaldi, he is caught in the act by the old* SERVANT, *who has noiselessly entered the room. The* SERVANT *looks at him, shaking his head contemptuously, until the* PHOTOGRAPHER *again busies himself with his camera.*

SERVANT *(watering flowers):*
    Don't keep His Honor the Count long
    or he'll send you packing.
    He hasn't even been told that the young master
    is back from Germany.
    When he knows, I can tell you right now,
    he'll have no time for you.
PHOTOGRAPHER *(flamboyantly emotional):*
    Who could forbid me to congratulate
    my old patron, His Honor the Count,
    on his receiving the Order of Christ!
    Moreover—his portrait is supposed to go
    on the front page! Moreover . . .
SERVANT: All right, all right, but now I'm closing the door.
    I'm not heating the garden, and the noise . . .

He closes the veranda door; the clang of the bells is considerably muted.

PHOTOGRAPHER: You'll have to open the door again in a minute.
    His Honor the Count is to stand outside,
    so that he'll have the dome of St. Peter's
    behind him.
SERVANT: I don't have to do anything. Here he comes.

Exit swiftly. The PHOTOGRAPHER *wipes his mustache and mouth as footsteps are heard in the next room. He nervously fingers his tie and retires behind his camera, where he assumes an "at ready" posture.*

FONTANA *(entering swiftly, nervously pleased):*
    Wonderful, what a surprise! When did he arrive, Vittorio! Let
      him sleep.

SERVANT *(following):* Barely an hour ago, sir. But he said
    I was to wake him straight off when you returned.
    He's so pleased too, our young master,
    He won't want to go on sleeping . . .
FONTANA *(has noticed the* PHOTOGRAPHER, *distractedly):*
    Ah yes, well, tell him that I'm here.

Exit SERVANT. *To* PHOTOGRAPHER:

Oh, do you have to? Good morning.
    Don't you have enough pictures of me?
PHOTOGRAPHER: But not a single portrait yet that shows Your
    Honor
    Wearing the Order of Christ. Permit me, Your Honor,
    to extend my most respectful congratulations!
    Besides, tomorrow's front page is supposed to . . .
    absolutely has to . . .
FONTANA *(who has greedily lit a cigarette, quite accommodating):*
    Well, all right. Where? Here? Go ahead.
PHOTOGRAPHER *(who has quickly opened the veranda door; the*
    sound of the bells comes very loud again):
    Here, if you don't mind, Your Honor, here on the threshold,
    so that besides the costume Your Honor
    will have St. Peter's dome at your back.
    The most effective . . .

He stands with a helpless air.

FONTANA: You've already set the camera, haven't you?
    What are you waiting for?
PHOTOGRAPHER: Permit me, Your Honor, if you don't mind . . .
    Do you think the cigarette and the court costume . . . ?
FONTANA: What's that—you want my hands
    to show as well? The whole paraphernalia?
    I thought, only a bust . . . ?

He lays the cigarette aside.

Very well, very well, get it over with.
PHOTOGRAPHER: Perhaps your hand on the sword and
    head a little higher—a little more to the left.

He squeezes the rubber ball.

Many, many thanks. Perhaps one more shot
at the desk, preserving for posterity
Your Honor in full exercise of business . . .
FONTANA *(trying not to laugh):*
Ah yes, preserved for posterity. Posterity
might even fancy that I opened letters
in this costume I'm wearing, with my sword.

He points to the SERVANT, *who has re-entered, picks up his cigarette and says merrily:*

Here, take a picture of our Signor Luigi.
He will be seventy soon.
The picture will make a nice gift to his wife
on his birthday. Go on, over there!
SERVANT: But Your Honor, that doesn't do!

Angrily to the PHOTOGRAPHER, *as he closes the door:*

Am I heating the garden? Keep the door closed.
FONTANA: Go on, Vittorio, your wife will be pleased.
Over there! Don't make such a face . . .

RICCARDO *enters.*

My boy, what a surprise!
RICCARDO *(embraces his father, who kisses him):*
Congratulations, Father! My, how grand!
(Nervously.) Why do the bells keep going on and on?
FONTANA: So good to have your company a while.
How long can you stay?
RICCARDO *(now, like his father, distracted by the scene between the*
PHOTOGRAPHER *and the* SERVANT *in the background):*
That's fine, Vittorio.
SERVANT: It's a waste. And my teeth
are being fixed . . .
PHOTOGRAPHER: One, two, three . . . One more picture
of Signor Riccardo, Count Fontana? I would suggest . . .
RICCARDO *(pleasantly):* Better not, I need a shave.
Some other time.
FONTANA: Thank you, thank you, do please pack up your things.
PHOTOGRAPHER *(while* SERVANT *is helping him fold his
equipment):* The thanks are all mine, Your Honor.

FONTANA: Are you ill, my boy? You look so worn.
Really, you do need looking after.
RICCARDO: I could not catch a wink of sleep while on the train.
It's only that this trip has tired me, Father.
There's really nothing wrong with me . . .
Why *(nervously and irritably)* do they go on ringing that way?
FONTANA: Because the Pope this morning consecrated
the world to the Immaculate Heart of the Blessed Virgin.
A very tiring ceremony. Right after came
my audience—and then the decoration
suddenly came my way—I had no idea.
RICCARDO: Mama would have been happy—how we miss her
in the house and everywhere . . .

Both look up at the portrait. The PHOTOGRAPHER *has by now
packed up and speaks.*

PHOTOGRAPHER: Much obliged, Your Honor
(To RICCARDO.) Your Honor!
Good day—good day!
FONTANA: Thank you. Good-bye.
RICCARDO: Good-bye.

PHOTOGRAPHER *leaves.*

SERVANT: God reward you, Your Honor.
FONTANA: Keep it a secret from your wife.

SERVANT *leaves.*

FONTANA *(as he prepares a cocktail, skeptically, ironically):*
Ah yes, my boy—the dogma of Mary's Ascension
may now, quite seriously, await us
when the war is over.
As a result, he'll merit an important chapter
in every history of the Popes . . .
RICCARDO *(bitterly amused, takes a glass from his father):*
The things they think about in Rome!
Take poverty, for instance, which, in practice, means
that as a nation's churches grow in number,
so do its prostitutes. Naples and Sicily—
centers of vice beneath the windows of the Vatican.
Instead of helping, we debate

how frequently a married couple may cohabitate.
Or if a widow may remarry.
And now, to top it off, the dogma of the Virgin.
Does he have nothing else to do?

FONTANA: Don't be too hard on him, my boy! An hour ago
the Pope, who almost always asks about you,
told me that nowhere in the world today
can you acquire the experiences
available at the Legation in Berlin . . .
Have you brought more bad news from the Nuncio?

RICCARDO: None at all. I left without assignment.
I could not stand it any longer. *(Reproachfully.)*
You must know that for months the Jews all over Europe
are being wiped out systematically.
Each day—Father, just think of it:
each day, six thousand!

FONTANA: I read that too, but it
must be enormously exaggerated.

RICCARDO: Suppose it is exaggerated!
(Despairingly.) I gave my word
the Pope would protest,
would raise a hue and cry
to stir the world to pity,
to outrage and to action!

FONTANA *(agitated):*
You had no right to do that, Riccardo.
Temerity—to dare to speak for him!

RICCARDO: Temerity, you say? Why, could I have thought
he would do otherwise?
The children of an entire people in all Europe,
from Narvik to the Don, from Crete to the Pyrenees,
are being born today only
to be murdered in Poland.
Hitler is systematically reducing
life itself to an absurdity. Just read
the ghastly details from Poland and Rumania
published two weeks ago.
How shall we ever find apologies
for our silence. And those bells!
(He almost shouts, hands clapped to his ears.)

They ring and ring as though the world
were Paradise. What sheer unfeeling idiocy
to offer *this* earth to the Blessed Virgin's heart.
Does not the Pope who holds
within his hand five-hundred million Catholics—
twenty per cent subjects of Hitler now—
does he not share responsibility
for the moral climate of this world?
How can he have the audacity . . .

FONTANA *(loudly, checking him):*
Riccardo, I will not have you use such language!
Is this the way you thank the Pope
for always—always favoring you?

RICCARDO: Father, please, what do personal affairs
matter here?

FONTANA *(warningly):* You are very ambitious. Lucifer,
the favorite of his Lord,
also fell from ambition.

RICCARDO *(smiling sadly):* Not ambition but disappointment
will make me an antagonist. Father:
(imploringly, as urgently as possible)
the greatest manhunt which the world has ever seen.
Divine creation—shipwrecked. Faith
locked in battle with the new ideologies,
with insights gained by science. And human wreckage
strewn upon the oceans, upon
the countries of the earth. Men sacrificed
on every front, slain in the fire,
on the gallows, in the gas—and God's ambassador
thinks he can *win,* yet venture nothing?
Suppose God has elected, in these days
unprecedented in all history,
to let *him* perish too.
Would *that* not be ordained as well?
Does no one in the Vatican grasp
this? They still cling
to the hope that *everything*
is preordained; the greatest pyres
ever reared, however, are made out to be
the whims of a dictator who is soon to pass.

Let us admit at last:
these flames are also *our* trial by fire!
Who will, in times to come, respect us still
as moral arbiters if, in *this* time,
we fail so miserably?

Both fall silent, worn out by contention; the ringing of the great bells of St. Peter's can still be heard, more muted. FONTANA *struggles to master his agitation; he tosses the ridiculous sword aside, lights cigarettes for himself and* RICCARDO, *and says appeasingly—*

FONTANA: Let's look at this realistically. I ask you
    as a member of the Secretariat of State
    how can the Pope, without surrendering
    his policy of neutrality,
    force Hitler not to deport the Jews.
RICCARDO: Let him exploit the fact
    that Hitler fears his influence.
    It wasn't out of piety
    that Hitler has refrained from all infringements
    upon the Church for the duration of the war.
FONTANA: That policy may change tomorrow. How many
    priests has he not killed already!
RICCARDO *(passionately)*:
    That's right—and Rome, despite that fact, has not
    called off her friendship. Why?
    Because Rome feels there is no cause to?
    The facts are there: the Pope
    chooses to look the other way when his own brother
    is slain in Germany. Priests there
    who sacrifice themselves do not do so
    on orders from the Vatican—rather, they violate
    its principle of non-intervention.
    And since Rome has abandoned them,
    their deaths cannot be counted as atonement
    for Rome's own guilt.
    As long as Rome permits her priests to go on
    praying for Hitler—praying for that man!—
    just so long . . .
FONTANA: Please, stick to the point. Why do you ignore
    the protests of the Bishop of Münster?

RICCARDO: Oh, Father, Galen's example proves my point.
  In the very heart of Germany he raised his voice
  against the murderers—in summer, '41.
  Hitler's prestige was at its height, but lo and behold
  they let the bishop speak out with impunity.
  He did not spend a single hour in jail!
  And his protest stopped the extermination of the sick.
  Only one bishop had to stand up
  and Hitler retreated. Why?
  Because he fears the Pope—the Pope
  who did not even back up Galen's speeches!
  There is no one Hitler fears now but the Pope, Father.
  In Potsdam I met Herr von Hassell—
  he sends his greetings to you. Almost
  his first question was: Why did Rome
  let Galen fight alone?
  And my question was: Why had Galen
  not also come forth to defend the Jews?
  Because the mentally ill were baptized?
  That is an ugly question, Father—
  let us admit it.
FONTANA: Riccardo, do not judge!
  You dare reproach a bishop for not
  risking his life for Jews as much as Christians?
  Do you know, Riccardo, what it's like
  to risk your life? I found out in the war.
RICCARDO: I admire Galen, I honor him.
  But, Father, we in Rome, here in the Vatican,
  which cannot be assailed—we must not
  be content with Galen's risk
  while in Poland . . .
FONTANA (*remonstrating*): My boy, your arrogance disturbs me.
  The Pope, daily contending
  with the world, with God, knows what he is doing.
  He knows why he must be silent.
  He will not always be. The tides of war
  are shifting. Time is on Great Britain's side.
  Once reasons of state permit
  the Pope to rise up against Hitler without
  imperiling the Church, then . . .

RICCARDO: Then not a single Jew will be alive
  in Poland, Germany, or France, or Holland!
  It's time you understood—every day counts!
  I gave my word. I guaranteed this officer . . .
FONTANA *(beside himself)*: Whatever made you do that?
RICCARDO *(flaring up, throwing moderation to the winds)*:
  Because—because I lacked the cynicism
  to cite reasons of state when
  things like these come to my ears.
FONTANA: How you simplify? Good God,
  do you believe the Pope could suffer to see
  even a single man hungry and in pain?
  His heart is with the victims.
RICCARDO: But his voice? Where is his voice?
  His heart, Father, is of no interest.
  Even Himmler, Hitler's police chief,
  could not tolerate the sight of his victims,
  so I have been assured.
  The orders sift down from bureau to bureau.
  The Pope does not see the victims;
  Hitler does not see them. . . .
FONTANA *(approaches* RICCARDO *threateningly)*:
  Enough—I'll cut this conversation short
  if you mention Pius XII and Hitler in the same breath.
RICCARDO *(scornfully)*:
  Confederates have to put up with that, Father.
  Have they not made a pact with one another?
  Pius the Eleventh would long ago
  have abrogated the Concordat.
FONTANA: That's not for you to say.
RICCARDO *(after a pause, softly, with a note almost of spite)*:
  Father, do you believe the Pope—
  are you quite *sure* the Pope
  is actually tormented by a conflict
  between reasons of state and Christian charity?
FONTANA: How do you mean that, Riccardo?
RICCARDO *(controlling himself with effort)*:
  I mean—he stands so very high above
  the destinies of the world, of men. For forty years
  he's been immersed in canon law, diplomacy.

He's never been—or only for two years—and that
in the last century—a priest, working with people,
entrusted with the care of souls.
He never condescends to say a word
to one of the Swiss guards at his door.
Neither in his garden nor at table
can he tolerate the face of a fellow man.
His gardener, remember, has strict orders
always to keep his back turned to the Pope!
Oh, Father—is there anything he loves
except his dictionaries and
the cult of the Madonna?
(Suddenly full of hatred, with flashing Roman mockery.)
I see the way he cleans his pen with utmost care—
and, worse yet, expatiating on that ritual—
and I ask myself whether—
or rather I no longer ask
if he was ever able to regard
a single one of Hitler's victims
as his brother, a being in *his* image.

FONTANA: Riccardo, please—that's hardly fair,
that verges on demagogy. Granted his coldness,
granted his egocentricity,
he still attempts to help, to understand. The victims . . .

RICCARDO: The victims—does he truly bring them to his mind?
Do you believe he does? The world press,
the ambassadors, our agents—all come
with gruesome details. Do you think
that he not only studies the statistics,
the abstract figures,
seven hundred thousand dead—starvation,
gassing, deportation . . .
do you think he is *there,*
that he has ever watched
with his mind's eye—has ever seen
the way they are deported from Paris:
three hundred suicides—before the journey even starts.
Children under five snatched from their parents.
And then Konin, near Warsaw:
eleven thousand Poles in mobile gas chambers—
their cries, their prayers—and the laughing SS thugs.

    Eleven thousand—but imagine
    you and I—that we were in it.
FONTANA: Riccardo, please—I know you tear at your own heart.
RICCARDO *(as if delivering an ultimatum)*:
    My question! Father, please, answer
    that question. Does the Pope—does he
    bring *such* scenes to his mind?
FONTANA *(uncertain)*: Of course, of course. But what of that?
    You know he cannot act according to his feelings!
RICCARDO *(beside himself)*:
    Father! What you are saying cannot be—
    how can you say it!
    Does nobody here realize—you, Father,
    surely you must realize . . .

The ringing of the bells stops. It is very quiet. Neither speaks. Then
RICCARDO, *extremely agitated but stressing every word, continues*
very softly at first, with slowly mounting intensity:

    A deputy of Christ
    who sees these things and nonetheless
    permits reasons of state to seal his lips—
    who wastes even one day in thought,
    hesitates even for an hour
    to lift his anguished voice
    in one anathema to chill the blood
    of every last man on earth—
    that Pope is . . . a criminal.

RICCARDO *collapses into a chair and is overcome by a fit of weeping. After some hesitation* FONTANA *approaches him. His indignation, which had at first left him speechless, is softened by the sight of his "prodigal" son.*

FONTANA: You see what talk like this
    can lead to. My boy, how can you . . .

The old SERVANT *enters quickly, but quietly, holds out a file folder and says:*

SERVANT: At last, Your Honor, here is . . .
FONTANA *(shouting, more intemperately than anyone would have
    thought him capable of)*: Let us be!

As the SERVANT, *shocked, slowly retreats toward the door,* FON-
TANA *manages to say:*

> Vittorio, not now—excuse me.
> I can see no one just now . . .

SERVANT *leaves.* FONTANA, *after a long look at* RICCARDO, *with
forced calm:*

> Your monstrous insult to the Pope
> as well as all who serve him . . .

RICCARDO *(still distraught):*
> My own share in the guilt—I, too,
> am guilty—this gives me the right . . .

FONTANA: You are not guilty.

RICCARDO: Yes, guilty as is any bystander.
> And as a priest . . .

FONTANA: Contrition can be pride as well.
> Your duty is *obedience*.
> You are far too—too insignificant
> to bear this guilt . . . aren't you aware
> that hard as you take all this,
> your point of view is superficial,
> humanely biased, distorted by the lenses
> of pity and contemporaneity.
> Proceeding as you do, you cannot grasp
> the meaning of this visitation.

RICCARDO: The meaning! It would take
> the sensibility of a meatgrinder
> to see a meaning in it.
> *(Springing to his feet.)*
> Would you have me look down,
> supercilious and serene,
> with the notorious glazed eyes
> of the philosopher,
> and dialectilize a meaning
> into this murdering?

FONTANA: No sacrifice is wasted, although history
> may fail to register the sacrifices. God does.
> How can you, a priest, doubt that?
> The Pope draws strength from that belief as well.

And he *can* act only when animated by
this confidence. And thus he also can refuse to
blindly grant the promptings of his heart.
He *cannot risk*
endangering the Holy See!
(After a pause.) Do not forget one thing, Riccardo:
Whatever Hitler may be doing to the Jews,
only he has the power
to save all Europe from the Russians.

RICCARDO *(wildly):*
A murderer is not a savior! What nonsense, all this talk
about the West, about Christianity!
Let the devil take us
if a murderer of millions
can be accepted by the Pope as a Crusader.
The Russians were defeated long ago.
Hitler stands at the Volga.

FONTANA *(firmly):*
History is not yet over,
a Russia occupied not yet a victory.
The Pope no doubt knows that his protest
would be without effect, or place
the Church in Germany in grave jeopardy.

RICCARDO *(violently):* He does not know that, cannot know!
Galen's success holds promise that a protest
from the *Pope* would certainly
stop Hitler in his tracks.
No doubt he would continue to oppress the Jews,
as slaves working in industry—but *kill* them?
That is highly questionable. And aside from mere
pragmatic grounds . . .

FONTANA *(quickly):* One cannot disregard these when one
is responsible for five-hundred million believers
on this globe.

RICCARDO: It is nowhere written that St. Peter's successor,
when he appears on Judgment Day,
will be the world's outstanding stockholder.
Suppose the Vatican forfeits its power
over banks, industries, and ministries
by fighting against Hitler—

surely the mission God has charged it with
would be fulfilled with greater honesty.
Don't you believe the suffering
and defenselessness of the Fisherman
who first held the key
are more becoming to the Pope?
In time, Father, it must come:
the Deputy of Christ's return to martyrdom.

FONTANA: Riccardo, you are a visionary!
You scoff at power, yet you ask us to
take measures against Hitler. The Pope as a
poor fisherman—think what Napoleon
would have done with him, let alone Hitler.
No, the Pope can only carry out his mission
as long as he stands at the victor's side.

RICCARDO *(passionately)*: On the side of truth!

FONTANA *(smiling, waving that aside, then dryly)*:
Truth *is* with the victor—who, as you know,
also controls the historians.
And since the history of the world—it's an old saw—
comes to have meaning only when
historians have assigned it one,
you can easily conceive for yourself
how many footnotes Hitler as the victor
would concede the Jews . . .
All of this, Riccardo, can only be endured
if we never lose our belief
that God some day will recompense the victims.

RICCARDO: These consolations!
Would Christ have turned away?

FONTANA: I am no priest—but I know
that the Pope is not, like you and me, an individual
permitted simply to obey his conscience
and his feelings.
He, in his own person, must preserve the Church.

RICCARDO: And yet it is this very Pope as an individual,
this twelfth Pius, whom Hitler fears.
Pacelli's prestige in Germany is greater
than anywhere else. Perhaps for centuries
no Pope has enjoyed such a reputation
in Germany. He is . . .

The SERVANT *has entered, still obviously cowed. He announces:*

SERVANT: His Eminence, the Most Reverend Cardinal . . .

The name is not heard, for FONTANA *swiftly, slightly alarmed, replies.*

FONTANA: Oh—yes, please show him in.
  (To RICCARDO.*)* Is it all right for him to see you here?
RICCARDO *(quickly):* He is bound to find out anyhow
    that I came here without official orders.
    Ask him to lunch.

Behind the stage, the sonorous, attractive laughter of a fat man is heard. Evidently His Eminence has condescended to jest mildly with the servants. The prelate, rotund, florid, but nervous, in fact irritable at work and in conversation, is a noted flower fancier. In addition he takes a lively interest in all the illnesses in his wide circle of acquaintance.

At first sight, but only at first sight, he looks like a clubwoman: with advancing age (although he is little older than FONTANA*) he has become visibly more female. But that is deceptive. The* CARDINAL *is a suave, even ruthless diplomat, and his blue eyes can suddenly assume the coldness of Göring's or Churchill's eyes, belying the grandmotherly amiability of his plump face. At such times his fondness for flowers seems as improbable as Göring's delight in toy railroads. He has another trick and that is to fall silent and by his engaging manner seduce his interlocutors into talking until they have said more than they can justify.*

The CARDINAL *is a man who has risen out of poverty. When he was still slim and straight, and his black curly hair formed a troubling contrast to his light, large, laughing eyes, he must have found it rather difficult to avoid women. He was reputed to have had affairs; these rumors were no doubt prompted by envy and were possibly an injustice to him. As long as the power of Eros disturbed him, he was feared for his biting wit. Now malicious sarcasm has given way to an effervescent gaiety.*

But the CARDINAL's *bent for sarcasm was always held in check by his remarkable intelligence, and his mind is still far too alert to reveal anything like its full brilliance in the presence of His Holiness. This prince of the Church always lags perceptibly behind the Pope, whom he refers to as "Chief" and of whom he is not espe-*

cially fond. He would rather appear stupid than ever show himself superior. He knows why.

His intellect, however, has never overcome one weakness—and like all such distinctive traits, it has grown stronger with the passing years: the CARDINAL *adores being the bearer of news. News as such fires him, no matter whether it is good or bad. And today a piece of news is burning on the tip of his tongue, a matchless news item, although unfortunately by evening the whole world will know it.*

Like many fat men, the CARDINAL *is extremely deft in his movements. He enters with characteristic vivacity, laughing infectiously.*

His huge head tilted to the right, hat still covering his zucchetto and wearing a light silk cape, the CARDINAL *spreads his arms wide to embrace Count* FONTANA, *who has come forward to meet him. In celebration of the day he is wearing his red hat. In his right hand he holds a choice orchid. He continues to laugh and goes on laughing as he says a few half-finished sentences during the casual embrace. He even laughs in between words as he becomes aware of* RICCARDO's *presence. This does not actually displease him, but is an annoying surprise. His noisy joviality instantly arouses liking, for it is altogether genuine. Here and now His Eminence is a very good man. Today, on this festival of the Blessed Virgin and the occasion of Count* FONTANA's *honor, he is quite uncomplicatedly delighted that his high blood pressure is not troubling him.*

CARDINAL: My dear Count—well, well, God
    bless you! We *should,* indeed, don't you think?
    Yes, this time it's gone to the right man! Well, well,
    I mean, I myself must—the Cross of Christ—indeed.
    No! It really—most cordially—indeed.
    I had no idea, really not, you know.
    Yes, straight from the heart. Here—this,
    my *Bletia verecunda,* you know.
FONTANA: Why, thank you, Eminence—how thoughtful.
    What an amazing flower!
    An orchid—what variety, did you say?
CARDINAL: Riccardo! Why, what a joy! Well, well,
    such a surprise. Punctually in Rome
    to congratulate your Papa, aren't you?
RICCARDO *(bending over the* CARDINAL's *ring):*
    Good morning, Your Eminence. Right after dinner

I intended to call upon Your Eminence
and ask for an audience.
FONTANA: You will stay for lunch, Eminence?
CARDINAL: What's that? Yes, oh yes, gladly. Look, Count,
the boy has his high blood pressure again—
well, well, Riccardo, such a flushed face.
Aren't there any doctors left in Berlin?

He talks on, as he gives the SERVANT *his hat and cape, alternately addressing father and son, without waiting for answers to any of his questions.*

Well, well, how splendid, what a surprise.
And today of all days—any time, for that matter,
now that your father is so much alone.
The Nuncio has not advised us of your arrival?
—Ah yes, the orchid interests you, Count.
Yes, you know, that is my belovèd
Bletia verecunda—oh, don't place it in the draft.
Plenty of light, you know, but no wind!
Yes, it rarely blooms for me—the only times,
so to speak, when the Order of Christ is conferred.
It's old in Europe—we first raised them
in England back in 1732.
FONTANA *(who obviously does not know quite what to do with the noble blossom, very courteously):*
So very thoughtful, so kind of you,
Eminence. And fascinating.
Did it not cost you a pang to cut it for me?
But please—let us sit down—please,
Eminence—here.

They continue to stand. FONTANA *hands the orchid to the* SERVANT *and gives him a word of instruction. His Eminence handles the cigar cutter with pleasurable fussiness.* RICCARDO *offers him a light—all this while the conversation continues.*

CARDINAL: Riccardo looks very worn, you know!
Yet Berlin has such marvelously clear air.
Here, in September, when no one can step outside,
why then, you know, I always wish

I were the Nuncio in Berlin.
What does your blood pressure read?
RICCARDO *(with extremely cautious irony):*
Why, Your Eminence, my health is good, very good.
I have not seen a doctor for more than a year.
FONTANA: But you should! He becomes
too agitated in Berlin, Your Eminence.
CARDINAL: He's too young for that! No other complaints,
heart, stomach—you're sure?
RICCARDO: Sound as a bell, Your Eminence.
CARDINAL: Then it must simply be the change of climate,
the difference in altitude. You felt congestion on the train?
RICCARDO *(politely):* Why yes, a little. But probably only
because I was lying down throughout the trip.
CARDINAL *(reassured):* Of course, I saw that, you know.
Well—you must restore the balance.
And how is your gall trouble, Count?
FONTANA: Oh, not worth mentioning—but please,
Your Eminence, lunch will be a while yet,
let us sit down.
CARDINAL *(holding big cigar, takes the Count's arm):*
Yes, let us sit, let us sit—that reminds me
of a soirée in Paris—I was then
as young as Riccardo, and no one looked at me.
I stood in a corner. Have you nothing to sit on,
the hostess called at last.
Indeed, Madame, I have something to sit on,
I called back across the room,
something to sit on, yes, but not a chair—well, well . . .

His Eminence enjoys his mot *for some time, while the Fontanas
laugh respectfully* RICCARDO's *restiveness increases. While the old
gentlemen are taking seats, the* SERVANT *brings champagne and a
precious Venetian glass vase for the orchid.*

CARDINAL: Your restlessness, Riccardo, also indicates
high blood pressure, you know. Sit down
over here beside us . . . Ah, yes,
a glass of *this* will go down well even before noon,
indeed. Well, then, Count,
once again: may you wear the Order for a long, long time!

FONTANA *(as they touch glasses):* It is really so kind of you
    to have come at once, Your Eminence . . .
RICCARDO *(after a bow):* Your Eminence! Your health, Father!
FONTANA: Thank you, my boy.
CARDINAL: To you, Riccardo!

The CARDINAL *finishes his glass of champagne before he replaces it
on the table. The* SERVANT *refills it immediately. Holding the glass
again, the* CARDINAL *now produces his piece of news, underplaying
it for dramatic effect:*

    London has just confirmed the claim
    that Moscow made last night, you know. In *Stalingrad*
    the fighting is over. A German field marshal now
    Stalin's prisoner! The Volga will not be crossed . . .
    Well, that is . . .
RICCARDO *(vehemently, surprised and overjoyed):*
    Capitulated? It's true! And in Berlin
    the Propaganda Ministry was saying,
    and everyone believed it,
    that not a German would surrender!
FONTANA: What else could they have done!
CARDINAL: Moscow says that ninety thousand Germans
    have surrendered—Hitler's field marshal,
    his twenty-two divisions, or rather all that's left of them.
    That is a nasty stroke, and not only for Hitler.
FONTANA: For Hitler militarily no catastrophe,
    Your Eminence, but psychologically . . .
RICCARDO: Psychologically wonderful for us!
CARDINAL *(vexed):* Riccardo, you are very frivolous, indeed.
    This victory at Stalingrad may be the very thing
    to pose a fearful threat to us as Christians!
    (With emphasis.) The West, you know, indeed . . .
    Hitler's entire southern front is shaken now.
    He needs the oil in the Caucasus.
    Ah well, perhaps he will become the master
    of the situation once again.
RICCARDO *(cautiously, aware of the need to tread with utmost
    care):* But Your Eminence, you must also wish
    to see Hitler humbled.

CARDINAL *(jovially, trying not to show his impatience)*:
> But hardly by the Russians, dear Riccardo.
> Let England beat him, and the USA, indeed,
> until he gets it through his head that he
> can't rule the whole world by himself, you know.
> *Defeats*—why, by all means! But let him stop
> oppressing and killing Poles and Jews,
> Czechs and priests. Oh yes, indeed, . . .
> Otherwise, peace is not conceivable, you know.

> FONTANA *signs to the* SERVANT *to leave.*

RICCARDO: Peace with Hitler, Your Eminence, can never be
conceivable.

CARDINAL *(first laughs amused at* RICCARDO's *rash statement;
then, as if he were on the point of weeping from sheer
vexation)*:
> *Never?*—Never say never in politics!
> Count, just listen to your son—such a bright boy,
> but he too, now, has caught this Casablanca nonsense.
> Well, well. Holy Madonna, who will *ever*
> persuade Hitler to surrender unconditionally!
> But, you know, must we go over all this
> today—here, on this beautiful morning, you know!
> I wanted to *congratulate* your father, Riccardo!

It must not be thought that the CARDINAL *is evading the argument
out of indolence. He simply feels it unseemly for his youngest assistant to be trying to lecture him.* FONTANA, *himself an old man, feels
that better than does* RICCARDO.

FONTANA *(mediating)*:
> Yes, Your Eminence, let us have one more toast—
> to what—let's say, that Stalingrad
> will be a lesson to Herr Hitler.

CARDINAL: Well, well, yes. Cheers and good health.

RICCARDO: Your health.

CARDINAL *(more amiably)*:
> The Chief—the Chief let Mr. Roosevelt know
> in no uncertain terms
> that he regards America's demand

for Hitler's unconditional surrender,
as absolutely un-Christian, you know.

FONTANA: And above all *ludicrous*, Your Eminence.
America is almost being bled to death against Japan.
And here in Europe? Why, there's no sign of them!
While Hitler can, at any rate, set
half a dozen victories like Cannae
against the drubbing he received in Stalingrad.
They will have to negotiate with him, certainly.

CARDINAL: I should hope so, although
Cannae clearly demonstrates, you know,
that victories in battle do not
necessarily decide the wars.
This time, again, the Germans might
conquer themselves to death because
they carry the fire everywhere instead
of concentrating on a single front.
Their megalomania, which was once our fear
today is our strongest hope, you know.
Already it has cost them so much blood
that even Hitler will grow temperate again.
Trouble is good for dictators, you know;
also the Kremlin, Heaven help us, last November,
just when the fight began for Stalingrad,
settled its conflict with the Church, you know.
Hitler, as soon as war began,
knew that when soldiers start to die
he could not do without the Church.

FONTANA *(who sees opportunity here)*:
May we hope, Your Eminence, that the Pope
will take advantage of Hitler's predicament
to threaten him with breaking off the Concordat
if he continues murdering the Jews?
I heard ghastly reports from New York yesterday
concerning Poland and Rumania . . .

CARDINAL *(smiling, suddenly nervous, rising)*:
Has Riccardo been besieging you as well, dear Count?
Lo and behold: Fontana *père et fils*
forming a single front!

FONTANA: Not quite, Your Eminence. Only Hitler's fiasco
    on the Volga gives me the courage to request
    that we denounce his infamy.
CARDINAL: Well . . . You know, Riccardo, I told you once before,
    last summer, when you and then the Nuncio
    in Pressburg and in Bucharest—and then the Poles
    in London reported, you know,
    the dreadful things occurring there: I told you
    the Concordat is intended to protect
    our fellow Catholics—the Chief will not
    expose himself to danger for the Jews.
FONTANA: Not even now, Your Eminence, when Hitler
    would have to be amenable?
CARDINAL *(with mounting earnestness and deep emotion; the huge
    cigar smokes heavily)*:
    Of course we do a lot, but on the quiet, you know.
    The Raphael Club has raised the money
    to help thousands escape abroad, you know.
    But three events in recent weeks
    must alarm every Christian, you know.
    First, the recklessness of the United States
    in leaving Europe to Stalin's divisions;
    second, the defeat of Hitler on the Volga;
    and third, Stalin's reconciliation with
    the Orthodox Church. That proves to me, you know,
    proves unequivocally to me, that Stalin's
    Communism is only a deceptive
    redemptionist ideal. Communist or not, you know,
    he *is* the Tsar, the Orthodox heart
    of all the Russians, the Slav,
    true to his nationality, who nurses
    the dreams of absolute sovereignty
    once cherished by Peter and by Catherine.
    Naturally he had first to make a reconciliation
    with those apostates from the Church of Rome,
    schismatics, anti-Latins, Pan-Slavists, you know.
    The soul of the East is alien to the Latin spirit.
    And if this war, you know,
    does not bring the old Continent closer
    to realization of the ancient dream

of a Holy Roman Empire, why then,
you know, the last Christians may as well
take to the catacombs again.
RICCARDO: Your Eminence, an incendiary like Hitler
who only squanders the power of Europe,
who lets Mussolini lure him into
futile adventures in Africa and Greece—
such a man cannot unite the West.
CARDINAL: Do you imagine then that the conceited
parliaments and debating clubs à la Geneva
would have the force to do it? Did not
the League of Nations perish from insincerity?
Ah, those representatives of narrow interests
from Warsaw to Paris, from Rome to London—
they *talked* Europe to her death.
Your father will tell you all about that, you know!
No, this continent is much too old,
too torn asunder, ravaged by prejudice,
for its inhabitants to unify in peace.
Did the cities of ancient Greece, for instance,
after all their quarrels, still have the strength
for unification?
What if God now were using Hitler
to chasten Europe's nations
deluded in their grandeur—
think of France, for instance—
so that after all this the old frontiers
which Hitler has overrun can never be restored again—
what of that?
Wars always bring about results
different from those that people fight for.
One need not be a general, you know,
to sense that any idea so formidable
as Europe's unification can only be
accomplished amid blood and agony,
on the battlefield—but not
by discussions among liberal democrats
who always merely serve as representatives
of special selfish interests, you know.
The fact that Scandinavians, Italians, Croats,

Rumanians, Flemings, Basques and Bretons,
Spaniards, Finns and Magyars, have formed
a single front with the Germans against Stalin—
(indignantly) that should have deterred Mr. Roosevelt
from giving the Kremlin leave to conquer Berlin . . .
Besides, you know, it is a vain and empty boast,
sheer megalomania, you know . . .

RICCARDO: Permit me, Your Eminence—the moral right,
surely, is on the Russian side, without a doubt.
They are waging a just war!
They were attacked, their country devastated,
their people carried off, slaughtered.
If they are threatening Europe now,
the blame is only Hitler's.

CARDINAL *(coldly, impatiently)*:
That may be—but when the house is burning,
the fire must be put out—the question
of who kindled it can be investigated
later on, you know.
(He laughs.) Be careful, Count. Your Riccardo
is an idealist, which is to say,
a fanatic, you know. In the end
the idealist always spills blood in the delusion
that he is doing good—*more* blood than any realist.

*He gives a lordly laugh; he wants both to conciliate and to change
the subject. Then, with ironic hauteur, which is designed to make*
RICCARDO *seem a figure of fun:*

Riccardo—you idealists are *inhuman.*
We realists are more humane, because
we take men as they are.
We laugh at their faults, for we know we share them.
An idealist does not laugh—can Herr Hitler
laugh? Has he personally any faults?
No, he cannot laugh at this world;
he wants to improve it.
Anyone who differs with his ideals is exterminated.
This rules out compromise, I fear.
He must first smash a world so that he can
confer *his* peace upon it. No, thanks.

We realists are compromisers, conformists—
very well, we make concessions.
But why not? It's a case of staying alive
or being consistent, you know.
Let us never forget that both the devil
and the saints were placed in this world by God.
Between them stands man, whose only choice
is always between two sins, you know, Riccardo.
(Casually.) Your fanaticism is no service to the Church.
Hitler exists, after all—we *must*
live with him, you know.
And be on your guard—an old man
may be allowed to say this, you know—
be on your guard against judgments that will
only damn us all in the eyes of history.
Hitler, you say, *attacked* Russia!
Your father and I—don't you agree, Count . . .
FONTANA: You are quite right, Your Eminence.
CARDINAL: We content ourselves with saying: Hitler marched in.
Marched in, you know. Let us not enter
into controversy. Do you imagine
that cunning chessmaster entered Russia *gladly?*
He could not help himself—not in thirty-nine
when he concluded the pact with Stalin
(before the English could make one)
and not in forty-one, when he broke the pact.
You really have no idea, you know,
to what extent a ruler is the slave
of the events that he has brought about.
When Hitler made an agreement with Stalin,
in order to be free to go at England,
he roused the tiger at his back. He *could*
not know how long Russia would play the part
of his grain supplier; and the prices—
the Baltic, the Straits and Besserabia—
were reaching the extortion point, you know.
But Mr. Churchill, you know, was sure
of his supplies from the United States.
I grant you Stalin did not directly threaten Hitler,
no more than Alexander let Napoleon

> provoke him into taking the offensive.
> But let us admit that scarcely anyone
> could have foreseen that Stalin would be able
> to resist the Wehrmacht nearly so long.
> Hitler was not alone in his mistake, you know.
> A *rapid* victory in the East would actually
> have made him invincible, you know. A blessing
> that he did not have it—but a blessing too
> that he will not be overthrown, you know.

RICCARDO (*terribly concerned, speaking as pleasantly as he can manage):* But Your Eminence, the Holy Father really must
> protest that hundreds of thousands of persons
> are being literally slaughtered—killings
> which have no bearing on the outcome of the war.

CARDINAL: Must, you say! Now, now, my boy,
> calmness alone disarms the fanatic, nothing else.
> The Chief, you know, would be risking a great deal
> if he took up cudgels for the Jews.
> Minorities are always unpopular,
> in every country. The Jews
> have long provoked the Germans, you know.
> they overdrew on the credit they'd been given
> there in Germany.
> Pogroms do not fall from Heaven . . .

FONTANA (*cautiously; he feels that* RICCARDO's *arguments are only having a negative effect):*
> I quite agree, Your Eminence—only,
> one really can scarcely speak of pogroms
> in Germany. Hitler's legal experts
> have drawn up whole collections of new laws
> to strip the Jews of civil rights, and now
> even physically to annihilate them.

RICCARDO (*with a quietness which makes its impression):*
> In times gone by we Christians
> were also in the minority, and perhaps
> we will be soon again. I believe that God
> has indissolubly linked us Christians to
> the people to whom Jesus belonged . . .

CARDINAL (*with a long laugh, adroitly):*
> But, but—my dear Fontanas,

to *whom* are you saying all this.

Count, do you think me an enemy of the Jews?

FONTANA *(quickly):* Certainly not, Your Eminence.

CARDINAL: I'm only saying, you know, that the share
 the Jews had of the leading professions in Germany
 before Hitler came to power, was certainly
 unhealthy. They provided too many
 doctors, lawyers, bankers and manufacturers.
 Newspapermen, too, you know—naturally
 because they were more capable. Members of a minority
 are always more capable; right from the start, in school,
 they take the whippings for the others, you know.
 That makes people unpleasantly capable, you know . . .

FONTANA *(determined to save the situation):*
 Too capable, at any rate, in a nation
 that has more than six million unemployed.

CARDINAL *(spontaneously, gratefully):*
 There you are—I meant no more than that.
 The chief problem, Riccardo, is, you know,
 the dreadful popularity of Hitler.

RICCARDO: Your Eminence must consider this: that since
 his entry into Paris two full years—
 war years—have passed. The people are tired
 and afraid. Then the Allied bombers . . .
 Berlin society has a wicked tongue.

CARDINAL *(animated, glad to digress, paces back and forth):*
 The people love rulers whom they can fear.
 Nero—I am not joking, you know—Nero
 was also highly popular with the mob.
 "But the people of Rome *adored* him!" Frightful, you know.
 He too was an "architect"! The Circus, the Party Days . . .
 The Reichstag Fire—and then the manhunts,
 not of Christians this time, but of Jews,
 of Communists—parallels, frightful, aren't they?
 (Half cynical, half downcast.)
 Society, Riccardo, it may be,
 sees Hitler as the parvenu—although they still rejoice
 when their sons receive his decorations,
 But the people—I would really like to see
 a people who did *not* adore a ruler

who offers it so many scapegoats, you know.
And where would the Church be, my friends,
if it had not ignited faggots for the mob
during the Middle Ages. Panem et circenses,
confiscations, indulgences and deaths by fire:
the people always must be *offered* something!
And Hitler, you know, also gave them bread.
Let us not forget that. Bread,
and a uniform and daggers.
Most of the rowdies who fought his beerhall battles
had long been running after the red flag
before the swastika was sewed on it . . .
Let us not ignore the fact, you know,
that the people gave him half of all their votes.
Or almost half—that was in thirty-three
during the last relatively fair election.
Granted, the noble Krupps and others like them
even then gave Hitler's unofficial cabinet
three million marks, you know.
He used them as bait for the rabble.
And then the bishops, you know, the bishops in Germany!
Of course we mustn't say this sort of thing—
but between ourselves, dear Fontanas, between ourselves
(with gustatory satisfaction, savoring the words like
oysters on his tongue)
that touches on the Chief's *point d'honneur.*
The great diplomat Pacelli, you know!
Hitler looked like a hairdresser—the Concordat
made him socially acceptable urbi et orbi.
And now you want the Chief to curse him ex cathedra?

He laughs; FONTANA *joins in.*

RICCARDO *(attempting to stand up for the Pope):*
    Your Eminence—did not the Concordat
    have to be concluded to protect our brethren?
CARDINAL *(laughs heartily, pats* RICCARDO *on the shoulder):*
    That's how history is made, you know, Riccardo.
    Let us hope it will seem so later on.
    No, ask your Papa—in those happy not-so-far-off days
    no one here believed Hitler would undertake

those dreadful things he'd trumpeted in his book . . .
It was there for anyone to read, you know,
that some time somebody ought to poison—
he's a rough one, you know—
a few tens of thousands of the Hebrews, as he put it.
I would have taken a look at the man first, you know.
FONTANA: The late eleventh Pius, Your Eminence,
told me the Concordat with Hitler would be
a platform from which to make protests
if necessary . . . Now it *is* necessary.
CARDINAL *(digressing again)*:
The old Chief was a fighter, I grant you that.
But above all Pacelli wanted to
top his Concordats with the biggest one of all.
And so, you know, the See went so far
as to advise the poor democrats in Germany
to give themselves up, you know.
Hitler was seen as a second Mussolini
with whom it would be so easy to do business . . .
(He laughs.) Ah yes, the democrats . . . some years ago, you
know,
I met in Paris one of Hitler's predecessors . . .
Oh yes, a very famous man, now exiled and embittered.
"We had the same intentions!" he said. He meant
the elimination of unemployment, the building
of the autobahns. The plans were his, he said . . .
FONTANA: Why didn't he carry them out?
I think, Your Eminence, I know who told you that.
CARDINAL *(laughs)*:
Yes, *why* not! That was my private thought as well.
You know, our singers in the old days, Count . . .
they also knew exactly how it's done,
only *they* couldn't, you know.
(Serious again, with steely opportunism.)
As long as Hitler is winning and has the people behind him—
Stalingrad alone will not topple his throne—
the Chief would only make himself unpopular
if he openly made an issue of the Jews.
Brother Innitzer has already tried that, you know.
The Cardinal was Hitler's mortal foe—until the day

the amazing scoundrel marched into Vienna.
Then the people roared a welcome—a
quantité négligeable, sixty thousand, I think,
were put behind bars—but the man in the street rejoiced.
Then the Cardinal did the only clever thing:
after the parade to the Hofburg he was
the first to congratulate Hitler, you know.
The Chief would lose a great deal of prestige
if he endangered his position for the Jews, Riccardo.

RICCARDO: Among the Germans—perhaps.
But what about the United States, Your Eminence?

CARDINAL *(firmly, conclusively)*:
Not only among the Germans, you know!
Among the Poles, the Dutch, the French,
the Ukrainians as well—among all those
who are actively participating in the manhunt, you know.
In the United States as well there are extremely militant
foes of the Jews, you know.
Men love butchery, alas, God knows.
And once they start, reason will not sway them.
No, Riccardo, I cannot advise the Chief
to challenge Herr Hitler at this juncture.
The defeat on the Volga is troublesome enough
for him at this time, you know.
How would it be if our Nuncio in Berlin
were to speak to Herr von Weizsäcker about the matter?

RICCARDO *(bitterly)*:
All that would come of that, Your Eminence,
would be a courteous exchange of words.
The undersecretary undoubtedly knows nothing
about the extermination of the Jews.
In the streets of the German capital
he manages to overlook completely
the fact that Jews are being sent away
like dangerous criminals.
And since nobody dares to suggest
to Herr von Weizsäcker that he might be lying
in the name of his Führer,
and since he so readily assures everyone
that threats will only aggravate the situation . . .

CARDINAL *(sharply, because he feels* RICCARDO*'s irony is arrogant)*:
  Can *you* guarantee that threats
  will *really not* aggravate the situation?
RICCARDO *(making his last attempt; his control is slipping and he
  speaks much too loudly)*:
  Your Eminence, a hundred thousand Jewish families in
      Europe
  face certain murder!
  It could not, could not, possibly be *worse!*
  (More quietly, fervently.)
  No, Your Eminence, please do not try
  to do anything through Weizsäcker, or through the Nuncio.
  It must be: the Pope to Hitler—
  directly and at once!
FONTANA *(agitated because he feels that* RICCARDO *is spoiling all
  chance by the tone he takes)*:
  Please, my boy—are you attempting
  to give orders here? I beg you . . .
CARDINAL *(places a hand on* RICCARDO*'s shoulder; but the gesture
  means nothing)*:
  He's tired from lack of sleep, you know . . .
  Riccardo—I do not care to hear
  such deprecating talk of Weizsäcker, you know.
  He is a man of honor, the tried and true
  familiar link between the Nuncio
  and the Foreign Office.
  In thirty-nine he was the *only* one
  you possibly could go on talking to.
  Though even he could not save the peace.
FONTANA *(making a feeble effort to appease)*:
  Yes, Your Eminence, that remains to his credit.
  But many a virtue, when employed by Hitler,
  is easily converted into vice.
CARDINAL *(smiling)*:
  It is always a virtue to speak of peace, Count.
FONTANA: While the freight cars crammed with deportees
  roll on toward the crematoria? I am,
  Your Eminence knows, no cynic . . .
CARDINAL: Yes, the problem is a difficult, an insoluble . . .

The SERVANT *has entered and reports to* FONTANA.

SERVANT: His Eminence is urgently wanted. An officer . . .
CARDINAL: Please!
    (*To* FONTANA.) Permit me? Naturally I want
    to go over the whole thing with the Chief once more.

An officer of the Swiss Guard enters and gives a highly military salute.

SWISS: Your Eminence, His Holiness urgently requests
    Your Eminence's presence in the Papal Palace.
    I have orders to drive Your Eminence at once . . .
CARDINAL *(extremely annoyed):*
    Now—before lunch? Very well,
    my hat, Vittorio . . . What a pity.
    I fail to see how anything we may discuss
    will change the course of things in Stalingrad . . . Well.

As he dons his hat and RICCARDO *takes his cape from the* SERVANT *to help His Eminence into it,* FONTANA *speaks.*

FONTANA: A fearful pity—can't we wait with lunch?
CARDINAL: Out of the question, Count. Too bad.

    Laughing intimately, as if the quarrel had been made up.

    I may as well confess I asked the servants,
    even before you mentioned lunch,
    what the menu was for today—ah yes,
    I'm without shame, you know.
    And now instead of specialità della casa Fontana—
    a conference on Stalingrad—it's sad, you know.
    Riccardo!

    He goes up to him. RICCARDO *again kisses his ring.*

    Take lemons to keep down that blood pressure.
    And if that doesn't work, foot baths, as hot
    as you can stand . . . This afternoon?
RICCARDO: Yes, Your Eminence, many thanks. When shall it be?
CARDINAL *(casually):* Let's say, five. I think
    you'd better go to Lisbon for six months.
    (*Quickly, without transition.*)

My dear Count, enough politics for today.
This is your day to celebrate. God bless you.
Arrivederla.
RICCARDO *(downcast):* Arrivederla, Your Eminence.
FONTANA *(bowing him out):*
    It was so good of you to come, Your Eminence.
    May I say, above all . . .

The SERVANT *closes the door behind them. All leave except* RIC-
CARDO.

    RICCARDO *(alone, crushed, to himself):* Lisbon! Sidetracked!

*He nervously lights a cigarette, opens the veranda door. His father
returns and says rapidly, before the* SERVANT *has completely closed
the door behind him—*

FONTANA: He's getting rid of you! He did not even ask
    why you returned from Berlin!
    Lisbon: that's your payment
    for having gone too far.
RICCARDO: But, Father, I kept back the very worst,
    hoping he might at least *try* to persuade the Pope
    to take a position.
FONTANA: What else?
RICCARDO: Weizsäcker is coming to *Rome.*
    He will soon ask for his *agrément!*
FONTANA *(incredulously):*
    Hitler is making his undersecretary of state
    ambassador to the Vatican?
RICCARDO: No doubt entrusted with a special mission!
    In the first place, he's to keep an eye
    on Mussolini. They're afraid that Italy
    will soon be liquidating Fascism.
    Secondly—and above all—Weizsäcker,
    as Hitler's pure and stainless front,
    is now supposed to keep the Pope in person
    carefully soothed. All the old stuff:
    mutual non-intervention;
    no discussions of principles, no intrigues.
    For Hitler knows what it would mean
    if the Pope should join the protests of the Allies

against his crimes.
It would scotch his last hope of the West's
agreeing on a separate peace
and giving him a free hand in the East . . .

Silence.

RICCARDO *(heartily):* I'm so grateful that you're backing me.
FONTANA: Stalingrad marks the turning point permitting us to act.
You are right, my boy—but you have no say.
RICCARDO: Father, I implore you:
We must act before
Weizsäcker arrives in Rome—immediately, Father.

The bells begin to ring loudly again. Both look up and then exchange glances. FONTANA *makes a resigned gesture.*

SERVANT: Luncheon is served.

CURTAIN

Act 3: The Visitation

The world is silent. The world knows what is going on here—
it cannot help but know, and it is silent. And in the Vatican,
the deputy of God is silent, too. . . .
FROM AN UNDERGROUND
POLISH PAMPHLET, AUGUST, 1943

Office of the Father General of a religious order. A few pieces of standard office furniture, a crucifix, not far from it and somewhat larger hangs a photograph of Pius XII praying, in profile. Four Renaissance chairs, reproductions, such as the Swiss Guardsmen use in their guardrooms. A prie-dieu. A large map of the world lit by a fluorescent light and punctuated with red dots to show the not very numerous sites of the order's missions. The longest wall of the room is dominated by an extremely ponderous baroque wardrobe with two large doors.

Downstage, near the telephone, an aged MONK *is reading his breviary. Hanging prominently near the door is a black cardinal's hat and red cape. The simple office clock strikes ten times; it is 10 P.M.*

*Footsteps are heard, reverberating loudly as if someone were walk-
ing across the thin board floor on an empty storeroom. The MONK
looks up; then he rises to his feet. Now the sonorous, likable laughter of a fat man is heard, muffled, as though it were sounding inside
a barrel. But it comes from the wardrobe, whose doors are opened
from within, heavily, with a creaking noise. His Eminence, amused,
worldly, emerges with considerable fuss. His left hand tucks up his
cassock—he is wearing red stockings and high, black, laced shoes—
and with his right arm he supports himself on the MONK, who has
hastened to the wardrobe door to help His Eminence out. The
CARDINAL laughs, talks and coughs all at once to the ABBOT, who
is still standing in the deep recesses of the wardrobe and sliding
shut the panel of its false back. Soon the ABBOT also emerges and
closes the doors. He is an elderly, white-haired man, slender, dry,
obedient, rather like an officer on an army general staff.*

CARDINAL *(with one foot still in the wardrobe, with the gaiety of
    royalty)*: Jonah, you know—Jonah
    in the belly of the whale.
    Thank you, my friend, thank you.

*He emerges completely. The MONK pats some dust from his cas-
sock, then fetches a clothes brush from the desk drawer and dusts
him more thoroughly, afterwards going on to the ABBOT.*

    A truly wonderful hiding place, you know!
    and right beside this wardrobe, my dear
    Father General, you negotiate with Hitler's henchmen?
    (He laughs again.) Priceless, you know. But just suppose
    one of your flock—up there *(he points to the ceiling)*
    should become deranged . . . as prisoners do . . .
    Suppose he could no longer stand captivity and ran off, you
        know—
    screaming and carrying on, you know,
    and came banging through the wardrobe and here, into your
        room,
    perhaps when you are sitting with the Gestapo chief,
    drinking Frascati. Might be somewhat ticklish, you know.

*The idea amuses him just as much as it horrifies him; he gives a
rather anxious, questioning laugh.*

ABBOT *(smiling):* No fear of that, Your Eminence.
    Besides, the Germans know quite well that I
    have the place full of deserters,
    full of Communists, Jews, royalists.
    They respect the peace of the cloister.
    (To the MONK *who is brushing him off.)*
    Thank you, Brother, thank you—no telephone calls?
MONK *(bows):*
    None, Reverend Father General.
    (Genuflects.) Your Eminence!
CARDINAL *(without interest):* Bless you, my friend . . .
ABBOT: Bring us a drop of wine.
    Red, Your Eminence? New wine?
CARDINAL: No thank you—I have
    the coachman and horse waiting in the piazza.
    I mustn't linger, you know.
    Oh well, a drop, red, you know.
    (To the MONK.*)* But please, my friend, not new wine.

MONK *bows, leaves.*

    And how is your rheumatism, Father General?
ABBOT: Thank you for asking, Your Eminence.
    I fear it will come with the November fogs,
    as it does every year. No sooner, but
    no later either. I don't suppose
    it will spare me this year.
CARDINAL: You know, tomorrow morning I'll send you
    my cat pelt. Start to wear it right away,
    don't wait until the pains come.

The CARDINAL *has taken a seat at the desk; the* ABBOT *has moved up a chair for himself.*

ABBOT: Very kind of you, Your Eminence.
    But don't you need the pelt yourself?
CARDINAL *(putting that suggestion far from him, with
    austere gravity):* Why no, I take the water cure—and then,
    the warm air in my greenhouse
    keeps ailments away, you know.

He points to the ceiling again and coughs—coughs himself into a tremendous coughing fit.

But up there—the storeroom is very dusty.
Where do *they* get fresh air,
the poor fugitives? This dust—ah.

He gradually stops coughing.

Yes, that dust up there, you know.
ABBOT: Very simple. Your Eminence, at night
they can go out on the roof, all night long
if they feel inclined.
By day they go into the garden
one by one. They help in the kitchen
and in the library also—why not?
Our secret entrance through the wardrobe, Your Eminence,
just gives a touch of color, for the present.
If, however, the Germans cease to respect
the extraterritorial buildings of Rome,
as they have done thus far so splendidly,
we will wall up the doors to the hiding place,
and then the wardrobe will be the only entrance.

The MONK *has silently returned with glasses and a bottle. He goes
out again.*

ABBOT *(pouring):* Thank you, Brother.
CARDINAL: Well then, Father General, to your protegés.
ABBOT: Many thanks! May God protect them.
with your visit and with your cordial talk
Your Eminence has brought a wonderful serenity,
a new and beneficent atmosphere,
into our refuge. Please, Your Eminence,
come often to see the fugitives.
CARDINAL *(touched):* Ah yes, I mean to visit also
the fugitives in the Campo Santo and the Anima . . .
The wine feels good, you know—it was
too dusty in the storeroom. I suppose,
Father General, that a good many of the Jews
(he points to the ceiling)
will be converted to the faith, you know.
ABBOT: A happy outcome, Your Eminence.
CARDINAL: And you know—you needn't tremble
for your guests. Herr Hitler will no more dare

to touch the monasteries of Rome
than touch our Chief. He is much too shrewd
to offer the world any such spectacle.
Although the Germans know that many a monastery
harbors a secret radio station . . .
they understand what lines they may not cross, you know.
Herr von Weizsäcker has even asked me
to confirm in the *Osservatore*
that the Germans are so handsomely
respecting the Curia and all its houses.
And yes, you know, we'll do it—
they've deserved it. But all the same,
we won't do it quite for nothing, eh?

ABBOT *(smiling):* Good, Your Eminence. Tomorrow morning
I'll offer the Gestapo chief a trade.
We'll publish the communiqué—
if he hands out to me a Communist,
the son of a noted Milanese scholar,
who has appealed to us for help . . .
The Pope is much concerned.
I think I can put that across.

CARDINAL: Splendid, that's fine.

The telephone rings. The CARDINAL *hands the receiver to the* ABBOT, *then stands up, puts his hat on over his zucchetto and drapes his cape over his shoulder while the* ABBOT *is speaking on the telephone.*

ABBOT: Yes, speaking—who? Hm, one moment.
Your Eminence, Father Riccardo asks
to be received at once, accompanied
by an officer of the SS. May I . . .

CARDINAL *(both curious and vexed):*
Riccardo Fontana? Oh, certainly, by all means.
Don't let me be in your way.

ABBOT: *(on the telephone):* Bring them up, Brother.

He hangs up and says to the CARDINAL, *who is striding rather angrily back and forth but cannot quite make up his mind to leave:*

Father Riccardo, Your Eminence, has urged me
several times to speak to His Holiness concerning . . .

CARDINAL *(offended, irritated):*
>Yes, yes, you know, that is Riccardo's
>everlasting subject. That seems clear by now.
>Six months ago, at the fall of Stalingrad,
>I had to remove him from Berlin
>because he was taking too much into his own hands.
>What is he doing back here in Rome?
>His place of work is Lisbon.
>He's spoiled because of his father's position, you know,
>and the Chief makes a pet of him,
>caresses him as if he were a nephew.
>He is too ambitious. Obedience
>is not at all his forte, you know.

Knocking at the door. The CARDINAL *has posted himself so that he will not be seen at once by the persons entering. The* ABBOT *opens the door.* RICCARDO, GERSTEIN *and the old* MONK *appear; the latter instantly withdraws.* RICCARDO *almost leaps down the two steps into the room.* GERSTEIN *hesitates in the doorway. Even before he introduces* GERSTEIN, RICCARDO *cries out—*

RICCARDO: *This* is how far we've let things drift.
>As of this evening Jews are being arrested
>right here in Rome! What a disgrace . . .

He sees the CARDINAL, *gives a start of great alarm, goes up to him and bends over the ring.*

ABBOT: What is that you say? Frightful!
CARDINAL: Well, well, Riccardo. Has
>the Nuncio sent you here from Lisbon? And who is . . .

He goes up to GERSTEN, *who makes a low bow, is very contrained, and also extremely suspicious.*

RICCARDO *(quickly):* This, Your Eminence, is our liaison man
>in the SS leadership. Best for us
>not to bother with his name.
>It was he who first asked the secretary
>of Bishop Preysing to describe
>the gassings in Belzec and Treblinka
>to the Holy See.
>*(Angrily)* That is now more than a year ago . . .

CARDINAL *(quite cordially, extends his hand to Gerstein):*
    Oh, indeed, we thank you, sir.
    We were terribly shocked to hear it.
    God will reward you for your having
    done such a service to the victims, you know.
    But, Riccardo, what did you just say?
    Arrests in Rome?
    (Uncertain, irritated, indignant.)
    Why, you know, we thought—those henchmen—
    my dear Father General, we felt certain they would not
    arrest the Jews right here in Rome!
    Let's hope that most by now
    have managed to get over to the Allies!
    They do hold Naples now, you know.
    (Self-justifyingly, to GERSTEIN.)
    And hundreds are concealed in monasteries . . .

In their excitement all four talk at once. The ABBOT *greets* GERSTEIN, *the* CARDINAL *goes on speaking to* RICCARDO *as well as to the others; the* ABBOT *addresses* GERSTEIN *alone, reassuringly.*

GERSTEIN *(nervously):* May I ask you, Monsignore,
    to make sure that—that no other German
    beside myself comes in here now . . .
ABBOT: No need to be concerned. If only you
    attracted no attention as you entered from the street—
    no one will see you here. At this time of night
    none of your associates ever visit me.
GERSTEN: Associates . . . Monsignore,
    I only wear the same uniform.
ABBOT *(with sympathy):* I know, I've already heard about you—
    although, you needn't fear, I wasn't told
    your name . . .

    The two now listen to the CARDINAL *and* RICCARDO.

RICCARDO *(while the* ABBOT *is speaking with* GERSTEIN*):*
    Your Eminence, we now have come to this!
    Citizens of Rome—outlaws!
    A manhunt for civilians underneath
    the windows of His Holiness! Will
    no action be taken even now, Your Eminence?

CARDINAL *(guilty and therefore highly offended)*:
    Action *has been* taken, Riccardo.
    (With emphasis). We have given asylum
    to unbaptized Jews as well.
    Father General, show your storeroom to Riccardo, please.
    (Threateningly to GERSTEIN*)*.
    You Germans! Yes, you frightful Germans.
    I'm so fond of you, you know, and the Chief
    is too—but why won't you stop
    that business with the Jews! You everlasting
    peacebreakers and Protestants! Now
    you've carried things so far that even the Pope
    must condemn you before the whole world!
    Here, under his very window,
    you drag away women and children, and
    everyone knows that none of them ever comes back!
    You're absolutely forcing us, you know,
    you're forcing the Pope publicly
    to take note of those crimes, you know.
RICCARDO: God be thanked! At last he must . . .
CARDINAL *(speaks sharply to* RICCARDO, *who receives the*
    rebuke with a sardonic air):
    I will not have that, Father Fontana!
    Are you so limited as not to see
    that any anathema against Hitler by the Curia
    will become a fanfare of victory
    for the Bolsheviks?
    Mr. Stalin is marching upon Kiev. Hitler's
    summer offensive has been a total failure . . .
    (To GERSTEIN, *plantively.)*
    Whatever are you doing, you Germans!
ABBOT *(to* RICCARDO*)*: I'll take you upstairs to my protegés.
    I'd like you to see that we are taking measures . . .
RICCARDO: I am aware you are, Father General.
CARDINAL *(imperiously)*:
    Nevertheless, go upstairs with the Father General.

He then turns to GERSTEIN, *while* RICCARDO *is led through the wardrobe by the* ABBOT. *The wardrobe doors remain open until the* CARDINAL *leans against them.*

GERSTEIN: Your Eminence, perhaps Hitler will
    draw back even if His Holiness
    for the present merely threatens,
    secretly and in writing,
    to abrogate the Concordat.
CARDINAL *(evasively, reserved):*
    It's possible, you know, it's possible.
    I'll speak to the Chief this very night.
    Tell me, sir—how could the Germans have forgotten
    the mission God assigned them
    as the fulcrum of the West?
GERSTEIN *(softly):* Your Eminence, that could not be. God
    would not be God if He made use of a Hitler . . .
CARDINAL: Oh yes, oh yes, most certainly, my friend!
    Was not even Cain, who killed his brother,
    the instrument of God? Cain said to the Lord:
    my sin is too great ever to be forgiven.
    And still, you know, God set a mark on Cain
    so that no one who came upon him would ever kill him.
    What is it your Luther says:
    secular rule derives from Cain, you know.
    Cain had his mission in the world, as Noah did.
    What can we know
    of the terrible detours of the Lord!
    (Enthusiastically.) But one thing we know, don't we—
    surely God has no wish to let
    the *West*, Christian civilization, perish, you know!
GERSTEIN *(repelled):* Why not, Your Eminence? If God
    did not desire us to perish, why would He
    strike us Christians with such fearful blindness?
    The Church, Your Eminence—may I speak frankly?
CARDINAL: Of course, certainly, have your say.
GERSTEIN: For sixteen months now Rome has known
    of Hitler's savage butcheries in Poland.
    Why not a word about it from the Pope—
    that where the steeples of his churches rise,
    Hitler's chimneys pour forth their ghastly smoke!
    That where on Sundays the church bells ring,
    on weekdays the flesh of men is burned.
    That is the Christian West today!
    Why, Your Eminence, should not God

send us a new Deluge?
Only Stalin's tanks can liberate
Auschwitz, Treblinka, Maidanek . . .

CARDINAL *(deeply horrified)*:
What is that you are saying! Surely
you love your country, do you not, sir?

GERSTEIN: Permit me not to answer, Your Eminence.
In my fatherland Hitler is
a very popular man. I love many Germans
who will die when the Red Army marches in.
Presumably I too will be killed—and nevertheless . . .

CARDINAL: And nevertheless! Surely you are not a communist—
do you really want the Red Army to come?
Can't you imagine what will happen:
altars pillaged, priests murdered,
women ravished?

GERSTEIN *(brutally)*:
Yes, Your Eminence, there will be grim scenes.
Like an apocalypse. And yet—the wildest band of soldiers
cannot wreak more outrages in a convent's dormitory
than the atrocities that Hitler's lawyers, doctors and SS men
have been practicing—wearing this uniform—
for years against the Jews, the Poles, and Russian prisoners.
Your Eminence, surely you can confirm these facts:
Tens of thousands from Western Europe—
tens of thousands of Jewish families
are being deported. Where to, Your Eminence, where to?
What do people imagine here in Rome?

CARDINAL *(haplessly, because he has been "caught out")*:
Naturally, yes, of course—and *nevertheless,*
dear sir, the smoke of the crematoria
has blinded you to the fact that there must be
an alternative to conquest of the territories
by the Red Army—*must* be, for the sake
of the West, you know . . .
Perhaps a landing in Normandy may . . .
But Stalin's entry into Berlin, why, dear God,
that is a price that Europe *cannot,*
that Europe *dare not* pay!

GERSTEIN: Your Eminence, after Napoleon
had senselessly led the Grand Army to its ruin,

he fabricated—in conversation with Caulaincourt
who did not believe a word of it—the legend
of the Russian colossus which, he would have it,
was aiming to annihilate Europe.
Hitler exploited this legend, which Bismarck
and Frederick and William the Second as well
had only treated as a joke. Hitler resurrected this legend
when he invaded Russia
and every criminal in Europe who greedily
looks to the East will always in the future
claim he is saving civilization.
The Vatican should never support such lies, Your Eminence!

CARDINAL *(happy to be able to go off on this tangent):*
We hope for no profit from aggression, you know,
But you simplify, sir. Frederick of Prussia
truly feared the Russian colossus, and so did Bismarck.
And because the king—like Napoleon, like Hitler—
saw no other recourse, he himself
incited Russian ambitions to expand
westward. Like Napoleon, you know, and Hitler:
an offer to collaborate, you know,
over the despoiled countries.
It is always the same, as long as it goes well.
It *never* goes well long, you know.

GERSTEIN: But Russia has never threatened the West,
Your Eminence, as gravely
as Hitler and Napoleon threatened it.
Both would have subjugated all of Europe
had not their march to Moscow
brought Russia into the fight.
Europe has been saved by *Russia* and
can fend off this dangerous rescuer
only if it agrees to live with him.

CARDINAL: With the Bolshevists too?

GERSTEIN: With any master of the Kremlin—
whether his name is Alexander or Stalin . . .

CARDINAL: Easy to say, but hard to do, you know . . .

RICCARDO *and the* ABBOT *return through the wardrobe. The*
ABBOT *closes the doors again.*

GERSTEIN: It was always hard, Your Eminence.
    Even for Bismarck, it was a feat of balancing,
    yet he did not permit himself even the *thought*
    of a preventive war against St. Petersburg.
CARDINAL: The Chief himself, as well, has never
    called for a crusade against Russia.
    Riccardo, I understand your deep distress, you know.
    But now you've seen, up there,
    that the Holy See is doing what it can.
RICCARDO: Your Eminence, those are the lucky few,
    a handful among millions, who reach the gate
    of a monastery. And if the Pope
    grants them a hiding place, he only does
    what many private persons in Berlin and Amsterdam,
    in Paris and in Brussels, are doing for
    the persecuted. But, Your Eminence,
    the doctor or the businessman,
    the workingman who gives asylum to a Jew,
    risks beheading. What does the Pope risk?
CARDINAL *(striving to repress his irritation, which is rising again):*
    Riccardo—here, today, you know,
    arrests in *Rome,* that changes everything, indeed.
    The Chief will not speak as a bishop,
    as other bishops did, you know.
    But we are losing time, while outside
    the reign of terror rages . . .
    Would you not prefer, for your protection
    (he lays his hand on GERSTEIN's *shoulder)*
    to stay here in this house—
    don't you agree, Father General?
ABBOT: I can guarantee you our protection as long
    as no bombs fall upon the monastery.
GERSTEIN: Your Eminence—Monsignore—I'm deeply touched.
    But I have a family I cannot
    leave alone in Germany.
CARDINAL: God protect you, and your family as well!
    I thank you. Let us pray
    for the persecuted, you know . . . My
    dear friend, I'll find my way out alone
    with Brother Irenäeus. Please stay
    here with your guests . . . Till we meet again!

ABBOT, RICCARDO, GERSTEIN *(simultaneously):* Your Eminence.
CARDINAL: Good-bye.

Starts off with the MONK, *but turns around to say to* GERSTEIN *impulsively*:

> One more question in haste, dear sir.
> I ask not out of curiosity but despair, you know:
> London, Madrid and Stockholm,
> and a good many visitors who come here
> are prone to talk of a German
> rebellion against Hitler . . .
> What is there to it? Anything at all?

> ABBOT *signs to the* MONK *to withdraw.* MONK *goes out.*

GERSTEIN: Alas, Your Eminence, a few defenseless people—
> pastors, socialists, communists,
> Jehovah's Witnesses—yes. In September
> they hanged one hundred-eighty on a single day
> in Plötzensee. The women were beheaded . . .
> It is a hopeless struggle.
CARDINAL *(agitated, very sympathetic; this is the first time
> he has heard about it):* Women, you say? Women too!
> Oh Blessed Virgin aid them!
> What about the military? London speaks of
> generals, you know. Could these officers
> carry the people with them—the people
> who after all love their Herr Hitler?
GERSTEIN: Only if they proclaim that *Himmler*
> has assassinated the Führer! Then they could.
> The rage of the people must be turned
> against the SS and the police.
CARDINAL: Satanic, isn't it? Satanic, you know!
GERSTEIN: That is the only way, Your Eminence,
> that revolutionaries might conceivably
> seize the rudder. Conceivably.
> But I do not believe that army officers
> are ready to sacrifice themselves.
> Not the German but the *Russian* army
> will dispose of Hitler.

CARDINAL: Unless Hitler does it himself, you know.
But what a frightful situation . . . I
thank you. Good night, gentlemen,
good night.

The ABBOT *accompanies the* CARDINAL *to the door, on the other side of which the* MONK *reappears.* CARDINAL *goes out with him.* ABBOT *returns and says to* RICCARDO, *who is leaning against the wall with an air of hopelessness—*

ABBOT: I am of your opinion. This evil
had to fall upon Rome too. Hitler
will now discover what it costs
to provoke the Holy Father.

RICCARDO *does not reply at once.*

GERSTEIN: Monsignore, are you certain
that he will now intervene?
ABBOT: Absolutely. Aren't you, Riccardo?
RICCARDO: I am not so certain.
Suppose the Pope does what he always does—
I mean, does nothing. *(Passionately.)*
Father General, what will we do then?
ABBOT *(curtly)*: Obey. As we must. You know that!
RICCARDO *(defiantly)*:
That would be only too easy! Look at him—
a German officer. If he were not disobedient,
breaking his oath,
he would be a murderer. And what about us?
(Urgently, trying to persuade.)
You have saved the lives of hundreds, Father General.
ABBOT: The *Pope* gave me the means to do so.
Don't forget that, Riccardo!
RICCARDO: I do not forget it. But consider,
this rescue work has not imposed
the slightest sacrifice upon the Pope,
aside from the financial one,
nor even the merest shadow of a risk . . .
And you, as I know you,
cannot stand idly by when

tomorrow—right here—
they load the victims into cattle cars . . .

ABBOT: Good God—a priest cannot use firearms!

RICCARDO *(softly, almost to himself)*:
No, but he can go along. He can go with them.

GERSTEIN *(does not suspect how long this idea has preoccupied*
RICCARDO): That would be utterly senseless!

ABBOT: And would not save a single Jew, not one.

RICCARDO *(still to himself)*: No, not a Jew. But one's own
superiors. When I saw Provost Lichtenberg
in prison hospital he was tormented
by the fact that none of us is with the Jews.
I shall go with them, he said; the Nazis had
already given their permission. Then
they broke their word, as always,
and shipped him off to Dachau.
Now none of us is with the Jews.

GERSTEIN *(firmly)*:
This SS would never permit an Italian priest
to accompany the deportees.
That would be far too interesting a matter
for Allied propaganda.

RICCARDO: What if the priest himself is Jewish,
like the monks transported to the East
from Holland?

He looks at the clock, then says with a smile:

By now he's sure to be in Naples,
safe among Eisenhower's soldiers—
I mean the Jew with whom I switched
passports this morning. *(To* GERSTEIN.*)* And I still have
the star of David that your lodger gave me.
I'd need only to let myself be seen with that,
and I would be arrested.

GERSTEIN *(aghast)*: Riccardo—you would not be treated
as a priest. You would be gassed like any Jew!

ABBOT *(frightened and also vexed)*:
Burn the star and the passport.
You are simply courting disaster!

RICCARDO *(to change the subject)*:
 How do you explain the fact, Herr Gerstein,
 that your protegé Jacobson has never been heard from?
GERSTEIN: He was so embittered, after the death of his parents.
RICCARDO: But not against me, after all.
GERSTEIN *(shrugging)*: Perhaps they caught him anyhow,
 and killed him on the spot.
RICCARDO *(after glancing once more at the clock, firmly)*:
 Father General, please tell me—
 you *must* have some idea: What are we to do
 if the Pope does not protest?

  Silence. Helpless gesture on the ABBOT'S *part. Silence.*

RICCARDO *(while* GERSTEIN *looks at the map of missionary posts,
 in a tone close to scorn)*: Nothing? Nothing at all?
ABBOT *(hesitantly; he feels that he must suggest something)*:
 In individual cases, offer help—as we are doing now.
RICCARDO: And look on? No, Reverend Father, that is—
 that cannot be your final word. To look on
 idly when tomorrow morning
 our fellow citizens—do not forget,
 the ranks of Jews hold many Catholics too—
 are loaded aboard cattle cars.
 Are *we* to stand by and
 (he gives a sudden laugh) wave our handkerchiefs to them?
 That is, if the kind Germans permit.
 *(He laughs again; then, with rhetorical shifts of tone as his
 irony and his arguments rise to their climax.)*
 And then—then we go home?
 Confess—what should we confess?
 That we have used the name of God in vain!
 And sit down to some journal, to read about
 the excavations in St. Peter's?
 And then on Sunday we ring the bells
 and celebrate our Mass—so filled with sacred thoughts,
 that nothing, surely, tempts us to consider
 those who are that very moment in Auschwitz
 are being driven naked into the gas.
ABBOT *(wearily, desperately)*:
 God in Heaven—what remains for us to do!

  Silence. Then—

RICCARDO: Doing nothing is as bad as taking part.
    It is—I don't know—perhaps it is
    still less forgiveable.
    (Screams.) We are *priests!* God can forgive
    a hangman for such work, but not a priest,
    not the Pope!

  Silence. Then he speaks more calmly, calculatingly, objectively.

    Please, Father General, tell me this:
    If God once promised Abraham that he
    would not destroy Sodom if only
    ten righteous should live there—
    do you think, Reverend Father,
    that God might still forgive the Church
    if even a very few of her servants—
    like Lichtenberg—
    stand by the persecuted?
ABBOT *(surprised and disturbed, but sympathetic):*
    Many of us are doing all in our power.
    But I do not see what this question . . .
RICCARDO: You see as well as I, Father General.
    You must see that the silence of the Pope
    in favor of the murderers imposes
    a guilt upon the Church for which we must atone.
    And since the Pope, although only a man,
    can actually represent God on earth,
    I . . . a poor priest . . . if need be

GERSTEIN *understands and attempts to still him.* RICCARDO *goes on undeterred.*

    can also represent the Pope—*there*
    where the Pope ought to be standing today.
ABBOT *(more shocked than outraged):*
    Riccardo, I shall keep your—your accusation,
    which is monstrous, like a secret of the confessional.
    (To GERSTEIN, *who makes a gesture of assent.)*
    Sir, may I ask you to do the same . . .
    But I am frightened for you, Riccardo.
    What justifies your words, which ought to plunge
    each one of us into the depth of shame . . .

RICCARDO *(alarmed)*: No! For God's sake, no, Father General.
    You and so many other priests—so many
    have already died on the scaffold—you have
    fulfilled your duty. You have . . .
ABBOT *(sharply)*: And the *Pope* has not?
RICCARDO *(firmly)*: Not to the limit of his power! Perhaps
    this very night, maybe tomorrow, he will
    at last fulfill the obligation he
    has long since had as spokesman of Christendom.
    Otherwise—otherwise one of our number
    must go along from Rome.
    And if in doing so he dies . . .
GERSTEIN: Yes, he will die!
    He will be gassed and burned . . .
RICCARDO *(undeterred)*:
    Perhaps this flame which will extinguish him,
    if only God looks on this penance with His grace,
    perhaps . . .
ABBOT: Riccardo!
RICCARDO *(with intense emotion)*:
    . . . perhaps it will annihilate as well
    the guilt of our superior. The concept of the Papacy . . .
ABBOT *(vehemently)*: . . . will outlive Auschwitz! Why do you
    doubt?
    Why lacerate yourself so, Riccardo. It is arrogance.
RICCARDO: Auschwitz is not in question now. The concept
    of the Papacy must be preserved pure
    for all eternity, even if temporarily
    it is embodied by an Alexander VI,
    or by a . . .
ABBOT *(grips him almost brutally by the shoulder)*:
    Not another syllable. Why, that is—
    Do you know Pius XII so ill?
RICCARDO *(shaken)*: Father General, the portrait
    of Cardinal Pacelli has hung
    above my bed since I was twelve years old.
    On his account I entered the priesthood,
    much as my . . . my mother begged me not to.
    I will spend the rest of the night praying
    that I misjudged the Pope,

that by tomorrow evening he will have
had the arrested families released—I'll pray for that.
I am afraid *(very softly, almost inaudible)*—
I have such horror of the camp.

The ABBOT *walks up to him in a paternal gesture, while* GERSTEIN *steps between them with determination.*

GERSTEIN *(vigorously)*:
> Forsaking us will only make you guilty.
> Forget the salvation of the Church.
> You would no longer have it in your power
> to aid a single human being. Riccardo,
> you'd only take on greater guilt yourself!

RICCARDO *(with disgust)*: I would only be keeping my word.
> Here I cannot do a thing.
> I have been trying—for more than a year.
> It's all been empty talk.

ABBOT *(it is impossible to say whether he believes his own words)*:
> Tomorrow morning, Father, you will see
> it has not been in vain. The Pope will intercede.

RICCARDO *(points to the clock)*:
> He *knows* what has been happening in Rome!
> And *you* are his liaison with the Gestapo.
> Why has he not talked with you hours ago?

ABBOT *(uncerntainly)*:
> He will not want to deal with the Gestapo here in Rome,
> but negotiate with Hitler himself.
> I'm confident he will present him with an ultimatum.

Silence. Pacing. GERSTEIN *gives* RICCARDO *a long look. Then he says, hesitantly, cunningly—*

GERSTEIN: I still see one last chance, but—
> no, no, I do not dare to say it.

RICCARDO: Please, speak out!

GERSTEIN: Who am I to tempt two priests
> into disobedience . . . ? No, I do not dare . . .

ABBOT: What do you mean by that?

GERSTEIN: Monsignore, if you and Father Riccardo
> could only take over the Vatican radio
> for half an hour . . .

ABBOT *(suspiciously):* What is the meaning of "take over"?
  I have free access to our radio station.
GERSTEIN *(quickly; but it can be sensed that this is no sudden*
  inspiration on his part):
    Then, Monsignore, instruct all the priests
    of Europe to follow the example of
    the prelate Lichtenberg—and rally
    their parishes from Narvik to Sicily
    to act for the rescue of the Jews.
ABBOT *(vexed):* Do you suggest a priest take it upon himself
  to speak in the Pope's name?
RICCARDO: Yes, when the Pope forgets
  to speak out in the name of Christ!
ABBOT: But that is monstrous wickedness!
  Is a priest in the guise of Pontifex Maximus
  to command his brother priests in Europe
  ex cathedra to submit to martyrdom?
GERSTEIN: Moinsignore, it would never come to that.
RICCARDO: Certainly not. All Hitler's fronts are crumbling.
  He will take care not to challenge
  all Europe's Catholics over the Jewish issue.
  There are millions, millions upon millions of us
  in his army and his industries . . .
GERSTEIN: Yes, Monsignore, Hitler would draw back.
ABBOT: But, gentlemen, not for a day, not for a single day
  could you maintain the fiction
  that the Holy Father himself had imposed
  the duty of resistance upon Catholics.
  The Pope himself would deny it!
  (To GERSTEIN, *now more vexed than agitated.)*
  Sir, be realistic. Suppose some shock troops
  were today to seize the Berlin radio station,
  and offer peace to England and the United States,
  allegedly in Hitler's name. How long
  would Hitler put up with such a sham?
  Thirty minutes? A full hour?
GERSTEIN: Monsignore,
  I am thinking of the Pope; you talk of Hitler.
  Surely there is no parallel between them.
ABBOT *(offended):* Certainly not. But naturally
  both would at once issue denials.

GERSTEIN: Oh, I see. No, Hitler would have to be
  prevented from doing that. First eliminate him,
  then the radio broadcast saying: the SS
  has killed your Führer—so that
  the fury of the people . . .
ABBOT *(self-righteously, repelled—he is incapable of lies—and
  firmly):* You have proposed this once before,
  this diabolic plan. But we ecclesiastics
  have no way of preventing the Pope
  from issuing denials. A priest, sir,
  this is a point you might know,
  does not "prevent" the Pope from doing anything.
  Absurd!
GERSTEIN *(as casually as possible):*
  Of course not, Monsignore, even though
  any "preventing" of the Pope, of course,
  in this case too, would automatically
  be blamed on the SS by all the world,
  as long as the SS in Rome continues
  arresting victims for Auschwitz . . .
ABBOT *(rises, clearly signalizing the end of the conversation):*
  Please, sir, let's put an end to this discussion
  here and now! Surely you do not wish—here
  in this religious house—you do not wish
  to discuss acts of . . . of violence against
  His Holiness. That would be monstrous!
GERSTEIN *(seemingly offended):*
  Monsignore, what are you attributing to me?
ABBOT: I attribute nothing. Your remark suffices:
  that anything done to the Pop right now—
  I dare not press you to be more specific—
  would automatically be blamed on the SS.
GERSTEIN *(hastily):* But it never occurred to me
  to suggest the use of violence against the *person*
  of His Holiness . . . Monsignore!
ABBOT *(ironically):* I see—you did not mean that?
GERSTEIN *(has regained his composure):*
  But, after all, in order to prevent denials,
  a priest would only have to
  temporarily put out of action

the Vatican broadcasting equipment.
For that, I meant, Monsignore,
the whole world would naturally
place the blame upon the SS—
especially if such destruction
comes after a radio protest
supposedly by the Pope against the SS.
RICCARDO *(fascinated by* GERSTEIN's *plan, speaks as if he has just awakened):* Father General, at this moment
such an act could mean salvation for thousands,
for hundreds of thousands.
Their last chance for rescue.
ABBOT *(coldly):* You, Father Riccardo,
would have no access to the broadcasting equipment.
That reassures me. You are tired, nervous;
please, let us get some rest now.
I must also have some words with you alone.
GERSTEIN: Monsignore, let me thank you
and take my leave.
ABBOT *(conciliatorily):* Live with more caution . . . Do not take
offense at this advice from an old man
who means to pray for you although
he cannot follow you. God be with you.
GERSTEIN: Monsignore, I thank you most sincerely.
Father—good night.
RICCARDO: Come to our house early, before
my father goes to see the Pope at nine!

> *The* MONK *is at the door waiting for* GERSTEIN

GERSTEIN: Good night—I'll come around eight.
RICCARDO: Good night.

> GERSTEIN *goes out with the* MONK.

ABBOT *(after looking in silence for a moment at* RICCARDO*):*
I was simply terrified, Riccardo,
to send you out into the night
with that strange person. His eyes! He virtually
hypnotizes you. He is marked, this man—he wears the mark
of Cain. What is his name?
RICCARDO: His name does not concern us, Father General.

ABBOT *(not offended)*:
>   You are right, forgive me. You did not
>   want to leave with him, did you?

RICCARDO: No, because I have one more request of you.
>   And then I still must make confession.

ABBOT: First a request from me: I am shocked
>   to see that you are wax in the hands
>   of this strange envoy, Father.
>   Be on your guard with him, I beg you.

RICCARDO: No need—don't be concerned.

ABBOT: Riccardo, this is a man who would be capable . . .
>   *(Extremely agitated.)* Why, I ask you, *why* did he twice,
>   needlessly, altogether without cause,
>   propose that diabolic treachery:
>   assassinating Hitler—and blaming the SS.

RICCARDO: A highly moral plan.

ABBOT *(with violent indignation)*:
>   A plan to lead to civil war! "Moral"—come now.
>   You are exhausted, Riccardo.
>   But that is not the issue for me, my boy,
>   nor is it for *him* either. The man is sinister,
>   believe me. I watched him closely and I tell you,
>   he had his reasons for voicing that idea to us.
>   *(His repugnance grows the more he thinks the matter
>   through.)*
>   Riccardo, that man has the power
>   to doom you, along with him, to hell
>   by suggesting to you—
>   more with his eyes than with his words—
>   that—I—I cannot say it outright,
>   it is so horrible . . . so . . .

RICCARDO *(still inhibited about uttering the truth)*:
>   *He* suggests nothing to me, Father General.

ABBOT: He does, he does!
>   He sowed in you the thought that the whole world,
>   all of mankind, could be lashed
>   to a ferocity of rage against Hitler
>   if Hitler's personal troops, the SS
>   could be accused of—of killing,
>   *(He repeats almost in a whisper.)*
>   of killing the *Deputy of Christ.*

RICCARDO *(groans, and in his agitation mentions* GERSTEIN's
name, although the ABBOT does not notice):
You are reading thoughts, Reverend Father—but . . .
they are *not* Gerstein's thoughts.
ABBOT *(so repelled that he cannot control his voice; he whispers
as he turns away abruptly):* Riccardo—what—I can think
of nothing more to say to you. Go.
(Silence. Then, with fervor.)
You do not know, you do not *know*
what you are saying . . . Come to the chapel.
You wanted to confess. You *must.*

*With trembling hands he lights a three-armed candelabra, then puts
out the desk lamp, takes the candelabra and starts to lead the way,
until he realizes that* RICCARDO *is not following him. The room is
now illuminated only by the candles.*

ABBOT: Why aren't you coming, Riccardo?
RICCARDO: I cannot. I cannot confess now.
You would have to refuse me absolution,
for I cannot *repent.*
Please understand me, Father General.
For the past three months, ever since Rome
has been occupied by the Germans, I have hoped
that at last the SS and the Vatican
would come together in a bloody clash.
Instead the most ghastly thing of all
is happening—they are not even
jarring one another.
They live together, harmoniously,
in the Eternal City—because the Pope
does not forbid the murderers of Auschwitz
to herd their victims into trucks
beneath his very windows.
(With madness in his eyes.)
How do we know if God has not
sent an assassin to the Pope only because He wants to
save him from—complete perdition?
ABBOT *(utterly uncomprehending, no longer capable of reaction):*
Riccardo—there is no limit to the sin
you have assumed.

RICCARDO *(as if obsessed):* He who said, I bring not
    peace but the sword
    (firmly) must have known there would be a time
    when the sword would strike the First of His own.
    The Church must know that, too,
    since she has always used the sword.
    (Tormentedly.) Am I to stand back from the struggle,
    Reverend Father? Do not resist the evil one—
    suppose we have been given this command
    because he is destroying us?
    No soldier is permitted to preserve his life—
    why then a priest?
    Could Judas have refused to play his role? He *knew*
    (with intense fear for his own conclusions)
    he would be damned for all eternity.
    His sacrifice was greater than the Lord's.

ABBOT *(crushingly):* Riccardo—you had better not compare
    yourself with Judas.
    For you want to commit your crime
    and shift the blame to others.

RICCARDO *(with wild passion):*
    Not *I!* Everyone, the whole earth
    would accuse Hitler and the SS.
    And it must be so. It must be.
    I myself would still atone
    on earth and before God.

ABBOT: Though you stumble, God still sustains you.
    Would you otherwise have opened your heart to me?

RICCARDO *(is matter-of-fact and nevertheless fanatical. The* ABBOT
    listens only because he is incapable of saying anything more):
    Because I cannot do the thing alone!
    Because I need you. You must announce over the radio
    that the SS took action
    because the Pope wanted to save the Jews.
    Once our radio has announced this news,
    once it has spread from Iceland to Australia,
    then for the remainder of his days
    Hitler would stand before the world
    as the adversary of the Creation
    which he is, as the greatest abomination.

No one, no Goebbels and no Cardinal,
could credibly repudiate the charge
before the fires were extinguished
in all the crematoria of Auschwitz.

He falls to his knees before the ABBOT.

Help me, Reverend Father.
You must help me.
ABBOT *(with icy horror):* Let me be—go.
You said the word—abomination,
the word applies to *you.*
Repent—begone—out of my sight—
or come to confession.
RICCARDO *(screams):* I cannot do it without you!
(Rising, making a last frenzied effort.)
If you won't help me, Father General,
then I must pray for you as well . . .
ABBOT: Go, go now,
if you persist in this criminal madness.
Go, this instant!

(He has turned his back on RICCARDO. *He gasps.)*
Go—get out—murderer!

RICCARDO *goes out. The door remains open. The candles flicker
wildly; then the draft blows them out. The* ABBOT *falls to his knees
on the prie-dieu.*

CURTAIN

Act 4: Il Gran Rifiuto

And I, who was gazing, saw a banner, that whirling ran
so swiftly that it seemed to me to scorn all repose, and
behind it came so long a train of folk, that I could never
have believed death had undone so many. After I had
distinguished some among them, I saw and knew the
shade of him who made, through cowardice, the great
refusal.
DANTE, *Inferno, Canto 3*

In the Papal Palace. A small, almost empty throne room which is often used as an intimate audience hall and as a place for discussions of business matters. It is draped in scarlet, the color of cardinals' robes, which, as is well known, are meant to symbolize readiness to suffer for the faith "even to the shedding of one's own blood." The POPE *wears white, of course. His cassock is as white as the dove with the olive branch in his coat-of-arms. This coat-of-arms, with tiara and the two crossed keys, is woven into the tapestry above the golden throne.*

The tapestry extends to the canopy, which hangs too high above the throne to be visible on the set. To both sides of the slightly elevated throne are tall, narrow doors, likewise hung with red and gold. On the wall at left is a baroque console table with astronomical clock and writing materials. Above hangs a large crucifix bound in brass. Several gold hassocks along the walls. No guards.

The CARDINAL *is conversing with* FONTANA, SR.

Count FONTANA, *a briefcase under his arm, is wearing the Order of Christ on the lapel of his tailcoat. His Eminence, although he is at home here, is more impersonal than he was on the occasion of his visits to* FONTANA's *house and to the monastery; he is quieter and more sparing of word and gesture.*

CARDINAL *(plaintively)*: At any rate, you know, it was not
    until September that Herr Hitler after all . . .
FONTANA: Ah yes, just recently . . .
CARDINAL: Exactly!
    He informed the Chief in confidence
    that he regarded bombers as the same
    as any other weapon, you know. He said
    the government of the German Reich
    had first applied this weapon, and hoped
    soon to retaliate with utmost force
    against the present Allied counterblow.
    Well, we will see, you know.
FONTANA: Naturally his pride prevented Hitler
    from asking the Pope to plead for him at the White House.
CARDINAL *(with some malice)*:
    But the Chief is so miffed, you know—
    he always is whenever his services
    as mediator are rejected.

He is so fond of writing letters to
Mr. Roosevelt with nothing in them, you know.
FONTANA *(impetuously):*
He should write to *Hitler*, Your Eminence!
Outrageous—what that scoundrel dares to do
to the Jews—even here in Rome.
CARDINAL: Do you think Herr Hitler has any idea
how that rabble of his are behaving here?
We shall also be discussing that today.
I have prayed for the Jews . . .
FONTANA *(coldly):* At least it saves our honor that the Pope
has protested at last. I heard about it
early this morning from the confidant
my son has in the SS.
CARDINAL *(extremely surprised, in fact alarmed):*
Protested? Out of the question.
The Chief most certainly did not protest, Count!
Here he comes, No, I know nothing about it.
FONTANA *(surprised and disturbed):*
But he did! This morning he . . .

The CARDINAL *and* FONTANA *have spoken these last words in a
whisper, for the right-hand wing of the double door has just been
noiselessly opened by a Swiss Guard. The* POPE *enters swiftly and
without speaking, and the door is closed again. At first His Holiness
appears only as an intense white gleam. He stands before the two
men, who bend their right knees and kiss the ring. The* CARDINAL
rises first; the POPE *graciously raises the Count to his feet and draws
him close and still closer to his cold, smiling face. After the Holy
Father's first words—he begins discussing affairs with out pream-
ble—*FONTANA *gradually withdraws a few steps. His Holiness more
and more turns to the Count, finally speaking almost exclusively to
him. After a while he seats himself on the throne, and cleans his
glasses while sitting there. When the* POPE *is seated, the* CARDINAL
*steps over to his left side. The actor who plays Pacelli should con-
sider that His Holiness is much less a person than an institution:
grand gestures, lively movements of his extraordinarily beautiful
hands, and smiling, aristocratic coldness, together with the icy glint
of his eyes behind the gold-rimmed glasses—these should suffice.
The rest should be largely conveyed by the uncommon, elevated*

language of the Pontiff. Pacelli is at this point sixty-eight, by no means an old man, and at the peak of his powers.

POPE: Dear Fontana! We are pleased to receive you, to hear your
    advice and that of Our venerable brother as well—for
    We are filled with burning concern for Italy's factories.
    Power plants, railroad terminals, dams, indeed every enterprise
    stands in imperative need of protection.
    Naturally We assess the chances of Our pleas being heard
    most realistically, where factories and mines are concerned.
    How different the situation of Our Eternal City:
    no one will dare to sin against Rome once more!
    Herr Weizsäcker has been so obliging and has requested
    Marshal Kesselring to reduce the German garrison
    down to some thousand men. Indeed, the Germans, one must concede,
    have on this point shown far more friendliness
    than the destroyers of San Lorenzo.
    But even the White House will now be chary
    of provoking Us once more. We have declared
    with utmost firmness that We, as bishop of this city,
    as spokesman for five hundred million Catholics
    who look toward Saint Peter
    will protest vigorously—and without delay.
    (Plaintively.)
    Yet the bombing of armaments plants
    is legitimate by the laws of war!
    You have recommended to Us, Count Fontana,
    that We invite the men around Roosevelt,
    industrialists and generals in the U.S. . . .

FONTANA: And also in London, Your Holiness.

POPE: Yes, very well—to purchase securities.
    But how will you persuade influential financiers, Count,
    to take shares in Italy's industries
    which are in such peril?

FONTANA: Good securities, the best we have,
    are as desirable as ever, Your Holiness.
    I am thinking principally of securities held
    by the Society of Jesus, which . . .

POPE *(as if fending off a physical danger)*:
 No, my dear Count, oh no—no!
 We do not wish to court
 any new conflict with the Jesuits. No, how fruitless.
CARDINAL: Heaven forbid, the Order of Jesus—you know!
 Why does it conceal its books from us!
 Eight thousand *patres* in America are refractory, you know.
POPE *(instantly placatory)*:
 Only as far as money is concerned.
 Otherwise they are devoted servants of our cause.
 The Lord preserve us from overlooking that, Your Eminence.
CARDINAL *(respectfully)*: Yes, otherwise, of course, certainly.
 And they are not stingy, you know.
 The diocese in New York alone—that one diocese
 contributes more to the Holy See than all
 the remainder of the West taken together, you know.
 But that they still refuse to show their books!
POPE *(astringently)*: We'll see those books yet, Eminence.
FONTANA *(smiling as he takes two checks from his briefcase)*:
 Your Holiness, there is no need to be ungrateful
 to the Jesuits, the Order my son belongs to.
 One of these two checks
 I have the pleasure of presenting to your Holiness
 in fact comes from the Order of Jesus—a sum

He hands the two checks to the POPE *who removes his glasses to read the figures.*

 which may well allay His Eminence's anger
 at the independent manner of those *patres.*
CARDINAL *(laughing, extremely curious to see the checks)*:
 Do I seem so implacable?
POPE *(expressionlessly returns the checks to* FONTANA. FONTANA
 hands him a pen and holds out the briefcase, on which the
 POPE *signs the checks, then passes them on to the*
 CARDINAL*)*:
 Dear Count—Eminence, will you both give the donors
 in Our name Our thanks for this Peter's pence.
CARDINAL *(who has added up the sums at a glance, looks at the*
 POPE *and then at* FONTANA*)*:
 Oh yes! Why, that comes to . . . really, you know!
 I shall thank Brother Spellman.

He returns the checks to FONTANA, *who replaces them in his brief-case.*

FONTANA *(insisting):* Something *must* be done, Your Holiness.
    Otherwise the Order's mines
    in Tuscany will be bombed.
    I must be permitted to ask the Jesuits
    to sell securities of Idria and Monte Amiata . . .
POPE: At a loss?
FONTANA: Not at a loss. The *patres*, after all,
    acquired the securities mostly at face value;
    they will still realize a profit.
POPE: Try it! You may try, Fontana.
    For Our feelings go out toward
    the families of the proletarians
    whom the destruction of the factories,
    and, above all, of the mines,
    would reduce to even greater poverty
    and still worse, radicalism—
    they would become anarchists—dreadful to conceive.
CARDINAL *(sincerely bothered):*
    Ah yes, you know—now, after the fall
    of Mussolini, who after all acted as a check
    to Communism and a guarantor
    of social order, a vacuum
    has certainly arisen, one that
    fills me with great anxiety, you know.
    Thank God the Germans are still in the country;
    they won't permit a strike or indolence, you know.
    But what will happen when their troops withdraw?
POPE: Then we shall have Americans here, Eminence.
    We intend to receive the President's envoy
    this afternoon. But unfortunately
    Mr. Taylor in his interviews with Us
    keeps reverting to Mr. Roosevelt's plea
    that we condemn Hitler's atrocities.
    It was not the Germans who bombed San Lorenzo!
    The Germans saved every book and every parchment
    from Monte Cassino and brought them
    safely to the Castle of St. Angelo.

(Fretfully.) Then Mr. Roosevelt's bombers came along
and reduced that place of peace to dust and rubble.
All the more *tactless* of the Germans now
to carry off the Jews of Rome as well.
(With great indignation.)
Have you heard about that, Count . . . Eminence?
It is extremely bad behavior!

FONTANA: Rome is shocked, Your Holiness.

CARDINAL: Yes, a wicked outrage, you know!

FONTANA: Permit me, Your Holiness—on behalf also
of those Israelites who have sought refuge
in my house, to express
most heartfelt gratitude for . . .

POPE *(full of kindliness, with spontaneous cordiality):*
Why, my dear Fontana, it is only natural
that We will do
all in the power
that God has given Us to aid, as always,
the unfortunates.

FONTANA: It is a veritable *salvation* that
Your Holiness has now so vigorously
threatened to take a public stand.
May I ask in all humility
whether the German City Commandant
has in any way reacted yet?

The POPE *looks at the* CARDINAL *with suspicion and incomprehension, then at* FONTANA.

CARDINAL: The German commandant? Reacted to what?

POPE *(suspiciously):* Reacted? But to what, Count?

FONTANA *(rather uncertainly; he already suspects what is to
follow):* Why, I heard from my son, you see,
that early this morning Bishop Hudal
warned the German commandant
that Your Holiness would make a *protest*,
for the first time since the beginning of the war.

POPE *(sharply):* The Bishop warned? In Our name!
Your Eminence, did you empower Hudal
to speak in the name of the Holy See
or even in Our name?

CARDINAL: God is my witness, Your Holiness!
    I have just this moment heard about the protest
    for the first time from the Count here.
    I will not, cannot believe, you know . . .
FONTANA *(nervously)*:
    I do not know the wording! Perhaps the Bishop
    did not make a protest *in the name*
    of His Holiness, but only announced
    that a statement from the Holy Father
    was to be expected. My son says . . .
POPE *(very angrily)*: Your son, Count Fontana—where
    is your son? Does he not belong in Lisbon?
CARDINAL *(alarmed, dutifully)*:
    The Minutante is expecting me downstairs,
    in the Secretariat of State, Your Holiness.
POPE *(extremely annoyed)*:
    Have him come up! We wish to be informed
    how it is he ventures,
    as a member of our Foreign Office,
    constantly to interfere in these affairs.
    The Jews and the Germans
    are matters for the two Jesuit fathers
    whom We have specially appointed for that purpose.

The CARDINAL *instantly goes to the door and whispers a command to one of the Swiss Guards. Confronted with the* POPE's *rage, his obedience goes so far that he now puts on a stony face toward* FONTANA.

FONTANA: Your Holiness, I ask forgiveness for my son.
    His zeal is desperation. He was
    an eyewitness in Berlin when the Nazis
    threw Jewish children on to trucks . . .
POPE *(angrily waves that aside; he now speaks naturally and*
    impulsively): Eyewitness! Count, a diplomat
    must see many things and hold his peace.
    Your son has no discipline.
    As long ago as July of last year
    the Nuncio in Pressburg learned
    that Jews from Slovakia were being gassed
    in the district of Lublin. Has he

run away from Pressburg for that reason?
No, he goes on doing his duty, and behold:
he managed to arrange that no more Jews
are being sent away to Poland.
Whoever wants to help must not
provoke Hitler.
Secretly, as our two Jesuit fathers,
silently, cunning as serpents—
that is how the SS must be met.
We have hidden hundreds of Jews in Rome.
Have issued thousands of passports!
Herr Hitler is no longer dangerous.
In Portugal and Sweden they are saying
that he is talking peace with Stalin. We are glad
to hear such rumors because We know
that there is nothing to them, but they may,
We hope, persuade the White House and Downing Street
to be somewhat readier for compromise.
They ought to negotiate, ought not
to play vabanque with all of Europe
and make Stalin into the heir of Hitler.
We leave it to the local parish priest
to use his own discretion on the spot
and to decide what measures of reprisal
to expect in the event there is a pastoral protest.
Even if We keep silent, dear Count,
We do so *also*
ad maioram mala vitanda.

FONTANA *(in agitation):* But after all, the Nuncio of His Holiness
in Pressburg did succeed in saving, by his protest,
the lives of countless victims,
without incurring the reprisals of the murderers.

POPE: Remember Our last Christmas message:
one single plea for brotherly love.
What was the end result? The murderers ignored it.

FONTANA: Your Holiness, I too was sadly disappointed
that it remained without effect.
However, in that message Your Holiness
did not, unfortunately, mention the Jews
expressis verbis—nor, I might add,

the terror bombing of open cities.
It seems to me that anything addressed
to Hitler and to Churchill requires
words so blunt as not to be misunderstood.

The POPE *impatiently turns from* FONTANA *to* RICCARDO *who has entered.*

POPE *(more friendly, smiling):* Your son! There he is, the hothead.

RICCARDO *is constrained because he assumes that the* POPE *has issued his protest after all, and therefore feels that he gravely misunderstood him last night. He kisses the ring. The* POPE *smiles.*

RICCARDO: Holy Father . . .

He bows to the CARDINAL, *who coldly refers him to the* POPE.

POPE: We are delighted with you, Riccardo.
and contemplate your zeal with affection. He who
defends the persecuted, always speaks as We would wish.
But—We have just heard with dismay
that you or Bishop Hudal in Our name
has protested the arrest of the Jews. Is that so?
Eminence—please send for the Father General.

CARDINAL, *at the door, gives a command to the Swiss Guard.*

RICCARDO *(still not understanding, very politely):*
I? No, Your Holiness, I heard
from my liason man in the SS
that Your Holiness through Bishop Hudal
has threatened to protest.
POPE *(angered):* What have you arrogated to yourself—
to conspire with the SS?
CARDINAL *(malignantly):*
The Holy Father, you know, has just heard
the first word of his alleged statement.
POPE: I am speaking to him, Eminence!
RICCARDO *(crushed, turns to his father, but does not lower his
voice):* So—after all—nothing whatsoever has been done!
(He still cannot believe it.)
But Your Holiness did threaten a protest.
I do not understand . . .

*(However, he has understood; he says passionately, almost
crying out.)*
Your Holiness, the Jews are being shipped out, murdered.
CARDINAL: Be still!
POPE *(smiling):* Why, no, Your Eminence . . . God bless you,
    Riccardo. Speak, your heart is good.
    Only you must not negotiate with the SS.
    The Father General will tell us what has happened.
    Hold yourself back!
    At your age modesty alone
    honors one.
RICCARDO: I am not concerned about my honor,
    Your Holiness.
    I am concerned for the honor of the Holy See,
    for that is dear to me . . .
FONTANA: Riccardo!

The POPE *remains silent; the* CARDINAL *answers swiftly for him.*

CARDINAL: Aha, he is concerned for the honor of the Curia!
    And have you never heard that we
    have set up whole bureaus,
    offices and committees,
    solely in order to help, to rescue—why, you know,
    it seems to me that we have several times
    discussed that very matter, haven't we?
RICCARDO *(more and more losing his self-control):*
    Such assistance reaches only some Jews in Italy,
    Your Eminence. That too has been discussed
    often enough. *(He now turns to the* POPE.*)*
    But the terror rages in the other countries!
    In Poland alone
    one million eight hundred thousand Jews
    have already been slaughtered! Since that figure,
    Your Holiness, was confirmed last July,
    and officially communicated
    by the Polish ambassador in Washington
    to the Papal Legate there—God cannot wish
    Your Holiness to ignore it!
CARDINAL *(indignantly):* Leave at once!
    What language in the Holy Father's presence!
    Count, say something to your son . . .

During Riccardo's *last words the* Pope *had risen, but he sits down again. A moment passes before he is able to speak, with utmost effort.*

Pope: "Ignore!" We do not intend to account for Our actions
to Riccardo Fontana—does his father make no comment?
Nevertheless, We would be pleased if We might also
be permitted to speak a word on the matter.
(With mounting bitterness, attempting to change the subject.)
Do you know, for example, my young man,
that weeks ago we were already prepared
to help the Jews of Rome, who were threatened with arrest,
out of their predicament with gold, considerable gold.
Hitler's bandits offered the Jews freedom
for a ransom.
They attempted to extort from Us a sum
that was no longer realistic.
Nevertheless we would have paid it!
Riccardo *(has turned, aghast, to his father; now speaks softly
to the* Pope): Then Your Holiness has already known—
for weeks—
what the SS here intended to do to the Jews?
Pope *(agitated, evasively):* What are you saying!
Father General can bear witness to
all that has already been accomplished.
The monasteries stand open . . .

The Father General has entered. The Pope *turns quickly toward him. Monsignore kneels, kisses the ring, bows to the* Cardinal, *and is promptly drawn into the conversation. The* Cardinal *avoids looking at* Riccardo, *who has gone over to stand beside his father. Before the Swiss Guard withdraws, the* Cardinal *claps his hands and has four hassocks brought from their places along the walls and grouped around the* Pope. *The* Cardinal *sits down, and his example is followed by old* Fontana, *who is intensely nervous and worn out.*

Pope *(coldly to the* Abbot):
Father General, please inform Us
what Bishop Hudal has done in Our name
about the arrest of the Jews.
Did he conceive this praiseworthy idea himself?

ABBOT: Herr von Kessel at the German Embassy
    called on me secretly at dawn and asked
    that His Excellency, the Bishop, threaten
    the German commandant with
    a forthcoming protest from Your Holiness.

POPE *(pleased, relieved)*:
    Well, well! A German does that—how gratifying.
    What times these are, when high treason is
    the last weapon of the righteous! A German
    is ashamed of the SS! Well—Kessel is the man's name.
    We will remember it. Now, then, this letter
    from the Bishop will do its work and save
    whatever there is left to be saved.

RICCARDO *(with the bluntness of one who has already lost
    everything)*: That letter will save nothing at all,
    Your Holiness. Only you yourself . . .

FONTANA *(steps between* RICCARDO *and the* POPE*)*:
    May I speak in my son's stead, Your Holiness?

POPE: What is it, Count?

FONTANA: Your Holiness, may I ask in all humility:
    Warn Hitler that you will *compel*
    five hundred million Catholics to
    make Christian protest
    if he goes on with these mass killings!

POPE *(senses that he must answer this seasoned adviser to the point.
    He is embarrassed, vexed; he speaks as if he has frequently
    explained the matter, and nevertheless he overcomes his
    irritation to the point of going up to* FONTANA *and placing a
    hand on his shoulder)*:
    Fontana! An advisor of your insight! How bitter
    that you too misunderstand Us. Do you not see
    that disaster looms for Christian Europe
    unless God makes Us, the Holy See,
    the *mediator?*
    The hour is dark. To be sure We know
    they will not touch the Vatican.
    (Hitler has only recently renewed his guarantee.)
    But what of Our ships out in the world, which We must steer?
    Poland, all of the Balkans, even Austria and Bavaria?
    Into whose harbors will they sail?

They may easily be shattered by the storms,
or else drift helplessly to land on Stalin's shores.
Germany today *is* Hitler. They are visionaries
who maintain that overthrow of the present regime
in Germany
would not result in the collapse of the front.
We expect less than nothing from
Hitler's generals who want to dispose of him.
They wanted to act as far back as the spring
of nineteen-forty.
And how did they act?
They let Hitler pin decorations on them
and smashed all of Europe into kindling wood.
We know that manner of men from Our own days in Berlin.
The generals themselves have no opinions.
When Hitler falls, they will all go home . . .

CARDINAL: And Stalin would then have an open road
to Warsaw, Prague, Vienna—even to the Rhine, you know.

POPE *(has sat down again):*
Do you think the President realizes that?
Stalin will not even talk about him.
Since Casablanca reason alone
no longer wields the scepter in the White House.
And Mr. Churchill is too weak. Moreover,
he too seems unwilling to establish
a second front in the West. He is pleased
if the Russians thoroughly exhaust themselves
against the Germans,
and the Germans against the Russians.

CARDINAL: We too would not be averse to that, you know.

POPE *(at every word pounding the arm of the throne):*
Hitler alone, dear Count, is now defending Europe.
And he will fight until he dies
because no pardon awaits the murderer.
Nevertheless, the West *should* grant him pardon
as long as he is useful in the East.
In March We publicly declared that We
have nothing, nothing at all, to do with the aims
of Great Britain and the United States.
Let them first come to an accommodation with Germany.

Unfortunately the Spanish Foreign Minister
proclaimed that view for all the world to hear.
However that may be: reasons of state forbid
our pillorying Herr Hitler as a bandit.
We have no choice.
Hitler's secret service here in Rome
has told the Father General of the Jesuit Order—
a pity, Signor Minutante, that you
know nothing of the efforts of your Chief . . .

RICCARDO: I know of that, Your Holiness.
But I cannot understand
how we so much as consider
using Hitler as a tool.

POPE: A tool that we will drop
as soon as possible . . .

CARDINAL: God be praised, Signor Minutante,
that you have no authority at all.

RICCARDO *(with hostility)*:
The Holy Father was addressing me, Your Eminence!
May I reply, Your Holiness?

POPE *(coldly)*: To the point, yes, to the point. To the point.

RICCARDO *(rushing ahead, with the sole result that nothing he
says makes any real impression)*:
Your Holiness, let me remind you that
for years we Jesuits have had in training
specialists for Russia whose mission is
to follow after Hitler, that is, the German army,
and preach the Faith among the Russians.

CARDINAL *(indignantly)*: Well—what of it? Would you, Signor
Minutante,
have known before Hitler attacked
that Stalin could hold out so long?

RICCARDO *(continuing to address the* POPE*)*:
Moreover, the remarks of many bishops
about this so-called crusade of Hitler
are—sheer blasphemies.
The Vatican must also share the guilt,
Your Holiness, if now the red storm
approaches Europe. Who sows the wind . . .
Russia was after all attacked!

The POPE *makes two uneasy gestures. He remains silent, either because he is so agitated that, as before, he cannot speak, or because he considers it beneath his dignity to reply.*

CARDINAL *(immediately after* RICCARDO *has spoken):*
 Your Holiness, please break off this conversation!
 Outrageous what the Minutante . . .
 (To RICCARDO.*)* I always thought you talented, you know.
 But we have precious little use
 for argumentative debaters in the Secretariat.
 You talk like—like a London newspaper, you know.
POPE *(his voice sounds as if it were coated with rust; then*
 with caustic irony): Count Fontana, it seems to Us your son
 is badly in need of a vacation.
FONTANA: Your Holiness, what Riccardo
 learned in Berlin from the arrested provost,
 Lichtenberg, and what he saw for himself . . .
POPE *(sarcastically, but still quivering with outrage):*
 Ah yes, we are concerned for him—Riccardo,
 you go to Castelgandolfo for three months,
 and catalogue our library—if your nerves
 are up to such a task. Above all take walks,
 go tramping for hours, and contemplate
 the Campagna and the water.
 A morning at Lake Albano soothes the spirit.
 The cool clarity of October days
 and the broad prospect out to sea provide
 many an insight into one's soul . . .
 Go right out there this very day.
 We gladly give you leave.
CARDINAL: Yes, you know, and very little reading,
 so that you spare your nerves. But read,
 I'd suggest, Ferrero's new masterpiece
 on the Congress of Vienna—disturbingly topical!
 (Seriously, to the POPE; *he becomes rather loquacious in his*
 effort to save the situation.)
 Those gentlemen in the Foreign Office and Washington
 should be set to reading it like schoolboys,
 you know. For *that* is what they must preserve
 in Germany, after all—a person

like Talleyrand. He, too, like everyone
who served Napoleon, had blood on his hands.
But nevertheless he was accepted as
a partner in negotiation. The way in which he, in Vienna,
split France's enemies, the Allies of those days,
and secretly ranged Austria and England
against Tsar Alexander:
this surely is his wisest counsel to our time.
Moreover—allow me, dear Minutante,
to enlighten you a bit, since
you are so concerned about the welfare of the Kremlin—
Russia also benefited by
restraint upon her craving to expand!
The peace of Europe lasted for decades.
The balance of power lasted for a century.

RICCARDO *(bows to the* CARDINAL *with barely perceptible irony.)*

POPE *(as though the Fontanas were no longer in the room; he
speaks with spontaneous ease, delighted to have another
subject)*: Yes, Eminence, those were indeed true diplomats,
there, at the Congress of Vienna! When we compare
their wisdom with the Casablanca formula,
that primitive unconditional surrender!
All that the Allies gain by that
is to force the poor Germans to identify
even more intensely than before
with that wretched Hitler of theirs.
Why don't the Allies proclaim they will make peace
as soon as Herr Hitler is eliminated?
That would be a basis permitting Us as well
to denounce Herr Hitler without necessarily
directing Our protest against Germany.
The Germans, if not Herr Hitler, must remain
acceptable partners in negotiations!

CARDINAL: Yes, Your Holiness, I have no doubt
that even a German Talleyrand might be found.
For example, Herr von Hassell, or . . .

ABBOT: The Allies will not deal even with *him,* Your Eminence.
The Germans have incurred far too much hatred.

POPE: Quite right, Father General—yet all the same
in Europe there can be no peace without the Reich

as central bulwark of the Continent,
holding East and West sufficiently far apart.
Great lords remain good friends
only when their lands do not adjoin.

CARDINAL: Yes, if the Reich is simply divided up,
as so much booty, you know,
the consequences would be the same
as the partition of Poland between Hitler and Stalin,
or as the Peace of Tilsit in 1807.
The seeds of a new war would be sown.

POPE: Exactly what We always tell the President's
Envoy, Eminence!
Herr Hitler must not be disposed of
unless the Reich survives his downfall
as a buffer state between the East and West,
a *small* but independent military power,
not strong but strong enough so that
it cannot be completely occupied
and torn to pieces.

CARDINAL: But the way the Germans are behaving now—
carrying off Catholics too, you know—
such impertinence should teach a lesson:
the Germans must be kept upon their knees!

FONTANA *(bitterly):* For decades, Your Eminence—forever.
The Germans must be kept on their knees forever.

CARDINAL *(coolly to* FONTANA. *His first sentence is addressed to*
RICCARDO, *whose mother was German, as all those present*
know. As he talks, he works himself up):
Why, you know, Protestantism—I mean,
megalomania—and good music:
these are their gifts to the world;
they must be taken in small doses,
or else we'll have them on our necks again, you know.
If the sole outcome of their war against Moscow
should be that the Russians march all the way
to . . . to Silesia and Stettin—
and now it very nearly looks that way—
the Germans will have lost the right
ever again to carry arms.
If that turns out to be the case, we should,

you know, do what was done during the days
before Bismarck, their barbare de génie:
allow them no more guns than they would need
to let each others' blood
while they indulge their passion
for war and slaughter.
For several thousand years, you know, that's been
their chief amusement, and Europe has
come off pretty well, you know . . .

POPE *(impatiently)*:

Tempi passati, Eminence. Very long past.
Certainly the terror against Jews is loathsome,
but we must not allow it to incense Us so
that We forget the duties that devolve
upon the Germans for the immediate future
as the present protectors and rulers of Rome.
Moreover, Germany must remain viable
not only to hold the frontiers against the East,
but also to hold the balance of power.
The balance of the Continent is more important
than its unity which hardly corresponds
to Europe's ancient national traditions.
Very seldom indeed has God guided the rivers of Europe
into a single bed or in a single direction.
When he did, the stream swelled to a raging torrent
flooding and washing away the older orders.
So it has been under Philip, under Napoleon, under Hitler.
No, let each land have its own river,
its own direction, to confine it and keep it within its confines.
That is the sounder pattern, more easily controllable.
Alliances, yes, but no unity.
We wonder indeed what God may have intended
when in the winter of nineteen thirty-nine
He prevented England and France, as they had planned,
from coming to Finland's aid in the war against Russia.
The plans were made but came to nothing.
Those days, so little noticed, settled the fortunes of the world.
France and England allied against Stalin—
that would have brought Hitler—who even then knew
he would break with Russia—to Britain's side.

The Continent, under Hitler's leadership,
would have emerged united from the struggle.
Great Britain would have kept her empire.
Why did God not wish it so?
Why did He permit it to come to this:
the West now rending itself asunder?
For a long time We failed to perceive its meaning—
however, now we know:
had Hitler triumphed, he would have crushed
everything, everything including Ourselves. It will be
just barely tolerable if he merely survives.
So that this hour too was God's hour.
The Lord had made his decision for Our salvation.
God be praised . . . We must now end this audience.
Our beloved congregation is awaiting Us.
We wish to further the canonization
of Innocent the Eleventh. It is indeed
a matter of great concern to Us to bring
that noble predecessor once more within
the range of vision of thinking Europeans.
Under his guidance Christianity concluded
an Alliance to resist the Turks.
God grant that this new assault from the East
will once more come to naught because Europe
has recognized in good time
that she must bury her internecine feuds
before *this* menace from without.

He starts to leave, but after a few steps, as if sensing that the Fontanas wish to block his way, he says:

And pray, all of you dear ones in the Lord,
pray for the Jews also, of whom so many
will soon be standing before the face of God.

FONTANA: Your Holiness, with all due respect
for the considerations that impose this silence on you,
I beg you in all humility, implore you . . .

POPE *(after a moment's embarrassment instantly recovering his
composure)*: Why, did you indeed believe, Fontana,
We would permit this sacrilege beneath Our very windows
to pass completely without comment? Of course not!

It goes without saying,
a proclamation shall attest it—the Pope,
in deepest sympathy, stands on the victims' side . . .
Eminence—we have time for *that*. Let us do it at once.
Send for the Scribe, please. No one shall say
We sacrificed the law of Christian love
to political calculations—no! Today,
as always, Our spirit dwells upon the unfortunates.

As though he had never intended to follow any other course, the POPE *now acts as if he were going to protest publicly against the arrest of the Jews. The* CARDINAL *has called in the* SCRIBE, *a tall, spidery monk with the gauntness of a Gothic painting, who seems as marvelously servile as a fourth-generation bureaucrat, and whose exquisite politeness would shame any normal man. He took his doctorate in Germany with a thesis on the symbol of the lily in the late Pre-Raphaelite painters. While this aesthetic Benedictine transforms the prescribed three genuflections into a ritual all his own, and then sits down at the console table and takes his pen in hand, the Deputy of Christ composes his thoughts. The coldness and hardness of his face, which Church publicists are fond of describing as "unearthly spiritualization," has virtually reached the freezing point. He strikes the pose in which he likes to be photographed, gazing over the heads of all around him, far into the distance and high up in the air.*

It is inevitable that the scene suddenly takes on an unreal, in fact a phantasmagoric atmosphere. Words, words, a rhetoric totally corrupted into a classic device for sounding well and saying nothing. It is a blessing that in this scene it is technically impossible to show some of the victims in the background: families in tatters, from infants to old men—several hundreds of thousands of European families, including Catholics, including a number of nuns and monks—on their way to the gas chambers, abandoned by everyone, abandoned even by the Deputy of Christ. So it was in Europe from 1941 to 1944.

POPE *(dictating):* Even more insistently . . . and awakening
ever greater compassion, there has come
to the Holy Father's ears the echo of
those misfortunes which protraction of
the present conflict . . . constantly increases.

CARDINAL: That will certainly be a blow to the Germans, you know.

The Fontanas silently look at one another. The ABBOT's *face is impassive.*

POPE *(begins pacing back and forth as he dictates):*
 The Pope, as is well known, in vain endeavored
 to prevent the outbreak of the war
 by . . . by warning the heads of all nations
 against resorting to arms, which today are
 so frightful in their power. Ever since he has not ceased
 to use all means within his power
 to alleviate the sufferings which . . . which are . . .
 in any form *whatsoever*
 consequences of the worldwide conflagration.
 With the augmentation of so much suffering,
 the Pope's universal and fatherly work of mercy
 has still more increased—semicolon. Increased; it knows
 —this is to be printed in italics—
SCRIBE *(in thin voice):*
 Very good, Your Holiness: to be printed in italics.
POPE *(with a grand gesture, raising his voice):*
 . . . knows no limits, comma, neither of
 nationality, comma, nor of religion
 nor of *race.*
 (To the Fontanas.) Content, you beloved in the Lord?
CARDINAL *(pretending to be impressed):*
 Race, too, Holy Father—ah yes,
 that is burningly relevant, you know.
 But ought we not also add, if I
 may suggest in all humility and gratitude,
 to add, you know *(Turning to the* SCRIBE, *in a
 declamatory vein:)*
 This varied and unresting activity
 of Pius XII
 (he bows, as does the ABBOT*)* has in recent days
 become still further intensified
 as a result of the arrests just undertaken
 in the Eternal city itself
 of Israelites who . . .

POPE *(vehemently checking him with a wave of his hand):*
    No, Eminence, absolutely not!
    Not so direct and not so detailed.
    That would amount to taking a position
    on military events. The Holy See must
    continue to shelter the spirit of *neutrality.*
    (Impatiently.) Not so direct . . . Now then, Scribe:
    what came before Rome and the Jews
    were spoken of so directly?
SCRIBE *(rising, bowing, thin voice):*
    This varied and unresting activity
    of Pius XII *(genuflects, then continues to stand)*
    has in recent days become still further intensified
    as a result of . . .
    of was the last word, Your Holiness.
POPE: Then let us say: of the aggravated . . . yes:
    of the *aggravated* sufferings of so . . .
    so *many* unfortunates.
    Eminence, We think that is more comprehensive
    than if We mention only the Jews.
CARDINAL: No doubt about that, Your Holiness.
    More comprehensive, certainly.
POPE *(appeased):* Since you, dear Cardinal and brother,
    have seen fit to speak of Our humble self,
    it is only fitting to speak with gladness
    of the prayers of all believers. Now, then, Scribe:
    (He now dictates very rapidly.)
    May this beneficent activity, comma,
    supported above all else by the prayers of believers
    throughout the world . . . my dear Count!
FONTANA *(goes to the* POPE, *who stands in the foreground, and
    says coldly):* Your Holiness?
POPE *(friendly and intimate):* One of those checks, Fontana,
    which you delivered to Us today, reminds Us
    of the securities of the Hungarian Railroads.
    Will you see to it, dear Count, that We
    suffer no losses even if
    the Red Army should occupy Hungary?
FONTANA: I am offering the shares in Zurich, Your Holiness,
    through intermediaries. Some have

been sold already, and on terms
not as bad as might have been expected.
Only it must not be bruited about
who is unloading them.
POPE: Of course, We understand. Dispose of them quickly.
No need to make a profit; just dispose of them.
Who knows if Hitler can protect Hungary . . .

RICCARDO *has meanwhile turned to the* ABBOT *and attempts to draw him away from the* CARDINAL, *downstage right. He succeeds in doing so while Pius continues to dictate and* FONTANA *steps back.*

POPE: Where were We?
SCRIBE *(bows, then repeats in a thin voice, almost singing):*
Prayers of believers throughout the world.
I thought, if I might humbly suggest a
phrase to Your Holiness . . .

The POPE *gestures assent.*

. . . believers throughout the world who
with hearts in one accord and with burning
fervor unceasingly raise their voices to Heaven.

The CARDINAL *and the* POPE *glance at each other.*

POPE: Yes, very much what We wish to say. Good.
How did you put it: raise their voices to Heaven—yes.
Comma, accomplish still *greater* results
in the future, and soon bring about the day
(With great emphasis, in an almost liturgical chant.)
when the *light of peace* will once more shine
over the earth, when men will lay down their arms,
all discords and resentments shall fade away
and men shall meet as brothers once again
to work righteously together at long last
for the common welfare. Period.

During this long last sentence the POPE *has approached close to the* SCRIBE. *After the phrase "lay down their arms" he goes up to the* CARDINAL *and* FONTANA, *almost singing the last words of his dicta-*

tion. Meanwhile RICCARDO *has been passionately urging his arguments upon the* ABBOT.

RICCARDO: These empty phrases! Father General,
 you know as well as I, he does not mean
 Hitler even to notice them.
 Please help! Today I must—
 we *both* must make a broadcast . . .
ABBOT *(already turning away from* RICCARDO, *in a low, harried
 voice)*: You are insane! Be quiet!
CARDINAL *(while* RICCARDO *is still speaking with the
 * ABBOT): This proclamation, Your Holiness,
 justifies, you know, the hope that . . .

The POPE *has heard the* ABBOT *talking insistently to* RICCARDO.
He turns away from the CARDINAL *and says, smilingly, but without
friendliness—*

POPE: Well, Signor Minutante, still not satisfied with Us?

The CARDINAL *also turns to* RICCARDO. *Before* RICCARDO, *who is
extremely perturbed, can reply, his father speaks.*

FONTANA: Your Holiness, this message,
 in which not one word mentions the arrests,
 cannot be construed as a reference
 to the Jewish problem.
POPE *(his patience exhausted)*:
 Have we not spoken expressis verbis
 of men *of all races,* Count Fontana?
CARDINAL: The proclamation will go down in history.
ABBOT: We do what we can.
FONTANA: Father General, as you well know,
 the Holy See has other means
 to command a hearing.
 Your Holiness, send Hitler an ultimatum,
 or even just a letter that Weizsäcker can deliver.

The POPE, *agitated, glances at the* SCRIBE *and signs to him to leave.*

SCRIBE *(bows)*: If I may humbly remind Your Holiness,
 Your Holiness has not yet signed.

The POPE *goes up to him and in extreme vexation reaches for the writing case which the* SCRIBE *holds out. Meanwhile* RICCARDO *takes out the yellow Star of David and pins it to his cassock. At this moment the* POPE *sees it. He is struck dumb. He reaches or rather gropes for the golden pen which the* SCRIBE *holds out to him, his gaze fixed on* RICCARDO, *intending to dip the pen into the inkwell. It should be a goose quill like the one with which, on November 1, 1950, the* POPE *signed the Dogma of the Assumption of the Virgin. Absently, he dips the pen into the ink, and as he starts to sign the* CARDINAL *speaks.*

CARDINAL *(breathless, furious):*
    Minutante, now you forget yourself!
    Remove—this—this thing.
    How dare you, in the presence of the Holy Father.
    Blasphemy—on a priest's robe—blasphemy!
FONTANA *(pleadingly):* Riccardo—please don't . . .
RICCARDO *(undeterred, passoinately):*
    Your Holiness, what you have set your name to
    grants Hitler unrestricted license to go on
    treating the Jews as he has always done . . .

While the POPE, *intensely agitated, swiftly traces his signature, the pen slips from his fingers; he smears ink over his hand and holds it our reproachfully so that the others can see.*

CARDINAL *(exclaims immediately after* RICCARDO *has spoken):*
    Be still! Holy Father, I humbly request
    that we end this discussion.

The POPE *has recovered sufficiently to find his voice again. He speaks haltingly, but without the stammer which frequently afflicted Pacelli as Cardinal, rarely as Pope.*

POPE: In the name of the victims . . . this . . . *this*
    arrogance as well! And this impertinence—
    the Star of David on the habit of Christ's servants!

He again looks at his inkstained hand, normally so painstakingly groomed, and deeply offended, shows it to the others like a wound. The CARDINAL *gives the* SCRIBE *an order and bustles him out. Then, turning to* RICCARDO, *he points with horror at his own chest, at the spot to which* RICCARDO *has pinned the Star of David.*

RICCARDO *(readily answering the* POPE's *reproach):*
    This star which every Jew must wear
    as soon as he is six years old,
    to show he is an outlaw—I shall wear it too
    until . . .
POPE *(quivering with rage):* He will *not!* We forbid him—
    forbid—on a cassock—this . . .

He stops, his voice failing him.

RICCARDO *(almost quietly, soberly):* I shall wear this star until
    Your Holiness proclaims before the world
    a curse upon the man who slaughters
    Europe's Jews like cattle.

The POPE *is silenced by his obvious inability to check* RICCARDO *or to find his voice.*

CARDINAL: Criminal folly! Get out!
RICCARDO *(his voice rising):*
    Folly? No, Your Holiness. The King
    of Denmark, a defenseless man,
    threatened Hitler that he would wear this star,
    along with *every member* of his house,
    if the Jews in Denmark were forced to wear it.
    They were not forced. When will the Vatican
    at last act so that we priests
    can once again own without shame that we are
    servants of that Church which holds
    brotherly love as its first commandment!
CARDINAL: Obedience, unconditional obedience
    is the Jesuit's first commandment, Minutante!
RICCARDO: Yes, obedience to God.
CARDINAL: Who speaks through the voice and will of
    His Holiness, you know. Obey!

The POPE *remains ostentatiously silent.*

CARDINAL: What vow did you take as a member
    of the Society of Jesus?
RICCARDO: Your Eminence, forgive me. Does not every Cardinal,
    true to the color of his scarlet robe,
    vow to stand by his faith even unto

the spilling of his own blood?
But our faith, Your Eminence, rests
upon brotherly love—remember the deportees
before you judge me.
CARDINAL: I do not judge you, I pray for you, you know.
But this sacrilege—on your cassock . . .
But now go—leave the presence
of His Holiness.
POPE *(makes an effort to leave; he is sincerely shaken, extremely agitated)*: Rebellion in *these* rooms!
Disobedience and arrogance—Protestantism.
Ugh! This is our recompense
for all the benefits we have conferred
upon the Minutante!
FONTANA: I ask permission to take my leave, Your Holiness.
POPE: Remain, Count. This son of yours
is trial enough for you. You need not pay for his folly.
FONTANA: Please, Your Holiness, permit me to go.
POPE *(with cold imperiousness)*:
You stay, and that is that. You, Father General

He turns to the Father General. The SCRIBE *has entered noiselessly carrying a large brass or copper basin of water and a towel.*

will be responsible to Us: make sure that this—
this scandalous behavior stops.
Accompany the Minutante to his home.
God watch over him, he knows not what he speaks.
We have forgiven him.
Of course he cannot return to his post,
nor to Lisbon . . .

RICCARDO *stands by as though all this has ceased to concern him; it is impossible even to tell whether he is listening. The* SCRIBE *approaches the* POPE, *carrying the basin.* FONTANA, *crushed, falls to his knees before the* POPE. *The* SCRIBE *looks as if he were dying of sheer horror.*

FONTANA: Your Holiness, please . . . I beg you, Holy Father . . .
POPE *(embarrassed):* Fontana, do stand up, you're not to blame.
Your son's behavior cannot make a breach
between the two of us.

(At last, with crystal clarity and hardness.)
Non possumus.
We cannot—will not—write to Hitler.
He would—and in his accursed self
the Germans *in corpore*—
only be antagonized and outraged.
But we desire them, and also Roosevelt,
to see in us impartial go-betweens.
Now, that is enough. Ad acta.

As he speaks the last sentence he returns to the throne and is about to begin washing his hands in the proffered basin. RICCARDO, *already at the door, says firmly and quietly—*

RICCARDO: God shall not destroy His Church
only because a Pope shrinks from His summons.

Speechless, the POPE *rises. He is unable to conceal the effect of these words which have struck him to the heart. All stare at the open door, through which* RICCARDO *has made an abrupt exit. All are stunned, but not a word, only gestures and expressions betray the shock.* FONTANA, *like the rest of course unaware of* RICCARDO's *intentions, feels that more is at stake here than an unforgivable "offence." Completely helpless, he takes three steps toward the door, in great anxiety, as though he intended to follow* RICCARDO, *then turns around and stands shattered. He looks down at the floor and supports himself by leaning against the console table. A Swiss Guard with a halberd appears at the door. The* CARDINAL *signs to him in extreme agitation; the door is closed again from outside. The* POPE *sits down once more and begins to wash his hands. He is incapable of speech; fortunately he can conceal the shaking of his hands in the basin. The* CARDINAL *watches him, taken aback; then he goes up to him and says in an intimate tone which he seldom uses—*

CARDINAL: Holy Father, you must not be . . .
so offended by such stupidities.
It is simply outright rudeness, you know!

The POPE *smiles painfully and gratefully at him. He has recovered his voice, and speaks to the* ABBOT, *somewhat appeasing his troubled conscience—*

POPE: Dear Father General, are the monasteries
    supplied with enough food for the fugitives?
ABBOT *(in the pacifying tone of one addressing a gravely ill*
    person): For the first few weeks, Your Holiness, there are
    undoubtedly ample provisions in all the monasteries.
POPE *(pained at having been so misunderstood)*: Summa iniuria!
    As though We did not wish to give succor to all, *all!*
    Whatever *has been granted Us to do was done.*
    We are—God knows it—blameless of the blood
    now being spilled. As the flowers
    (He raises his voice, declaims.)
    in the countryside wait beneath winter's mantle of snow
    for the warm breezes of spring,
    so the *Jews* must wait, praying and trusting
    that the hour of heavenly comfort will come.
    (He has dried his hands; now he rises.)
    We who are here assembled in Christ's Name
    will pray in conclusion . . . Fontana, please,
    you too come into our circle . . .

FONTANA *reluctantly moves forward between the* ABBOT *on the left and the* CARDINAL *on the right, who have knelt at the steps of the throne. The* SCRIBE *has placed the basin and towel on the table and is kneeling there, almost prostrate. The* POPE *descends the two steps and leans toward* FONTANA, *saying mildly—*

POPE: Fontana—who should know it better than We,
    to be a father is to wear a crown of thorns.

FONTANA *must kiss the proffered ring. Then the* POPE, *once more completely stage manager of the situation, steps back to the throne. "The gaunt, tall figure straightened up . . . and turned his eyes to Heaven . . . With arms outstretched the Pope seemed to wish to close all mankind in a fatherly embrace."*

POPE *(while the curtain falls)*:
    Exsurge, Domine, adiuva nos, et libera nos
    propter nomen tuum—
    sit super nos semper benedictio tua—

CURTAIN

Act 5: Auschwitz; or,
Where Are You, God?

When the weather was bad or the wind strong, the smell
of burning was carried for many miles. The result was
that the entire population of the vicinity talked about
the burning of the Jews, in spite of the counter-
propaganda of the Party and the government
authorities. Furthermore, Air Raid Defense objected to
the nocturnal fires, which were visible for a great
distance from the air. However, the cremations had to
continue at night, rather than stop the incoming
transports. A timetable conference of the Reich Ministry
of Transportation had drawn up a precise schedule of
the various operations, and this schedule had to be
maintained in order to avoid clogging and confusion on
the railroad lines involved. This was especially
important for military reasons. . . .

STATEMENT BY HÖSS, COMMANDANT OF
AUSCHWITZ

*The most momentous events and discoveries of our time all have
one element in common: they place too great a strain upon the
human imagination. We lack the imaginative faculties to be able to
envision Auschwitz, or the destruction of Dresden and Hiroshima,
or exploratory flights into space, or even more mundane matters
such as industrial capacity and speed records. Man can no longer
grasp his own accomplishments.*

*For that reason the question of whether and how Auschwitz
might be visualized in this play occupied me for a long time. Documentary naturalism no longer serves as a stylistic principle. So
charged a figure as the anonymous Doctor, the monologues, and a
number of other features, should make it evident that no attempt
was made to strive for an imitation of reality—nor should the stage
set strive for it. On the other hand, it seemed perilous, in the drama,
to employ an approach such as was so effectively used by Paul
Celan in his masterly poem* Todesfuge, *in which the gassing of the
Jews is entirely translated into metaphors, such as:*

Black milk of the dawn we drink it at evening
we drink it at noons and mornings, we drink it at night.

For despite the tremendous force of suggestion emanating from sound and sense, metaphors still screen the infernal cynicism of what really took place—a reality so enormous and grotesque that even today, fifteen years after the events, the impression of unreality it produces conspires with our natural strong tendency to treat the matter as a legend, as an incredible apocalyptic fable. Alienation effects would only add to this danger. No matter how closely we adhere to historical facts, the speech, scene and events on the stage will be altogether surrealistic. For even the fact that today we can go sightseeing in Auschwitz as we do in the Colosseum scarcely serves to convince us that seventeen years ago in our actual world this gigantic plant with scheduled railroad connections was built especially in order that normal people, who today may be earning their livings as letter carriers, magistrates, youth counselors, salesmen, pensioners, government officials or gynecologists, might kill other people.

SCENE 1

Throughout the entire scene the light is never bright; it remains dusky. The "cloud," present in almost all the existing drawings made by prisoners, hung continually above Auschwitz, as did the pestilential stench of burning flesh and the swarms of flies. Passengers on the rail line from Cracow to Kattowitz would crowd to the windows when the train passed by the camp.

The pall of smoke and the glow of fires visible to a distance of thirty kilometers, the showers of sparks from the crematoria and from the ten vast pyres on which a thousand corpses could be burned at once in the open air—all this created the infernal atmosphere which surrounded even the railroad yards and outer reaches of this death factory. What took place in the interior of this underworld, at the crematorium itself, exceeds imagination. There is no way of conveying it.

It is, however, that constant pall of smoke and fire which makes the stage setting characteristic of Auschwitz. The audience must sense that the dreary hut with its little garden represents a comparatively human façade—but a façade that rather exposes than conceals what goes on behind it.

Unfortunately we cannot reassure ourselves with the thought that a camp like Auschwitz was run by madmen or pathological criminals. Ordinary human beings regarded this as their "place of work." To remind ourselves of that, let us begin with a detailed picture of HELGA.

She is well-endowed with the specifically feminine abilities to adopt the opinions of those who impress her, and to see nothing that might disturb her. Like all distinctly feminine traits, those qualities are so innate in her that she would find even Auschwitz "all right," if she ever gave it any thought. Of course she never does. Hence, she is a particularly tempting opiate for the men here, who sometimes see ghosts at night. She has nothing in common with the witches who serve as female guards in the camp. But of course she knows perfectly well what "program" her services at the switchboard and teletype machine further. Far more than such a person as Commandant Rudolf Höss, HELGA *unconsciously demonstrates, simply by her warmth and physical attractiveness, how human even professional murderers remain. She proves, indeed, that "human" is a far too equivocal word to be useful any longer.* HELGA'S *favorite game, when she is not thinking about some man or other, is to daydream of living far away from this place—in the Lüneburger Heide, say. For she would like to be a happy, faithful wife; she wishes she did not have to repeatedly betray her fiancé, a handsome, utterly unimaginative crematorium drudge with the rank of lieutenant. But she is so completely under the spell of the* DOCTOR *that she overcomes formidable fears and scruples solely in order to come to his bed during the lunch hour. She hates him because she is helpless to resist his lascivious charm—and because she hates all evil and all unusual intelligence. Given her craving for purity and decency, she would even be repelled by the slaughter of the Jews if it had ever occurred to her that such a thing could be as reprehensible as adultery or listening to the BBC. But she is totally malleable, like most young girls; not only is she molten material in her lover's hands, but after the fashion of secretaries, she will parrot her boss of the moment even to his most personal likes and dislikes.*

Consequently, two years later, in 1945, she will quickly understand without in any way being an opportunist that what was done to the Jews was "not nice." But it will take a virile Jewish officer of the army of occupation to make that clear to her. Moreover, even in bed she will be careful not to admit that she knew what she was helping to do in Auschwitz, down to the most horrifying details. "Of course" she had no idea that people were being systematically killed there. And the American officer will believe her, not just because she is charming. He will in all seriousness think her avowal quite plausible—just as his fellow-countrymen on the judges' bench in Nuremberg could credit Julius Streicher when he maintained that he knew of no killings.

The DOCTOR *enlisted the services not only of sweet young things without principles, but of sour, highly principled solid citizens—in keeping with Prince Talleyrand's incontestable observation that a married man with family will do anything for money. Whom God assigns as task, he also assigns a task force.*

Let us take the man in uniform: Lieutenant Colonel Dr. FRITSCHE *is pallid and bespectacled, resembling his superior Heinrich Himmler as an amateur photo resembles a portrait by a master. His job is to allocate the healthy "inmate material" of both sexes from the transports among the industrial plants which have settled in the immediate vicinity of Auschwitz, receiving a receipt in return. A few months later, after honorable firms such as I. G. Farben have mercilessly drained these workers of all strength,* FRITSCHE *takes back the worn-out human wrecks, returns the receipt, and delivers them to the gas chambers. Herr* FRITSCHE *has never felt any compunctions about this work, for he took his doctorate in jurisprudence and knows that nothing is being done illegally. The whole procedure is according to official decree. He has never had the impulse to beat a prisoner, and he hopes that his subordinates use the lash only if prisoners make themselves legally eligible for corporal punishment by malingering or laziness. All illnesses are considered malingering unless the prisoner proves otherwise by dying.*

Herr FRITSCHE *on principle neither sees nor hears the infliction of corporal punishment. He also avoids looking at the crematorium, for he sometimes fears "going soft and relapsing into our bourgeois notions." To offset such fits of weakness, he takes long walks accompanied by two wolfhounds, and reads the Nazi Party political education pamphlets, though politics scarcely interests him. He went through the university at the cost of considerable self-denial, married a girl without money, and consequently is anxious to do well in his career financially. But he would never enrich himself illegally; the gold watch once belonging to a cremated Amsterdam Jew has arrived on his wrist in a strictly official manner. Since the Führer has recently castigated all legal experts as stupid simpletons, Dr.* FRITSCHE *no longer cherishes hopes of becoming a judge.*

A lawyer's career seems to him totally absurd. Not that he would be conscious of the grotesquerie of people of his sort sitting in judgment on a man who has stolen a bicycle, for example—a situation frequently to be enacted in West Germany after 1950. But Lieutenant Colonel FRITSCHE *tells himself that after Final Victory modern legal practice will hardly admit more than two punishments: death, or transportation for service in the occupied Eastern Territories. Greater Germany will not want to be burdened with superfluous mouths in prisons. Reasoning thus, Herr* FRITSCHE *talks of a subject which greatly pleases his family: the broad lands in the Ukraine (temporarily lost again, alas) which he will certainly receive for his services. Naturally, he knows nothing whatsoever about farming. He lacks the ability to come to grips with any living thing— including* HELGA, *for example. He even keeps a safe distance from horses, for fear of being kicked. In 1952 he will be a financial expert for one of the most prominent German building and loan companies and by 1960 a judge in a State Superior Court, and eligible for a pension—having changed his profession after a heart attack and put up with a temporary cut in salary out of concern for his family's security.*

It has grown somewhat brighter, insofar as that is possible in the fog and pall of smoke. While HELGA *is making coffee,* FRITSCHE *appears in winter coat, warm cap and earmuffs, and starts to enter the guardroom to warm up. From the left a savage-looking* OFFICER, *equipped with steel helmet, whip, lantern and wolfhound, approaches him.*

OFFICER: Lieutenant Colonel—report!

He ties the dog to the bench.

FRITSCHE: So early in the morning? What's up?
OFFICER: Quite a surprise at the outer platform, sir.
    The Pope in person has sent us a priest . . .
FRITSCHE: What's this about the Pope?
OFFICER: The Pope has sent a priest along
    to keep the baptized Jews company.
    These Jews are from Rome, you know. He was
    sent right with them, as their pastor, of course.
    And . . .
FRITSCHE: And what?

OFFICER: And some damned moron in Rome
 put the man aboard with the rabble,
 right in the middle of the lot,
 in the middle of a freight car, although
 the fellow's wearing a cassock, is an Italian, not a Jew,
 and even said to be related to the Pacellis.
FRITSCHE: Goddam! Goddamned idiocy!
OFFICER: He spoke to me. It was still dark.
 Lucky I didn't set the dog on him right off.
FRITSCHE: Where is he now?
 Has he seen anything of the camp?
OFFICER: No, not yet. He's still out there on Platform One.
 I turned him over to the military police
 who took charge of the transport from Passau on,
 and to the railroad men. They're to take him back.
 He's having some breakfast with them now and . . .
FRITSCHE: What a mess! Don't guard him too closely.
 He must be allowed to move around
 fairly freely on the outer platform,
 so that he doesn't get too nosy and
 make trouble for us, like the Red Cross people.
OFFICER: I'm afraid, though, that he's
 seen too much on the train already.
FRITSCHE: Come on in. We need a drink after this shock.

They cross the small garden. FRITSCHE *knocks rather timidly.*

HELGA: Come in.
FRITSCHE *(embarrassed):* Uh, *Heil und Sieg.* May we
 warm up here for a minute, Fräulein Helga?
HELGA: Of course, good morning. Cold, isn't it?
 Help yourself, Heinz—here are cigarettes.
 Herr Fritsche, please help yourself.
OFFICER *(taking a cigarette):*
 Thank you, Helga, how are you?
 I don't need a drink now—I'm off duty.
HELGA: What about you, Herr Fritsche? Coffee?
FRITSCHE: No thanks, better a brandy—I'm due at the platform.
 (To the OFFICER, *while* HELGA *folds blankets.)*
 We have to get that priest out of here.

I'll telephone Berlin at eight sharp.
Does the man want to go back to Rome?
He's all we needed!

OFFICER: He wants to go to Breslau, at our expense.
He says he's supposed to visit the Bishop there.
Then he's going to see the Nuncio in Berlin.

FRITSCHE: What's that? Does he mean to make a complaint?

OFFICER: No, he's said nothing about that.
He used to work there.
Of course he was furious at the idiots
in Northern Italy or Rome
who shipped him off like some Jewboy.
But he's calmed down now.

FRITSCHE: The man responsible for the slip-up
will soon have the pleasure
of getting a good look at Russia from the front lines.
An irresponsible moron!
To pick this of all times, when our situation
in the south is so precarious,
to act down there as if it were the Ukraine!
Incredible, when only recently the Führer
made a point of warning that the Church
is not to be attacked before the Final Victory!
And Himmler—have you heard about that?

OFFICER: No, sir.

FRITSCHE: Himmler recently had his mother buried
with the blessings of the Church! Pretty rich, eh?
All right then—get that black crow out of here!
Ship him off to Berlin—there they know
how to behave toward an envoy from the Vatican.
Well—another drink to make up for the shock.
Helga, please pour me some consolation.

HELGA: I'm always the one to console—who consoles me?

FRITSCHE: Ah, that's good—I'll call Berlin later.
Well, Heil Helga, and thank you.

HELGA: See you later.

OFFICER: I'll go along, I want to get some sleep.

HELGA: Heil, Herr Fritsche. Heil, Heinz—sleep well.
I have to catch up for last night, too . . .

She yawns and laughs. FRITSCHE *and the* OFFICER *go out.* HELGA *switches out the desk lamp and raises the blackout shades on the window at the rear. A circular saw whines; this noise from one of the camp workshops from time to time forms the background for significant remarks of the* DOCTOR.

From the right, jumping gallantly over the beds of the small garden and up the two steps to the door, swagger stick in hand and a book under his arm, the "handsome devil" appears. He lithely enters the room, tall and slim, laughing and genial, crafty and engaging. HELGA *is frightened to the bone, but the audience senses that she loves this fear more than her soul's peace. She starts back, but he has already pulled her to him and kisses her on the mouth between phrases.*

HELGA: You! Go away, let me be, you devil.
    I hate you, I *hate* you—stop!
    People can see us—don't!
    The window—you beast—go back to your Jewess!

After his first kisses she tries to push him away. He laughs softly and tenderly; they wrestle a bit, and while she flails about, resentfully but hopelessly, he clamps her in his arms as in a vise.

HELGA *(tormented, weak, already snuggling close to him as he bites her ear)*: You'll get us all in trouble—all three of us.
    Go sleep with the prisoners, till you're hanged for it.
DOCTOR *(with tender irony, which at last forces her to smile)*:
    Jealous of that poor woman?
    Do I make a fuss because at night
    you do your duty as a bride-to-be
    with Günter, and only have time for me at noon.
    Today, at noon? Who comes knocking at my door,
    who slips into my hut to ask—that's
    the only reason—just to ask whether
    Herr Doktor can lend her *Anna Karenina?*
HELGA: You don't need me, you have the Jewess now.
DOCTOR: But you'll only be coming, my puss,
    to ask whether I have that trashy book . . .
    there's no harm in that.
    How would you know that I just
    happen to be taking a shower?

HELGA *(frees herself; moves three steps away from him)*:
    Let me alone—people can see.
DOCTOR: Quite right—let's keep away from the window.

He picks her up; she kicks out and he whirls her twice around in a circle:

    Why, you're wearing stockings, for the first time!
HELGA *(now passively clinging to him)*:
    It's so cold this morning. Oh, you—

He quickly lays her down on the cot and props his left knee between her feet.

DOCTOR *(tenderly)*: I'm looking forward to this afternoon.
    Look here . . .

He takes a string of pearls from his pocket and dangles it above her face. She pays no attention to it, but says tormentedly:

HELGA: He'll report you! He'll kill us.
DOCTOR: Nonsense! Your Günter has quite enough
    of killing, in the normal course of things.
    He's on duty at the crematorium this afternoon
    while we'll be keeping warm in our bed.
    Why not? You'll be so timid and so small,
    my little naked puss—
    (softly) and then all at once wild,
    so wild that you'll be able to forget
    whom you're being wild with.
    Look here.

He swings the necklace.

HELGA: You're horrible.
DOCTOR: Doesn't the necklace excite you? I found the pearls
    yesterday morning when we scooped out
    a fat Jewish oyster.
    I'll give them to you for your wedding.
HELGA: I don't want any of those things.
    What would I tell Günter?
DOCTOR: Just say you inherited them.
    We'll consecrate the necklace this afternoon.

He stands up, paces the room nervously, says ironically but winningly:

> Then you needn't be shy
> in broad daylight. I'll dress you in the pearls.
> Besides, your left hand will be wearing something too:
> your engagement ring.

HELGA: It's worse when you make fun of me!
>> I don't want to, I don't want to any more,
>> I don't want to!

DOCTOR *(calmly):* It's good for you—I see that by the way you look:
>> like a dirty mirror after it's been polished.

She shakes her head vehemently, and smiles involuntarily; then she embraces him and draws him down on to the bed.

HELGA: You're a devil!

DOCTOR: How do *I* look after we've had our fun?

HELGA: Very peaceful, no longer nervous, and
>> not so wicked—especially not so wicked.

DOCTOR: Wicked? What do you mean by that?

HELGA *(embracing him more tightly):*
>> That easy laugh of yours
>> is no more real than my faithfulness to Günter—
>> and than my love for you, this abominable love!
>> I really don't know whether I love you at all.
>> Sometimes I'm mad about you, but then—
>> then the hate comes back, then I hate you
>> with all my heart, I really do . . .
>> Please, let's be honest—I'll break the engagement.

DOCTOR: But you sleep with him every night!

HELGA *(beginning to cry):* Stop it—not every night!
>> And only so that I can be with you afternoons.
>> Why do you send me away again every time?
>> I don't want to know whether I love you.
>> All I know is that I'm helpless to resist you.
>> I must be with you. Please, let's get married . . .

DOCTOR *(has gradually been freeing himself from her embrace.*
>> *Now he stands up and resumes his restless pacing):*
>> Marriage, propagating children—good God!

That's the one sin I won't commit,
never, I swear that.
Stick to your Günter, sweetheart.
My climate is too harsh for you.
Günter is better.
Present the Führer with soldiers and
joyfully fecund girls.
(Sardonically, his irony directed at himself.)
By the time your daughters are nubile
I'll have seen enough twins here
to learn how they're begotten. And then
I'll prescribe for our blond beasts,
our master race, the recipe for twins,
so they can multiply like rats.
I'll have my name in encyclopedias—
that's my last ambition, and the silliest.
Isn't that enough for you, my pet?
Do I myself have to plow, harrow, and sow
in marriage? I'm already doing enough
to perpetuate racially pure humanity.
I cremate life,
I create life—
and always I create suffering.
Some suffer when I steer them into the gas,
others because I turn them back to life.
But Uncle Doctor, my puss, is far too fond
of his own children to expose them to
history's tender mercies.
(He draws her close to him and says almost passionately.)
Don't worry, in our tumbles
I'll see to it you do not get knocked up.
HELGA: Please stop, you make me feel so queer. Oh . . .
(Softly, so haltingly that she barely brings out the words.)
Tell me, why did you pick on just this Jewess
whose—who had two children. Does she know
that you're the one who sent her children . . .
DOCTOR *(releases her, but remains undisturbed. In a
matter-of-fact tone):*
I don't care to talk shop with you.
Enough of your infantile jealousy . . . Oh,

some nice rolls. Small and fair-skinned like you,
and just as tasty. I'm hungry.
(He kisses her, takes a roll, eats, and starts toward the door.)
We have some Italians to sort out.

HELGA *(blocks his way; for the first time she shows a degree of firmness, but it does not last long):*
I won't be jealous if you'll tell me
why you chose this woman of all people . . .

DOCTOR *(impatiently):*
It stimulates me, that's all, it stimulates me.

HELGA *(silly and feminine):*
I suppose I don't stimulate you enough?

DOCTOR: Little fool—my little sugarbun, I mean.
Can't you understand? I want to find out
whether this woman will go on sleeping with me
after I've told her where her children went—
and that I am the lord of life and death
in this place. That's what I want to find out.

HELGA *(moving away from him):* How cruel you are. Let her live.
The least you can do is let her live . . .

DOCTOR: What good would it do her, with her family dead?

HELGA *(loudly, indignantly):* But that's what she hopes for.
That's why she comes. That's the only reason!
Any woman would—I would, anyway.

DOCTOR: Maybe that is why she came at first.
Perhaps just for a hot bath and
a bite of supper—that may be.

HELGA: What do you get out of it, if you know that!

DOCTOR *(smiling):* Things aren't quite so simple any more.
Now she also comes . . .
(He laughs and breaks off.)

HELGA: You make me more uneasy all the time. You know—
(Haltingly forces out the words:)
If you're the same to her as—as to me,
then she simply can't help loving you
even if she curses you—and herself
to all eternity.

DOCTOR: Eternity!

HELGA: I'll never come to you again, never.

DOCTOR *(kisses her, smiles):* Fine, then, as usual—half past one.
We'll play pretty pussycat, all right?

HELGA *(screams, tears in her eyes):*
    Never again, I said, never again.
DOCTOR *(takes her in his arms again, softly, tenderly):*
    Get some sleep first. Don't bother to knock.
    Look around. If anyone is following you,
    just walk right on—once round the house
    and in at the door.
HELGA *(humbly):* I'll have to think it over carefully.
DOCTOR *(smiling):* We'll think it over together. So long.

HELGA *has accompanied him to the door. Unobserved by either of
them, a dim wall of deportees has assembled upstage left.*
    *A Kapo moves away from the group waiting in the background,
silently counts six deportees of all age groups, and sends them
down the ramp to the right. For a moment* HELGA *and the* DOCTOR
*look at these first victims, who creep forward, almost paralyzed
with fear, until they disappear at upstage right. Then the glow of
the fire flares up; the concrete mixer grinds more softly. The monot-
ony of its sound is in keeping with the stereotyped procedure of the
killings.* HELGA *is now in a hurry to get away. Suddenly she points
to the left and says:*

HELGA: Look—over there—look!
    Back there—the priest.
DOCTOR *(takes two steps away from her to the right):*
    Well, what about it? Take your nap now, Helga.
HELGA: No, listen—Fritsche gave orders
    that the priest—I guess it must be that one—
    wasn't to set foot inside the camp.
    He was deported by mistake!
DOCTOR *(turning around):* They all were. What's the difference!
HELGA: It seems he's not a Jew.
DOCTOR: I decide who's a Jew—as Göring says.
    So long—I know all about it.
HELGA: See you soon . . . How strong the smell is today. Horrible.
DOCTOR: The smoke can't rise on account of the fog.
    Sweet dreams, sugarbun.

HELGA *quickly goes across the garden. She turns to the left around
the hut, her head briefly appearing behind the window, and then
disappears. The* DOCTOR, *tapping his swagger stick against one of*

his extremely smart, supple riding boots, looks at RICCARDO *who stands with Signora Luccani, her father-in-law and the children.* RICCARDO *can just barely be discerned. We hear the sharp noise of an approaching truck. The oppressive "light," the gaseous smoke and the glow of fire, concentrate the gaze upon the* DOCTOR *who stands with his back to the audience, legs wide apart, but nevertheless graceful. He stares fixedly at* RICCARDO, *who glances over once, shyly and timidly, as though he felt the look, and then quickly takes the Luccanis' small daughter in his arms.*

DOCTOR: You there! Your Holiness.
    The one in black over there—come here.

Signora LUCCANI *draws her son closer to her. All the deportees look at the* DOCTOR *except* RICCARDO. *It has become very quiet.*

    Get a move on, come here!

Impatiently he goes upstage, left, toward the group, beckoning to RICCARDO, *who can now no longer evade him. Carrying the little girl in his arms,* RICCARDO *hesitantly steps forward out of the line. The* DOCTOR *silently retraces his steps, going as far as possible downstage, right, signing to* RICCARDO *to follow him. Uncertainly,* RICCARDO *follows. Signora Luccani watches him walking away with her child and screams wildly.*

JULIA: Don't go away. Stay here, stay with us!

She weeps. Her father-in-law takes her arm reassuringly and talks to her. At her scream, RICCARDO *stands still and looks back. He is frightened.*

DOCTOR *(threateningly, as if speaking to a dog)*: Come here, I say.

RICCARDO *again follows him a short distance. They now stand face to face, far downstage.* RICCARDO's *forehead and face are bleeding. He has been beaten.*

DOCTOR *(in a sarcastically friendly tone)*:
    That pretty brat your own?
RICCARDO *(with pent fury)*: The Germans beat her father to death.
    They thought it funny because he wore glasses.
DOCTOR: Such brutes, these Germans.

With his stick, which he handles with the air of a dandy, he gives
RICCARDO *a brief and almost comradely tap on the chest.*

> Where is your yellow star?
RICCARDO: I threw it away because I wanted to escape.
DOCTOR: What's this about your not being a Jew?
> On the railroad platform, I am told, you claimed
> the Pope assigned you to care for the Jews.
RICCARDO: I said that only to escape.
> They believed me and let me go.
> I am a Jew like the others.
DOCTOR: Congratulations. A subtle Jesuit trick.
> How is it they caught up with you again?
RICCARDO *(contemptuously):* Nobody caught me.
> I joined my companions of my own accord,
> when nobody was looking.
DOCTOR *(scornfully):* My, how noble!
> We've needed volunteers. Priests too.
> Just in case someone should die here.
> The climate can be nasty in Auschwitz.
> Of course you're not a Jew . . .

RICCARDO *does not answer. The* DOCTOR *sits down on the bench.*
He says sarcastically:

> A martyr, then.
> If that's the case, why did you run away?
RICCARDO: Wouldn't you be afraid if you were sent here?
DOCTOR: Afraid of what? An internment camp.
> Why should a man so close to God as you
> be afraid!
RICCARDO *(insistently): People* are being burned here . . .
> The smell of burning flesh and hair—
DOCTOR *(addressing him more as an equal):*
> What foolish ideas you have.
> What you see here is only industry.
> The smell comes from lubricating oil and horsehair,
> drugs and nitrates, rubber and sulphur.
> A second Ruhr is growing up here.
> I. G. Farben, Buna, have built branches here.
> Krupp will be coming soon.

Air raids don't bother us.
Labor is cheap.
RICCARDO: I've known for a year what this place is used for.
Only my imagination was too feeble.
And today I no longer had the courage—to go along.
DOCTOR: Ah, then you know about it. Very well.
I understand your ambition to be crucified,
but in the name of God the Father,
the Son and the Holy Ghost,
I intend to have a little sport
deflating your self-importance.
I have something quite different in mind for you.

RICCARDO *has placed the child he was carrying at his side. She snuggles close to him.*

DOCTOR *(to the child):* Uncle Doctor has some candy for you.
Come here!

He takes a bag from his pocket. The child reaches out eagerly.

THE GIRL *(shyly):* Thank you.

The DOCTOR *picks up the little girl and attempts to seat her on the bench. But the child scrambles off and clings to* RICCARDO.

DOCTOR *(scornfully):* So affectionate!
(Pleasantly, to the child.) What's your name?

The child does not answer.

A pity the little girl has no twin brother.
Research on twins is my special hobby.
Other children here never live
more than six hours, even when we're rushed.
Nor their mothers either—we have enough workhorses
and we're sufficiently accommodating
to gas children under fifteen
together with their mothers.
It saves a lot of screaming. What's wrong?
You did say you knew what we do here.
RICCARDO *(hoarse from horror):* Get it over with.
DOCTOR: Don't tell me you want to die right now!
You'd like that, wouldn't you:

inhaling for fifteen minutes, and then
sitting at God's right hand as saint! No!
I cannot give you such preferential treatment
while so many others
go up in smoke without that consolation.
As long as you can *believe*, my dear priest,
dying is just a joke.

*A scuffle in the background; the deportees are being made to move
forward. The line advances. Signora Luccani tries to break out of
it, to go to* RICCARDO. *She screams:*

JULIA: Let us stay together.
I won't.—My child!

A Kapo *runs up and tries to push her back into the line.* LUCCANI
clumsily intervenes.

LUCCANI: Don't! Don't hit the women. Don't hit their children.

The little GIRL *tries to pull* RICCARDO *over to her mother.* RIC-
CARDO *hesitates. The* DOCTOR *interferes.*

DOCTOR: Let her go!
(To JULIA.*)* What's this weeping over a brief separation?

The deportees move forward; old LUCCANI *tries to stay back, is
pushed on. He calls out in a feeble voice:*

LUCCANI: Julia—Julia—I'm waiting—do come.

*He is pushed out of sight. The whole group disappear off right. The
back of the stage is left empty. Soon the cement mixer falls silent.*

JULIA *(pleading with the* DOCTOR*)*:
Let us stay with the priest! You can see
how attached the child is to him.
He calmed us so on the train. Please,
let us die together, the priest and us—
DOCTOR *(to* JULIA*)*: Now, now, nobody's dying here.
(To RICCARDO.*)* Tell the woman the truth!
That those are factory chimneys over there.
You'll have to turn out work here, work hard.
But nobody will do you any harm.
(He strokes the little boy's hair reassuringly.)

Come along, my boy. It's time for lunch,
and there's pudding for dessert.

JULIA *(A moment before half-mad with fear, is now full of confidence in the* DOCTOR):
Do you know where my husband is?
Where my husband was taken to?

DOCTOR: Run along now. Here, take your sister with you.
Your husband? Still in Rome, I think.
Or perhaps in another camp.
I don't know everybody here.
(To RICCARDO.*)* Let go—give the woman her child!
(To JULIA.*)* Here, take your little girl.
The priest and I have some things to discuss.

JULIA *(To* RICCARDO): Stay with us, please stay!
You disappeared so suddenly this morning,
were gone so long.
I was so relieved when you returned.

RICCARDO *(strokes the little girl, kisses her and gives her to her mother):* I'll come afterwards—I'll come,
as surely as God is with us.

DOCTOR: Please, now—in fifteen minutes
Your friend will be with you again.

> *He beckons to the Kapo, who herds the family along.*

Those who don't keep up
get nothing more to eat.
Hurry—move on!

All go out except DOCTOR *and* RICCARDO. RICCARDO *sways. The* DOCTOR *addresses him patronizingly:*

You're very tired, I see.
Do sit down.

He points to the bench and walks back and forth with little tripping steps. RICCARDO, *exhausted, sits down.*

RICCARDO: What a devil you are!

DOCTOR *(extremely pleased):* Devil—wonderful! I am the devil.
And you will be my private chaplain.
It's a deal: save my soul.

But first I must see to those scratches.
Oh dear—however did it happen?

While the DOCTOR *goes into the hut,* RICCARDO *remains seated on the bench, holding the bloodstained handkerchief to his forehead to check the flow. The* DOCTOR, *in the doorway, calls:*

Come here. I have great plans for you,
Chaplain.
RICCARDO: What do you want of me?
DOCTOR: I mean my offer seriously.
Do you really know what awaits you otherwise?

He goes inside the hut, and is rummaging in a medicine chest. RIC-CARDO *has dragged himself up the steps. He drops into the nearest chair. The* DOCTOR *applies a dressing and adhesive tape to his wounds, meanwhile saying reassuringly, and almost seriously:*

Not long ago the brutal idiots here
had their fun with a certain Polish priest
who said he wanted to die in place
of another prisoner—a man with a family.
A voluntary offering, in short, like yours.
They kept him in a starvation cell ten days,
then even put a barbed wire crown on him.
Oh well, he had what he wanted, what your kind wants:
suffering in Christ—and Rome
will surely canonize him some day.
He died as an individual,
a fine, old-fashioned, personal death.
You, my dear friend, would be merely gassed.
Quite simply gassed, and *no one*,
no man, Pope or God, will ever find out.
At best you may be missed
like an enlisted man on the Volga,
or a U-boat sailor in the Atlantic.
If you insist on it, you'll die here
like a snail crushed under an auto tire—
die as the heroes of today do die, namelessly,
snuffed out by powers they have never known,
let alone can fight. In other words, meaninglessly.

RICCARDO *(scornfully):*
>Do you think God would overlook a sacrifice,
>merely because the killing is done
>without pomp and circumstance?
>Your ideas can't be as primitive as that!

DOCTOR: Aha, you think God does not overlook
>the sacrifice! Really?
>You know, at bottom all my work's concerned
>entirely with this one question. Really, now,
>I'm doing all I can.
>Since July of '42, for fifteen months,
>weekdays and Sabbath, I've been sending people to God.
>Do you think He's made the slightest acknowledgment?
>He has not even directed
>a bolt of lightning against me.
>Can you understand that? *You* ought to know.
>Nine thousand in one day a while back.

RICCARDO *(groans, says against his better knowledge):*
>That isn't true, it can't be . . .

DOCTOR *(calmly):* Nine thousand in one day. Pretty little
>vermin, like that child you were holding.
>All the same, in an hour they're unconscious or dead.
>At any rate ready for the furnace.
>Young children often go into the furnaces
>still alive, though unconscious. An
>interesting phenomenon. Infants, especially.
>A remarkable fact: the gas doesn't always kill them.

RICCARDO *covers his face with his hand. Then he rushes to the
door. Laughing, the* DOCTOR *pulls him back.*

DOCTOR: You cannot always run away.
>Stop trembling like that. My word of honor,
>I'll let you *live* . . . What difference does it make
>to me, one item more or less
>puffing up the chimney.

RICCARDO *(screams):* Live—to be *your* prisoner!

DOCTOR: Not my prisoner. My partner.

RICCARDO: I assure you, leaving a world
>in which you and Auschwitz are possible,
>is scarcely harder than to live in it.

DOCTOR: The martyr always prefers dying to thinking.
    Paul Valéry was right. The angel,
    he said—who knows, you may be an angel—
    (laughs) is distinguishable from me, the devil,
    only by the act of thought that still awaits him.
    I shall expose you to the task of thinking
    like a swimmer to the ocean.
    If your cassock keeps you above water
    then I promise I'll let you fetch me
    back home into the bosom of Christ's Church.
    (Laughs.) Who knows, who knows. But first you have to practice
    the celebrated patience of Negation.
    First you can watch me for a year or so
    conducting this, the boldest experiment
    that man has ever undertaken.
    Only a theological mind like my own—
    (he taps RICCARDO's *clerical collar)*
    I too once wore the iron collar for a while—
    could risk loading himself with
    such a burden of sacrilege.
RICCARDO *(beating his forehead in despair, cries)*:
    Why . . . why? Why do you do it?
DOCTOR: Because I wanted an answer!
    And so I've ventured what no man
    has ever ventured since the beginning of the world.
    I took the vow to challenge the Old Gent,
    to provoke him so limitlessly
    that He would have to give an answer.
    Even if only the negative answer
    which can be His sole excuse, as
    Stendhal put it: that He doesn't exist.
RICCARDO *(bitingly)*: A medical student's joke—for which millions
    are paying with their lives. Can it be
    that you are not even a criminal?
    Are you only a lunatic? As primitive
    as Virchow when he said he had dissected
    ten thousand cadavers and never found a soul?
DOCTOR *(offended)*: Soul! Now *that's* what I call primitive!
    What utter flippancy to be forever

taking cover behind such empty words!
(He imitates a priest praying.)
Credo quia absurdum est—still?
(Seriously.) Well, hear the answer: not a peep
came from Heaven, not a peep
for fifteen months,
not once since I've been giving tourists
tickets to Paradise.

RICCARDO *(ironically):* So much sheer cruelty—merely to do
what every harmless schoolmaster manages
without all this effort,
if he happens to be stupid enough
to want to prove that the Incomprehensible
isn't there.

DOCTOR: Then do you find it more acceptable
that God in person is turning the human race
on the spit of history?
History! The final vindication
of God's ways to man? Really?
(He laughs like a torturer.)
History: dust and altars, misery and rape,
and all glory a mockery of its victims.
The truth is, Auschwitz refutes
creator, creation, and the creature.
Life as an idea is dead.
This may well be the beginning
of a great new era,
a redemption from suffering.
From this point of view only one crime
remains: cursed be he who creates life.
I cremate life. That is modern
humanitarianism—the sole salvation from the future.
I mean that seriously, even on the personal level.
Out of pity, I have always buried
my own children right away—in condoms.

RICCARDO *(attempts mockery, but shouts in order to keep himself
from weeping):* Redemption from suffering! A lecture
on humanism from a homicidal maniac!
Save someone—save just a single child!

DOCTOR *(calmly):* What gives priests the right to look down on
   the SS?
   We are the Dominicans of the technological age.
   It is no accident that so many of my kind,
   the leaders, come from good Catholic homes.
   Heydrich was a Jew—all right.
   Eichmann and Göring are Protestants.
   But Hitler, Goebbels, Bormann, Kaltenbrunner . . . ?
   Höss, our commandant, studied for the priesthood.
   And Himmler's uncle, who stood godfather to him,
   is nothing less than Suffragan Bishop in Bamberg!
   (He laughs.) The Allies have solemnly sworn
   to hang us all if they should catch us.
   So after the war, it's only logical,
   the SS tunic will become
   a shroud for gallows birds.
   The Church, however, after centuries
   of killing heretics throughout the West
   now sets itself up as the exclusive
   moral authority of this Continent.
   Absurd! Saint Thomas Aquinas, a mystic,
   a god-crazed visionary like Heinrich Himmler,
   who also babbles well-meant nonsense,
   Thomas condemned the innocent for heresy
   just as these morons here condemn the Jews . . .
   But you do not cast him out of your temple!
   The readers that they use in German schools
   in centuries to come may well reprint
   the speeches Himmler made in honor of
   the mothers of large families—why not?
   (He is royally amused.)
   A civilization that commits
   its children's souls into the safeguard
   of a Church responsible for the Inquisition
   comes to the end that it deserves
   when for its funeral pyres it plucks
   the brands from our furnaces for human bodies.
   Do you admit that? Of course not.
   (Spits and pours a glass of brandy for himself.)
   One of us is honest—the other credulous.

(Malignantly.)
Your church was the first to show
that you can burn men just like coke.
In Spain alone, without the benefit of crematoria,
you turned to ashes three hundred and fifty thousand
human beings, most of them while alive, mind you.
Such an achievement surely needs the help of Christ.

RICCARDO *(furious, loudly):*
I know as well as you—or I would not be here—
how many times the Church has been guilty,
as it is again today. I have nothing more to say
if you make God responsible
for the crimes of His Church.
God does not stand *above* history.
He shares the fate of the natural order.
In Him all man's anguish is contained.

DOCTOR *(interrupting):* Oh yes, I also learned that drivel once.
His suffering in the world fetters the evil principle.
Prove it. Where—when have I ever been fettered?
Luther did not fool himself so badly.
Not man, he said, but God
hangs, tortures, strangles, wars . . .

Laughing, he slaps RICCARDO *on the back.* RICCARDO *shrinks from him.*

Your anger amuses me—you'll make a good partner.
I saw that right off. You'll help in the laboratory,
and at night we'll wrangle
about that product of neurosis
which for the present you call God
or about some other philosophical rot.

RICCARDO: I don't intend to act your court jester,
to cheer the hours when you are
face to face with your own self.
I have never seen a man so wretched,
for you know what you do . . .

DOCTOR *(painfully jarred):*
Then I must disappoint you once again.
Just as your whole faith is self-deception

and desperation, so is your hope
that I feel wretched. Of course
boredom has always plagued me.
That is why I find our dispute so refreshing,
and why you are to stay alive.
But wretched? No. At present I
am studying *homo sapiens.* Yesterday I watched
one of the workers at the crematorium.
As he was chopping up the cadavers
to get them through the furnace doors
he discovered the body of his wife.
How did he react?

RICCARDO: You do not look as if this study
    made you especially cheerful . . .
    I think you too feel
    no easier than that worker.

DOCTOR: Don't I? Well then, I still have my books.
    Napoleon, as you know, remarked to Metternich
    he did not give a damn about
    the death of a million men. I've just been
    investigating how long it was before
    that scoundrel became the idol of posterity.
    Quite relevant, in view of Hitler's . . .
    Of course, that disgusting vegetarian has not,
    like Napoleon, seduced all of his sisters.
    He's quite devoid of such endearing traits.
    All the same I find him more likeable—

He picks up a book; the name "Hegel" is on the cover.

    than the philosophers who squeeze
    the horrors of world history
    through countless convolutions of their brains,
    until at last they look acceptable.
    I was recently rereading Nietzsche,
    that eternal schoolboy, because a colleague of mine
    had the honor of delivering to Mussolini
    Herr Hitler's present on his sixtieth birthday.

Laughs piercingly.

    Just think: The complete works of Nietzsche
    on *Bible* paper.

RICCARDO: Is Nietzsche to blame
    if weak-headed visionaries, brutes and murderers
    have stolen his legacy?
    Only madmen take him literally . . .
DOCTOR: Right, only madmen, men of action.
    It suits *them* perfectly that Nietzsche
    looked to the beasts of prey for his criterion
    of manly virtues—
    presumably because he himself
    had so little of the beast in him,
    not even enough to lay a girl.
    Grotesque: the Blond Beast, or,
    The Consequences of Crippling Inhibitions,
    comes down to: a massacre of millions.
    (He chuckles.)
    No, what captivated Hitler was certainly not
    the finest critical mind in Europe.
    What Hitler fell for was the Beast, the
    beautiful beast of prey.
    No wonder, when the inventor of that monstrosity
    wrote in language so intoxicated,
    and with such sovereign arrogance, it seemed
    he had champagne instead of ink in his pen.
    (Abruptly.)
    You can have champagne here too, and girls.
    This afternoon when those people there,
    the ones you came with,
    burn up in smoke,
    I shall be burning up myself
    between the legs of a nineteen-year-old girl.
    That's one amenity that beats your faith
    because it's something a fellow really has,
    with heart, mouth and hands.
    And has it here on earth, where we need such things.
    But of course you know all that . . .
RICCARDO *(casually)*: Oh yes, a fine amenity . . .
    only it doesn't last too long.
DOCTOR *(draws on his gloves, smiles with something close to*
    triumph): We understand each other splendidly.
    You'll have two nice girls in the laboratory.

I suppose the newest books will interest you more.
Habent sua fata divini—the saints
fall on their faces.
The light of reason falls on the Gospels.
I made a pilgrimage last year to Marburg,
to hear Bultmann. Daring, for a theologian,
the way he throws out the clutter in the New Testament.
Even evangelism no longer asks men to believe
the mythical cosmogony of the past.

During these last sentences the rumble of the cement mixer resumes. As yet, no more deportees are visible. But upstage, far right, the glare of a mighty fire rises once more, high and menacing. Shrill whistles. RICCARDO has leaped to his feet. He wrenches the door open and runs outside. He points to the underworld light and cries out contemptuously, as the DOCTOR slowly follows him—

RICCARDO: Here—there—I'm in the midst of it.
    What need have I of believing
    in Heaven or Hell.

He comes closer to the DOCTOR, speaks in a lower voice.

    You know that. You know that even St. John
    did not see the Last Judgment as a cosmic event.

Loudly, flinging the insult at the DOCTOR.

    Your hideous face
    composed of lust and filth and gibberish
    sweeps all doubts away—all. Since
    the devil exists, God also exists.
    Otherwise *you* would have won a long time ago.
DOCTOR *(grips his arms, laughs ebulliently)*:
    That's the way I like you. The idealist's St. Vitus dance.

He grips him by both arms as RICCARDO attempts to run off to another group of deportees who have appeared and are now standing silently, with only a KAPO prowling around them. The DOCTOR forces RICCARDO, whose strength quickly deserts him, down on the bench. RICCARDO covers has face with his hands, resting his forearms on his knees. The DOCTOR places his foot on the bench beside RICCARDO and says chummily:

All tensed up. You're trembling. So scared
you can't stand on your feet.

RICCARDO *(shrinks back because the* DOCTOR's *face has come too
close to him. Sick at heart, he says):*
I never said that I was not afraid.
Courage or not—in the end
that is only a question of vanity.

DOCTOR *(while* RICCARDO *scarcely listens, for he has his eyes fixed
on the waiting victims):*
I gave my word that nothing would be done to you.
I need you for a purpose of my own . . .
The war is lost; the Allies will hang me.
You find me a refuge in Rome, a monastery.
The Commandant will even thank me
if I personally return to Rome
the Holy Father's guest, whom we
did not exactly invite to come here. Agreed?
One moment.

He goes toward the hut, looks around.

RICCARDO *(as in a dream):* To Rome? I am—to go back to Rome?

DOCTOR: We'll have a fine drive to Breslau.

*He goes to the telephone in the hut, dials, listens, hangs up, mean-
while saying, half to* RICCARDO, *half into the receiver:*

With a girl as blond as sunlight
and our own personal deputy of Christ.
Helga, hello! Helga? Asleep already . . .
And you'll be back with Pius.

He leaves the hut. RICCARDO *is shaking with emotion.*

RICCARDO: No—never! You only want me to try to run away.
I would not get a hundred yards. You want
to say I was shot trying to escape.

DOCTOR *(takes out his wallet and shows him a passport):*
Only natural for you to mistrust my offer.
But look at this. Is this a passport from the Holy See?

RICCARDO: So it is—where did it come from?

DOCTOR: Only the personal data are missing.
I'll fill those out as needed. Now our agreement:

You find me a place to stay in Rome
until I can escape to South America.
RICCARDO: How can you hope to desert?
Rome is occupied by the German army.
DOCTOR: For that very reason it's so easy
for me to make a pilgrimage there.
With a perfectly legitimate travel order.
I'll be there in a week—then with your help
I go underground. Agreed?

RICCARDO *remains silent.*

DOCTOR *(impatiently, insistently, persuasively):*
Why—are you still thinking only of yourself,
of your soul, as you call it?
Go to Rome and hang your message
on St. Peter's bell.
RICCARDO *(haltingly):* How could I tell the Pope anything new?
Details, of course. But that the Jews
are being gassed in Poland—the whole world
has known that for a year.
DOCTOR: Yes—but the Deputy of Christ
should speak out. Why is he silent?
(Eagerly). You couldn't yet have heard the news:
last week two or three bombs
which killed nobody, fell in the Vatican gardens.
For days that's been the great sensation
all over the world!
The Americans, the British, and the Germans
are all desperately trying to prove
that they could not have been the culprits.
There you have it again: the Pope is sacred
even to heretics. Make use of that.
Demand that he—what's wrong with you?
Sit down.

He grips RICCARDO'*s shoulder.* RICCARDO *has collapsed on to the
bench.*

You're whiter than the walls of a gas chamber.

Pause.

RICCARDO *(on the bench, with effort):*
　　I *have* already asked the Pope to protest.
　　But he is playing politics.
　　My father stood by me—my father.
DOCTOR *(with infernal laughter):*
　　Politics! Yes, that's what he's good for,
　　the windbag.
RICCARDO *(for a moment seems to be elsewhere. Then,*
　　still lost in thought): Let us not judge him.

During these last sentences the cement mixer has stopped. Upstage right, from the direction of the fires, comes the shrilling of whistles. The KAPO *drives the waiting victims off to the right—the procedure should be exactly the same as the last walk of the Luccanis and the other Italians. The* DOCTOR *blows his whistle to summon the* KAPO; *the deportees have vanished down the ramp; the reflection of the flames leaps very high.*

KAPO *(comes back, stands at attention):* Major!
DOCTOR *(indicating* RICCARDO*):*
　　This fellow goes along to the crematorium.
　　No jokes with him, understand.
　　He is my personal patient.
　　He's to work there.
　　(Ironically, to RICCARDO.*)*
　　I will not forget you, Father.
　　You'll have plenty to eat,
　　and a normal workday of about nine hours.
　　You can engage in studies there,
　　theological studies. Find out about God.
　　In two weeks I'll take you into the laboratory,
　　as my assistant, if you wish.
　　I'm sure you will.
　　(To the KAPO.*)* On your ashes: not a hair,
　　not a hair of his head is to be touched.
　　I'll talk to your superior later.
　　Now beat it.
KAPO: *Jawohl, Sturmbannführer!*

He goes off, right, with RICCARDO, *down the ramp. The* DOCTOR *stands motionlessly watching them.*

CURTAIN

SCENE 2

The same set. It is again early in the morning, about a week later. Snow is falling. We hear the cement mixer. HELGA *is standing in the guardroom, holding a hand mirror and combing her hair.* FRITSCHE *enters accompanied by civilians carrying briefcases: Baron* RUTTA *and Chief Engineer* MÜLLER-SAALE.

FRITSCHE: So early, gentlemen! I'm sorry
    I cannot take you to the officers' mess yet. Please.

He lets the civilians precede him.

RUTTA: We have all day, Major, and we are
    looking forward to being shown around.
    Herr Müller can go over the contract with you.
    Once you've checked its details, we can have it
    all wrapped up by lunchtime.
FRITSCHE *(at the door of the guard hut)*:
    We'll find a table here, and something to drink.
    All at once it's winter. I don't
    like to think about our Eastern Front.

He knocks and opens the door rather shyly.

HELGA: Come in.
FRITSCHE *(embarrassed)*: Please, step in . . . I have visitors from
        Essen.
    The gentlemen will be going over to the mess—
    we just wanted to have a drink together.
    They've had a long drive. Please come in.
RUTTA *(courteously)*: Are we a bother? I hope
    you've rested well? Good morning.
HELGA: I was on night duty, not much sleep—it's all right.
MÜLLER: Heil Hitler, Fräulein. Good morning.
FRITSCHE: Herr von Rutta and Herr Müller-Saale—
    This is Fräulein Helga, our loveliest assistant,
    if I may say so. We're on duty
    and freezing, Helga dear.
RUTTA *(with exaggerated gallantry)*:
    We know each other! From Berlin, don't we?
    Where was it that we met? How delightful . . .
HELGA: In Falkensee, at the tavern there—of course.

RUTTA: Why yes! And now you're in Auschwitz.
    Do you enjoy your new job?
HELGA: A job's a job.
    But my fiancé is here too.
MÜLLER: Aha, so it was love that lured you here.
    An enviable fellow, your fiancé.
    No doubt about it.
HELGA: Shall I make coffee—or would you prefer schnapps?
RUTTA: So kind of you, Fräulein Helga.
    Herr Müller will have schnapps, if I know him . . .
MÜLLER: You wouldn't be wrong. It's turned
    damnably cold overnight.
RUTTA *(laughs pointlessly)*: As for me, though I'm no wet blanket
    I really would prefer a cup of coffee.
HELGA: Gladly. The water will be hot in a minute.

FRITSCHE *gives her a rather inane smile; he is trying to be gallant,
but does not know how. She puts out glasses and cups. The men
take off their coats;* RUTTA *has been wearing a fur coat and wool
leggings.* MÜLLER-SAALE *takes a file from his briefcase,* RUTTA *a
set of blueprints which he spreads out on the bench. He indicates*
HELGA.

RUTTA: Congratulations, Herr Fritsche! I hardly
    expected to find such attractions in Auschwitz.
FRITSCHE *(smiling as if* HELGA *were his fiancée)*:
    Yes—Strength through Beauty!

The telephone rings. HELGA *lifts the receiver.*

MÜLLER *(half-humorously, half-seriously, as* HELGA *goes to answer
    the telephone)*: After working hours, I should think,
    that's a sight for sore eyes, isn't it?
HELGA: Inside Platform One, yes. He's here. Certainly.
    Herr Fritsche, for you.
FRITSCHE *(still utterly vapid and humorless, listening to*
    HELGA *at the telephone)*:
    Yes, we're lucky—a few of the gentler sex . . .
    Excuse me . . . Thank you, Fräulein Helga.

He takes the receiver as RUTTA *is spreading the map out on the cot.*

    Fritsche speaking. Yes sir, Commandant. *Gerstein?*
    Oh, *he* is to fetch him?

But I have visitors from Essen—
I can't go for the priest.
I suggest we have him brought here
and Gerstein himself can take charge of him.
Yes, sir. Of course. The whole thing was totally unnecessary.
Incredible carelessness.
Just what I said right off. Thank you, sir.
(He hangs up, murmurs:) A fine mess.
(Abruptly, turning toward the cot, respectfully:)
By God! The fuse plant!
RUTTA: Ideal, isn't it? Capacity
five hundred thousand fuses every month.
When in your opinion can Krupp
begin production here in Auschwitz?
You certainly should have enough labor.
FRITSCHE: More than enough! One moment, please.

He listens to sounds from outside. All listen. HELGA *brews the coffee. A distant loudspeaker comes on:* "Attention, an announcement: Inmate Riccardo Fontana No. 16670 is to report at once to the guardroom at Inside Platform One. End of Announcement."

That is a priest from Rome, an Aryan.
The Church sent him along with the Italians
since some were Catholic. Now he's to be released.
We've had him here ten days—just by mistake.
MÜLLER *(incredulously):* And now you're releasing him, just like
   that?
Isn't that pretty risky?
FRITSCHE: We'll saddle his conscience with hostages,
two Polish priests we have as inmates here.
If he talks—they die.
He'll keep his mouth shut all right.
RUTTA: Ah! Yes, they use hostages
in Essen too: French or Belgian workers
whom we cannot refuse a visit home
must give a hostage to the firm,
a fellow-countryman.
MÜLLER: That does the trick, just like in Schiller's poem.

Everyone laughs.

FRITSCHE *(stupidly):* Haha, Damon and Pythias—I see.
But can the workers from the East—Polacks,
Ukrainians, also go home on leave?
MÜLLER: What a fine mess that would be! Naturally not.

The coffee is now ready. The announcement comes through on the loudspeaker again. While MÜLLER-SAALE *chats with* HELGA, FRIT-SCHE *makes a telephone call.*

MÜLLER: What part of the country are you from, Fräulein Helga?
FRITSCHE *(to* RUTTA *as he lifts the receiver):*
Excuse me, Baron . . . yes? This is Sturmbannführer Fritsche.
Bring Bundles 16670 to the guardroom Inside Platform One—
a cassock. What's that? You know, the thing a priest wears.
Can't find it that quick? Are you crazy, 16670 was delivered
last week. I made a special point that that piece was to be
put aside. Kindly look around. I should think so. Good.
At once.
MÜLLER: Is your mother Saxon? Or did someone from Saxony
teach you to brew perfect coffee like this?
HELGA: Glad you like it. We make pretty good coffee
in Hamburg too.
RUTTA: Really tip-top. Herr Müller, please
read the draft aloud to us, will you?
Then we'll go to Herr Fritsche's office . . .
MÜLLER *(reading aloud):*
Very well, then, to make it short and sweet:
subject of the contract, the Auschwitz building,
one hundred and twenty by one hundred eighteen meters,
will be leased by the SS to Friedrich Krupp.
Secondly: the electrical substation,
to be built and equipped by Krupp,
will be transferred to the SS administration.
FRITSCHE: Transferred to us?
RUTTA: Only the substation, Herr Fritsche. The machines,
am I not right, Herr Müller, remain Krupp property?
MÜLLER: Yes. Point Three: machines
remain the property of Krupp.
Fourth: a year's notice is required
to terminate the contract.
I think it just as well, Major,

if we say nothing in the contract
about the daily fee Krupp pays the SS
per inmate?

FRITSCHE: Of course not, Herr Müller, of course not.

RUTTA: For the rest, our Lieutenant Colonel—
I mean Herr Doktor von Schwarz of Army High Command—
looked the plans over last week and approved them.

FRITSCHE: Fine. I guess that's it. One more cigarette,
then I must go.

They smoke and drink.

RUTTA: Many thanks. My colleague, Streifer,
of I. G. Farben was not exaggerating,
God knows, when he praised the exemplary
cooperation of SS and industry
in Auschwitz.

FRITSCHE: Yes. Siemens, too, is using forced labor
from some of the camps.

MÜLLER: Back in September Alfried Krupp von Bohlen
wanted to send a man to Auschwitz.
And Herr von Bohlen knows that his Breslau office,
which is in charge of technical affairs,
has kept in closest contact with Auschwitz.

RUTTA *(abruptly)*: The people here are easy to control!

FRITSCHE: Here, yes! But how does Krupp keep in check
the twenty thousand foreigners in Essen?

RUTTA: They're fairly docile. If not—there's the Gestapo,
Mother's little helper. They pick up
a few troublemakers every now and then.
We even allow a certain amount of correspondence.
Not to the East, of course. Their mail
has to be burned twice a week.
They're quite a bother, that rabble.
A pity we have to make do with them.

*They laugh; HELGA does not join in. Outside, wearing a steel hel-
met, looking about tensely, GERSTEIN has appeared. He peers surreptitiously into the hut, and hesitates. His expression is gloomy
and depressed—he knows this is to be the greatest risk he has yet
taken. Now he forces himself to assume an expression of calm superiority, knocks, enters, salutes.*

GERSTEIN: Major—the Commandant has sent me to you.
>   Am I intruding? I have orders
>   to fetch a certain Father Fontana from here.

FRITSCHE *(amiably):* Heil Hitler, Gerstein . . . Excuse me,
>   gentlemen.
>   I'll be along shortly. Fräulein Helga, will you
>   be so kind as to show them the way.
>   I know all about it, Gerstein.

HELGA: Yes, I'm due there, anyhow. Good morning, Herr Gerstein.

GERSTEIN: Ah, Fräulein Helga, how are you—good morning.

RUTTA: Well, many, many thanks, Herr Fritsche.

MÜLLER *(while the three are helping one another into their coats):*
>   It's been nice in your wigwam, Fräulein Helga.
>   I wouldn't mind having you make my coffee
>   every morning. Heil Hitler!

RUTTA *(to* GERSTEIN*)*: Heil Hitler.

GERSTEIN: Heil Hitler.

HELGA *(calling back as she goes):*
>   There's some coffee left, Herr Gerstein.

FRITSCHE *(to the civilians):* I'll be right along.
>   *(To* GERSTEIN.*)* The black crow will be along soon.
>   Our Doctor, it's incredible, amused himself
>   putting the priest to work at the crematorium.
>   As a dentist—just for a joke! He wants, he says,
>   to give the priest this chance for a second communion.
>   It's all the Doctor's fault that the man
>   ever set foot inside the camp.
>   I wanted to send him straight back home.

GERSTEIN: Where is the Doctor now?

FRITSCHE *(laughs disapprovingly):* He was going strong last night.
>   Still sleeping. Everyone's sleeping late. I could have used
>   a few extra hours sleep myself. We threw
>   a farewell party for Höss last night—
>   *(confidentially)* till four in the morning. You know about
>   that?

GERSTEIN: Yes, of course. But they don't hold it against him.

FRITSCHE *(sniggering):* The Doctor says that from now on Höss
>   can wear the Iron Cross with fig leaves and balls.
>   Seriously, though, he's getting a promotion.
>   He's to be inspector of all the camps in Germany.

All the same, it was going pretty far
for the Commandant to shack up with a Jewess.
You know, that was his consolation—
since he inspected the ovens every day.
At bottom he's a *terribly* good fellow.
GERSTEIN *(without sounding in the least sardonic):*
Yes, Höss has a heart. You'll miss him.
He's right at his post today, as always.
(As casually as possible.)
Has the Jewess been liquidated?
FRITSCHE *(eagerly)* No—imagine that—she's still alive. Odd, eh?
I suppose that Kaltenbrunner
means to keep the dame on ice
so that he has a hold on Höss for good.
Oh well, you'll bring the priest over?
GERSTEIN: To you, Major?
FRITSCHE *(rejecting that suggestion):* No, not to me! I want
(firmly) nothing at all to do with this affair.
Take him to Höss. See that the fellow signs a statement
that he's seen nothing in the camp but flower beds.
GERSTEIN: He'll sign anything to get out of here.
FRITSCHE: Nobody's ever been released before.
GERSTEIN: I've wondered about that myself. Oh well,
I suppose they know what they are doing.
I happened to be at the phone when the Nuncio called.
Then I went straight to Eichmann, who
was just as much upset as I was.
FRITSCHE: Terribly reckless of the Doctor
to let that black crow come in here at all.
He really goes too far, I think. Last night
he did a take-off of Ley and Heydrich. I found it disgusting.
After all, there's a limit to everything.
GERSTEIN: Heydrich—well, that certainly is tasteless.
Ley is really a marzipan pig, but Heydrich!

A KAPO, *timorous and careworn, brings a bundle of clothing tied
with string, to which a number is attached:* 16670. FRITSCHE *and*
GERSTEIN *leave the hut. The* KAPO *takes the bundle inside. A factory siren screeches.* FRITSCHE *looks at his watch and sets it.*

FRITSCHE *(laughing):* Marzipan pig is right. And always soused.

    The cassock! Just drop it in the hut.

    Well then, Gerstein, the black crow . . .

KAPO: Yes sir.

FRITSCHE: . . . will be along in due course. After all,

    we're a good two kilometers from the crematorium.

GERSTEIN: And still the smell of flesh is so sharp?

    What do the local people say?

FRITSCHE: They know what's up, of course.

    What you smell now doesn't come from the furnaces.

    That's from the open burning pits.

    We can no longer manage with furnaces alone.

    I must go now, I really don't want

    to have *anything* to do with this affair.

    It can only lead to trouble.

CARLOTTA *shyly passes by the two men in uniform. Carrying a pail of water and a scrubbing brush, she approaches the hut, enters, and begins scrubbing the floor on her knees. She sees* HELGA's *hand mirror lying on a chair. Still on her knees, she pushes her kerchief back slightly and examined her shorn hair, her dirty, haggard face. This seems to have been her first opportunity to do so since the deportation. She begins crying silently. Later, when* GERSTEIN *enters the hut, she makes an effort not to show that she has been crying.*

FRITSCHE: Please tell them in Berlin that I

    had not a thing to do with it.

    I guessed right off he wouldn't stay here.

    (He points to the bundle of clothes.)

    That's why I did not have his costume there

    thrown on to the big heap. *(As he walks off.)*

    So then, it's not my fault. Heil, Gerstein.

    And feed him up a bit at the canteen.

GERSTEIN: Thanks, Heil Hitler, Major, many thanks.

    (Gritting his teeth.) Asshole!

His nervousness keeps him pacing about. He lights a cigarette, then notices the girl scrubbing and goes into the hut, trying to flee from his own uneasiness. As he enters, the girl shrinks away; her every movement betrays her terror of any man in uniform. GERSTEIN *takes a piece of bread wrapped in newspaper from his pocket, un-wraps it and offers it to* CARLOTTA.

GERSTEIN: Where do you come from? Here, eat this.
  Have you been here long?
CARLOTTA *(not standing or taking the bread)*:
  From Rome—no, thank you, for a week.
GERSTEIN: From Rome? Then you know the priest,
      Father Fontana?
  Go on, take the bread.
CARLOTTA: We all know him.
  (Refusing, for fear of a trick.)
  Why do you give me bread?
GERSTEIN *(placing the bread on the chair)*:
  Why? You're hungry, aren't you?
  Would you like me to send a letter out for you?
CARLOTTA *(after a pause, coldly)*: No, thank you.
GERSTEIN: You don't trust me.
  But give a message to the Father.
  He's being released to go back to Rome.
CARLOTTA *(overjoyed, then abruptly sad)*:
  Released? He, too. But of course he
  doesn't really belong—to us.
GERSTEIN *(takes a sheet of paper and an envelope from the
    typewriter table, unscrews his fountain pen, and lays all these
    objects on the chair)*:
  Write in here, so that no one will see.
  The Father will take the letter to Rome.
CARLOTTA *(continuing to refuse, but with a touch of Italian pathos;
    her voice at the end subsides into tears)*:
  I have no one to write to!
  My fiancé died in Africa—for Germany,
  at the capture of Tobruk. To prove your gratitude
  you Germans have deported
  my parents and me, my sister and her children.
  Don't offer me bread—tell me, are they . . . dead?
  Tell me that. We arrived on October 20th.
  We were separated on the platform.
  Only a hundred or so entered the camp here.
  The others were taken away in trucks.

Where? Trucks with Red Cross markings.
You must know where they were taken!
GERSTEIN *(helplessly):* I'm not one of the camp guards, really not.
I don't know. I never go inside.

*The cement mixer begins to grind. She listens for a moment to the
sound. He attempts to distract her.*

Your fiancé wasn't Jewish. Then write
to his parents. Ask them to try, through the Vatican . . .
CARLOTTA: No. It's because of my in-laws
that I became a Catholic.
GERSTEIN: You regret that—why?
CARLOTTA: Catholics, Catholic Fascists were the ones
who handed me over to the Germans,
who took away my last picture of Marcello
and my engagement ring. Perhaps that was
my punishment for deserting my own people
and going over to the Catholic Church.
GERSTEIN: You must not say that! Catholics
are being persecuted too. Many priests
in Poland and in Germany have been murdered.
And Father Riccardo, coming with you voluntarily . . .
CARLOTTA *(still hostile):* There are just a few like that. Exceptions.
GERSTEIN: Of course. And yet—the majority of Italians,
the great majority, are against this terrorism.
Both Church and people.
CARLOTTA *(ostentatiously turning back to her work):*
Against this terrorism—like you, I suppose.
But do nothing or little against it, like you.
Christians! They're all Christians.
Marcello—he was a Christian. He could
respect a different religion, and let me keep mine.
But I listened to his parents instead—
they were after me to become a Catholic.
(Bitterly.) As a Catholic I felt safe in Rome.
That's the only reason I did not hide.
Can't you please find out
whether my family is still alive?
GERSTEIN: Really, I have no way to.
At least write down your name for Father Riccardo.

CARLOTTA *(suddenly taking heart):*
  I'd like to write a letter after all.
  Thank you. And forgive me.

She crouches on the floor and begins hurriedly writing, using the chair for a desk. Later, alone in the hut, she cries again and tears up what she has written. She puts the scraps of paper into the pocket of her smock.

GERSTEIN *(smiling at her, goes to the window, says rapidly to himself, but quite loudly):*
  Here he comes—why, it's Jacobson!

He wrenches open the door and rushes to meet JACOBSON. JACOBSON, *at the shock of finding him here, is incapable of doing more than cry out his name, while his skeletal face widens in a smile that threatens at any moment to disintegrate into sobs.*

JACOBSON: Gerstein! You!
  (Softly.) Sometimes I hoped for this.
GERSTEIN *(has retreated three steps to close the door to the hut):*
  Good God, Jacobson! You here. I thought
  you were in England. Where were you caught?
  Why, you had Riccardo's passport.
JACOBSON: At the Brenner.
  They looked too carefully at the passport photo.
  But I stuck to my story
  through thick and thin.
  Otherwise they would have killed me outright.
  I kept insisting that I was the priest.
  You understand, my name here is Father Fontana.
  I *am* the priest, you see.

As he speaks, he looks around several times to make sure he is not being overheard. One can sense that he has almost completely identified with his part, which is his sole salvation. Feverishly and hoarsely:

  I work at the outer platform sorting the belongings
  of those who have been gassed. Sometimes I find
  jewelry that I swap with the railroad men
  for bread. That's why I'm still alive.
  And because I hate. I want to get out.

Otherwise I would long ago
have run into the wire.
And now you've sent for me!
GERSTEIN: Not you, Jacobson!
  (Despairingly.) Don't you see: Riccardo Fontana's in the
      camp.
  I've come on his account.
  How could I have dreamed
  that you were here.
JACOBSON *(not understanding)*: What's that? The Father here?
  But he's no Jew. How could he . . .
GERSTEIN: They deported the Jews from Rome,
  and he went with them, of his own volition.
  He's been in Auschwitz for a week.
  Now they're releasing him.
JACOBSON *(incredulous—then with an effort to respond
  generously)*: Released—from Auschwitz? Incredible!
  But . . . I'm glad for the priest's sake.
GERSTEIN: To think that we should meet here, Jacobson!
  How painful it is to be powerless to free you.
JACOBSON *(unable to hide his mounting bitterness)*:
  Yes, I am no priest, Gerstein.
  A priest is worth an ultimatum.
GERSTEIN *(gives a short, harsh laugh)*: Ultimatum? From whom?
  Believe me, this order for Riccardo's release
  is only something I've invented.
JACOBSON: Then invent another—to get that girl,
  or me or any of us wretches out of here.
GERSTEIN: You know I can't, Jacobson.
  I'm only a lieutenant, nothing more.
  At this moment I stand closer to the brink
  of death than you, Jacobson!
JACOBSON *(looking away)*: Forgive me—you wear that uniform.
GERSTEIN: How else could I have come here?
  That I can never shed this uniform
  is my part-payment of the debt of guilt
  that burdens all of us. Our resistance movement . . .
JACOBSON: Resistance? Why, Gerstein, can't it even
  tear up the railroad tracks to Auschwitz?
  Why doesn't your resistance show itself?

(Softly, fervently, despairingly.)
Or are you still a lone wolf?
How can you people go on living, knowing
what day after day, for an entire year,
has been happening here?
You live, you eat, you beget children—
and you know—you all know about the camps.
(He grasps GERSTEIN's *shoulders, his voice tearful:)*
Make an end, make an end of it, somehow!
(Disjointedly.)
Why don't the Allies drop arms for us?
God knows, Gerstein, I don't mean to accuse you;
it's only thanks to you that I'm alive . . .
It's only that—I was numbed enough to forget.
Seeing you has made me realize
there's still a world outside the camp.
Gerstein, you can do something for me, after all.
GERSTEIN: If there's anything . . .
JACOBSON *(rapidly):* Just say I claimed to be the priest
   and then attacked you when—the real priest came.
   Shoot me.
GERSTEIN: Jacobson!
JACOBSON *(pleadingly):* Shoot me, Gerstein.
   Say I attacked you—they'll believe that.
   Please, Gerstein, do this for me. I no longer
   have the courage to run into the fence—
   the current doesn't always kill at once.
GERSTEIN: You've survived for a whole year—surely
   you'll make it to the end. Jacobson—
   just one more year—at most one year.
   Then the Russians will be here to free you.
JACOBSON: A year!
GERSTEIN: They've already retaken the Ukraine.
JACOBSON: Gerstein, why won't you do it? Why not?

GERSTEIN *shakes his head, unable to reply.* JACOBSON *turns away.*

   Then I'll go, so that I don't
   put you and the priest in greater danger.
GERSTEIN *(helplessly, deeply moved, stops him):*
   Not this way, Jacobson, don't leave this way.

JACOBSON: Four thousand, five thousand—some days
    even more are gassed here.
    Nothing frightens me any longer except
    the world that permits such things.
    (More composed and matter-of-fact.)
    And the most devilish thing of all is
    that if one man escapes he dooms
    ten others to the hole. That happened once,
    and ten were sentenced to death by starvation.
    We listened to their crying for a week.
    Father Kolbe was the last to die, they say.
    It's knowing that which held me back
    a while ago, when I could have escaped—
    out there on the platform—in one of the cars
    that take the shoes
    of those they've gassed to Breslau.
GERSTEIN: They think the priest is being freed
    officially. There'll be no reprisals,
    except for me, if ever the truth comes out.

RICCARDO, *shocked speechless at seeing* GERSTEIN *here, has appeared behind* JACOBSON, *whom he does not immediately recognize.* RICCARDO *has been terribly marked by the work he has had to do at the crematorium for the past week.*

GERSTEIN: Riccardo!
    The Nuncio sent me to take you back.
RICCARDO: Gerstein! You should not have tried to find me.
    Jacobson—you!
JACOBSON: How could you come here, Father?
    I'm living under your name, you know.
RICCARDO: Jacobson—forgive me, I thought
    you'd come through safely that time.
JACOBSON: To come here voluntarily, unarmed—
    whom did you think you could help?
GERSTEIN *(insistently, since* RICCARDO *has obviously not
    understood)*: Riccardo, you are being released!
RICCARDO: Released?

Suddenly done in, he sits down on the steps leading up to the guard-room.

I can't go on.
I've already told myself a hundred times
that it was sheer presumption to come here.
I can't bear it, I can't bear it.

He cries silently; none of the others can speak.

For the past week
I have been burning the dead ten hours a day.
And with every human body that I burn
a portion of my faith burns also.
God burns.
Corpses—a conveyor belt of corpses.
History is a highway paved with carrion . . .
If I knew that He looks on—
(With revulsion.) I would have to—hate Him.

GERSTEIN *(uncertainly, pulling* RICCARDO *to his feet):*
None of us understands Him any longer.
But now at least He wants to save you, Riccardo.

RICCARDO *(wearily):* How do you know that? And why me?
I was not speaking of myself—the families . . .
(Murmuring disconnectedly.)
I am—I would be frightened of rescue
by Him . . . The Monster that devours its young.

JACOBSON *(speaking more vigorously and resolutely):*
Father, speak for us, help us!
Tell the Pope that he must act.

RICCARDO: I could never get to the Pope again.
(Suddenly.) What were you thinking of—return to Rome?

GERSTEIN *(feverishly):*
You have to survive, Riccardo—to live, somewhere.

RICCARDO: Live? No one can
come back from here to go on living.
(Points to JACOBSON.)
And what about him? And all the others?
I came here with a mission; that must sustain me.
Whether it's meaningful, I'm no longer sure.
I do not know. But if it's not,
my life, too, is no longer meaningful.
Let me be.

JACOBSON: Father, if you do not go along
    you will endanger Gerstein. He only
    invented the order for your release.
GERSTEIN: You shouldn't have said that.
JACOBSON: I did to get him out of here—now hurry!
RICCARDO *(starts convulsively):*
    So—I rather thought as much, Gerstein,
    you used to go about things
    so cautiously, for all your daring . . . *(Despairingly.)*
    Why this insanity now, to come for me?
GERSTEIN *(gloomily):* Because I have you on my conscience.
    I turned you first onto this fatal path.
RICCARDO *(quickly going up to him):*
    What would I have on my conscience, if I weren't here?
    And shall I shrink from it now that I am? No,
    God knows it's not your fault that I am here.
    But it is not my fault either, is it,
    if something happened to you through my staying?
    Please understand, I have no right to go.
    Why lead me into temptation—that makes it worse.
    You see I hardly have the necessary strength.
    (Softly.) I'm doing penance, as I must.
GERSTEIN *(excitedly):* You've done your penance long ago.
    You've just come from the fires, Riccardo.
RICCARDO: Gerstein, please, take *him* with you.
JACOBSON: Me?
GERSTEIN: And suppose he is killed?
JACOBSON *(firmly):* Father, I won't accept that.
RICCARDO: Jacobson, I'm not staying in your place.
    It's not a question of me or of you.
    I am here to represent the Church.
    I could not go even if I wanted to.
    God knows, I did want to.
    You will owe me nothing, Jacobson.
    If you don't go, then no one will at all.

While GERSTEIN, *who feels it is unendurable to leave the two behind, stands by passively, although with dark forebodings,* RICCARDO *says slowly, with heavy pauses:*

    Put on my cassock one more time—
    if Gerstein agrees . . .

JACOBSON: I can't accept that—not from you,
and certainly not from him.

He indicates GERSTEIN, *and the two wait for* GERSTEIN *to reply.*
GERSTEIN, *to hide his fear of such a risk, fends off the decision.*

GERSTEIN: I say nothing. Decide it for yourselves.
RICCARDO: You can do all the things that I cannot.
You can use a gun, can sabotage.
It's not a case of simply saving your life.
Gerstein is not going to set you free
so that you can hide out till the end of the war.
GERSTEIN *(unable to forebear commenting):*
The practical side—do any of the high camp officers
know either of your personally?
JACOBSON: No.
RICCARDO: Only the head doctor knows me.
GERSTEIN *(starts back, aghast):* The Doctor!
No! If the Doctor knows you, Riccardo,
that makes our game so much more difficult
that we must ask ourselves: can we afford to risk it.
His house is at the entrance to the camp.
He's too much for me.
RICCARDO *(undeterred):* The Doctor—and nobody can prove
that you knew me, Gerstein,
or that you already knew Jacobson.
GERSTEIN: *(with extreme impatience):* Yes, that's *my* outlook.
(He indicates JACOBSON.*)* But what chance has he
if the Doctor finds him with me.
We'd only be endangering Jacobson.

Pause. Both look at JACOBSON. *He hesitates, then says softly—*

JACOBSON: Rather one more risk—even if I lose—
than stay on with the railroad squad until the time
they automatically count me off for gassing.
Gerstein, I swear to you, those bandits
will never learn from me that you knew me.
GERSTEIN: I'm not worrying about myself now,
but about you. Make up your mind:
Either back to your work—
for there on the platform you might possibly
come through after all—
and in that case I'll tell the Commandant

that the priest refused to give his pledge
to keep his mouth shut after his release,
and therefore it's all off—
or else we go straight to the gate,
to the Commandant—a course that may
lead us right into the Doctor's arms.
You know what that would mean.
The odds are about fifty-fifty.

JACOBSON: But what would happen to you then?

GERSTEIN: I'll talk myself out of it. Perhaps. Probably.
Decide for yourself alone.

JACOBSON *(quickly, firmly):* Then I will try it.

From this point on to the end GERSTEIN *reacts swiftly, unsentimentally and consistently, although he has no hope at all.*

GERSTEIN: Good. Let's try it.
The cassock's in the hut. Get into it!

RICCARDO *(with forced dryness):*
Is my breviary there? Let me have that.
Then I'll go . . . Carlotta!

RICCARDO *and* GERSTEIN *enter the hut.* JACOBSON *hangs behind, suddenly frightened.*

CARLOTTA *(warmly):* Father, you're going free!

GERSTEIN *(insistently to* JACOBSON*):* Come in, hurry, Jacobson.

RICCARDO: I'm staying with the rest of you, Carlotta.
Your father is still living. I saw him
last night at roll call . . .

GERSTEIN *(to the still hesitant* JACOBSON, *irritably):*
Change your clothes, man, change your clothes!

CARLOTTA: How did he look? And my mother,
my sister, the children . . .

JACOBSON *now removes his jacket and puts the cassock on over a dirty, torn undershirt. While* RICCARDO *takes the breviary and rosary from the pocket of his cassock, he tries to hide his face from* CARLOTTA—*he knows that her mother and sister have already been cremated.*

GERSTEIN: I'll take your letter with me—is it ready?

RICCARDO: No, Carlotta, I don't see the women.
Your father is holding out bravely.

CARLOTTA *(fumbles the scraps of paper from the pocket of her*
smock): Thank you, I . . . could not write the letter.
Take these, please—so that
they aren't found on me.
GERSTEIN *(helplessly)*: The Father is staying with you.

RICCARDO *offers* CARLOTTA *the rosary.*

CARLOTTA *(embarrassed, does not want the rosary, but also does*
not want to reject him): No, Father, no—keep it for yourself.
You're staying?
RICCARDO *(who does not understand her refusal, smilingly places*
the rosary in her hand): Yes.
GERSTEIN *(to* RICCARDO, *in fear)*:
If we run into the Doctor, Riccardo,
you'll see us both again—there—tomorrow.

Silently, RICCARDO *shakes hands with* GERSTEIN. JACOBSON, *al-*
ready wearing the cassock, grips RICCARDO*'s shoulder.*

JACOBSON: Thank you.
(Fanatically.) Hold out. We'll come. We will avenge you.
RICCARDO *(trying to smile)*: Then you'd better hurry . . .
Goodbye Gerstein. Don't let my father know
where I am. Tell him my life
has been fulfilled.
You know the truth.
Carlotta!

He leaves quickly; just outside the hut he makes a broken gesture
that betrays the depths of his emotion. GERSTEIN *accompanies him*
to the door, then turns around. A long silence.

GERSTEIN *(urgently to* CARLOTTA*)*:
Don't let yourself fall sick. Keep fit for work.
Above all keep fit for work.
They cannot finish off all of you.
JACOBSON: I feel ashamed
because I am going and you stay.
CARLOTTA: I'm glad for you anyhow.
JACOBSON: Stave off despair. If you start
weeping here, you're lost.

CARLOTTA *nods mutely to him and goes out quickly to refill her pail, but chiefly to make their departure easier. With spasmodic self-control,* GERSTEIN *raps out his instructions.* JACOBSON *has just drawn the black trousers over his striped ones and now kicks off his wooden sandals and puts on* RICCARDO's *shoes.*

GERSTEIN: We're going to the Commandant now.
 Talk as little as possible.
 You've been here a week, is that clear, one week.
 You must sign a statement
 pledging your silence by the lives of two priests.
 Do so. All right, let's go.
 Talk as little as possible.
 Remember, you were working at the crematorium.
 Let's try it.
JACOBSON: He was here a week? I have
 (pointing to his forearm) an altogether different number . . .
GERSTEIN *(gloomily):* No one will ask your number. Ready!
 (Already at the door, he starts violently.)
 Over there—the Doctor! Hurry past now.
JACOBSON *(in a harsh whisper):* He's coming here. Done for.
GERSTEIN *(in the same manner):* Pull yourself together.
 (In tone of command.) Walk ahead of me, Father.

The DOCTOR *approaches, wearing a jaunty fatigue cap and accompanied by a helmeted SS man who holds a submachine gun at the ready. Flexing his swagger stick between his hands, the* DOCTOR *plants himself in front of* JACOBSON *and* GERSTEIN. *He is smartly dressed, from the big, soft gloves to the high, supple boots and the wide black cape. The sound of a circular saw, very close by, has accompanied his entrance.*

DOCTOR: What's the hurry, Gerstein? How are things?
GERSTEIN: Heil Hitler, Major—I'm here to pick up
 Inmate Fontana, the priest.

Abruptly, making a pointless attempt at distraction, in a forced, confidential tone:

 Incidentally, Doctor, you've got a girl here . . .
 (He looks around in embarrassment.) She comes from Rome.
 Where is she? Oh, she's gone for more water.
 Her fiancé was killed fighting for Germany.

DOCTOR: Then he won't have to cry over her.

GERSTEIN: *(in the jargon):* Keep the girl on ice, Doctor.

DOCTOR *(laughing):* I don't mind, if she's attractive,
  I'll take her into my private lab.
  A Roman girl who has survived our recent
  Feast of Tabernacles, our grand harvest-home,
  is certainly a rarity in the camp.
  But the reason I left my soft bed, Gerstein,
  was to say goodbye to our priest.
  (Yawns widely.)
  In a hurry, isn't he? Touching, touching.
  Since when do Hebrews belong to the One True Church?

GERSTEIN *(harshly, with a good pretense of assurance):*
  Hebrews? What do you mean by that?
  Major Fritsche told me . . .

DOCTOR: *(irritated by the mention of Fritsche):*
  Oh, don't give me any of that Dr. iuris neutrum Fritsche.
  What business is it of Fritsche's!

GERSTEIN: I have orders from Lieutenant Colonel Eichmann . . .

DOCTOR *(scornfully):* Really!

GERSTEIN: To take this Jesuit, a diplomat from the Holy See
  who was sent here by mistake . . .

DOCTOR: By mistake—they're all sent by mistake.
  What does that matter?

GERSTEIN: *(undeterred):* . . . to the Nuncio in Berlin.
  Well, here he is.

DOCTOR: Who? The Nuncio? Is he the Nuncio?
  (With an elaborate bow to JACOBSON.*)*
  Your Excellency—is it true that God is sick?
  It's said he's having those depression fits again—
  as he did the time his Church was burning up
  the Jews and Protestants in Spain.

GERSTEIN: This is Father Riccardo Fontana.

JACOBSON *(trying to play along):*
  I also think God suffers great grief now.

DOCTOR *(playing with his stick, enjoying every word):*
  Or maybe he has syphilis, like so many female saints
  who were prostitutes on earth—and sodomites
  like St. Francis. . . .
  You've stuck your hand right in the shit this time,

Gerstein, old fox—I've seen through you
ever since our drive to Tübingen.
But Christians as ingenious as you are
delight me.

GERSTEIN *(indignantly)*: Major, I will not stand for that.
I demand an explanation.

DOCTOR: So, you demand! You demand
that I make a fool of myself.
You think I am another Adolf Eichmann?
I'll make you pay for thinking me a fool, Gerstein.

GERSTEIN: I don't understand you at all.

DOCTOR: You understand perfectly well; I know the priest.

GERSTEIN *(to* JACOBSON*)*: Do you know the Major, Father?

DOCTOR *(thrusting* JACOBSON *aside with his stick)*:
I know the *real* priest, the real one.
When he arrived here a week ago
he wanted to convert me, then and there.
A charming master of ceremonies for Christ
who'll amuse me as my private chaplin
(points to the glow of the fire)
as soon as the incense from the furnaces
tickles his nose enough to make him puke
and spew all over his faith.
(He taps JACOBSON *in the face with his stick.)*
Tell me what's so attractive about this fellow
that you're determined to have him?
Nice, warm, Christian, brotherly love?

GERSTEIN: It's a cheap joke, Major,
to go on mocking me all the time
because I go to church. That's my affair.

DOCTOR: Really touching: a member of the Confessing Church
comes here to swindle a priest free
and instead smuggles a Jew out of camp.

GERSTEIN *(seemingly bitterly amused)*: Smuggle? Ridiculous!
Smuggling an inmate past Höss in broad daylight!
I'm taking him to the Commandant now.
Of what are you accusing me?
Did I have the inmate summoned?
How am I supposed to know
if he is not the man they're looking for?

DOCTOR *(blows his police whistle; laughs malignantly):*
How? How are you supposed to know?
You'll get your chance to explain how . . .

CARLOTTA *returns with the pail of water and resumes her work inside the hut.*

GERSTEIN *(feverishly interrupting him):*
Was I the one who insisted
on taking the priest to the camp gate?
I wanted to wait outside. It was only because
Major Fritsche was busy with visitors from Essen—
Fritsche asked me, and Höss too,
to wait for the priest here at the platform.
—By the way, there's that girl again.

He points to JACOBSON. *The* DOCTOR *has blown his whistle once more.*

If you have any doubts . . .
DOCTOR: Doubts! I'm arresting you, Gerstein.
All three of you were standing here just now
and cooking up your little plot.
I've bided my time patiently to hear
how idiotic you expect us to be.
Rome hasn't asked for the priest at all
or you would never have swapped him for that fellow.
There, his belt! Arrest him!

These last words are addressed to the guard. GERSTEIN *draws his pistol; it is impossible to say whether he intends to shoot. The guard knocks it from his hand and kicks it to one side. The guard grins.* GERSTEIN *hesitantly hands over his belt. Immediately after his last words the* DOCTOR *turns to* RICCARDO, *whom another guard has brought in.* RICCARDO *has come to a halt some steps away.* CARLOTTA, *inside the hut, senses the terrible events outside. She opens the door and begins scrubbing the three steps.* RICCARDO, *endeavoring to grasp the situation, scarcely pays attention to the* DOCTOR's *chatter.*

Well, well, hello, my dear Father. Have you now
reconciled reality with the ideal
there at the furnaces? This baptism of fire
enters you in the ranks of the great *testes veritatis.*
I hope, as my private chaplin, you will show

appreciation for my giving you the chance
to study the Golgotha of Absolute Spirit
at closer quarters. A little stunned, eh?
Well, anyone who, like you,
sees history as a therapeutic process . . .
(He laughs challengingly.)

RICCARDO *(calmly and contemptuously):*
You'll never win; that makes you so talkative.
Your kind can only triumph temporarily.
What have I been brought here for?

JACOBSON *(has come to the decision to give up quickly, so that*
GERSTEIN *at least may be exonerated. He steps forward):*
Wish to report that I tricked the lieutenant.
I pretended to be the priest.
Since he didn't answer, I reported to the guardroom.
He wasn't there . . . didn't come, so . . .

DOCTOR *(flies into a rage after this last sentence, which too*
obviously attempts to give information to RICCARDO*):*
One more word and you'll go into the furnace *alive.*
About face—about face, I say!
*(*JACOBSON *obeys.)*
Kneel—on your knees.
And now your face in the filth.

JACOBSON *lies on the ground, face down. The* DOCTOR *says trium-*
phantly to GERSTEIN*, pointing to* RICCARDO*:*

I suppose he did not want to come?
Or didn't you want to take him?
(Ironically.) You know he is the man the Pope
blubbers over, night after night, in the Sistine Chapel.

GERSTEIN *(indicating* RICCARDO*):*
This is the first time I have ever seen him.
How should I know which is the real priest.
It isn't my affair to check on that.

DOCTOR *(looking at* CARLOTTA*):*
Oh well, let's see what the bit of skirt here has to say.
Come over here, you! Come here!
Oho, the Spiritual Exercises of
Ignatius Loyola. Crematorium reading!
Always used to be read aloud at the stake.

Reaching out quickly, he has snatched the breviary from RICCAR-
DO's *pocket. With his other hand, he takes hold of* CARLOTTA, *who
has approached falteringly.*

RICCARDO (*addresses her rapidly, then the* DOCTOR):
    Carlotta—*you!* We were deported together . . .
    Do you still remember me?
CARLOTTA (*trying to play along*):
    Father, it's good to see you're still living.
DOCTOR (*paying no attention, speaks to the girl while, stick tucked
    under his arm, he eagerly leafs through the* Exercises):
    You came from Rome, with your family? Are you Catholic?
CARLOTTA: Yes.
DOCTOR: Where's that passage about the girls . . . ?

*Reads aloud, savoring the words; the background and the man
himself give vividness to Loyola's text.*

> The devil on the throne of fire and smoke
> lures as the tempter—yes, yes, we know.
> Aha, here it is: "I see with the eyes
> of imagination the tremendous glow of flame
> and the souls locked in the *burning* bodies.
> I smell with the sense of smell smoke, sulphur,
> excrement and rotting things."
> And that about the girls, Father, where is it?
> The sin of fleshly lust, my love of the flesh
> (*laughs*) of the world—you ought to be exposed
> to that, too, Father.
> Shall I put the two of you together?
> (*Abruptly to* CARLOTTA *as he closes the breviary.*)
> You've been cleaning here since seven o'clock?
> Were you on time today?
CARLOTTA (*frightened*): Yes, right on time.
DOCTOR: Your fiancé was killed?
CARLOTTA: Yes, at Tobruk.
DOCTOR: I see—what is—what was his name?
CARLOTTA: Marcello.
DOCTOR (*very rapidly*): So, you were here on time!
    But still you came later than the priest, eh?
CARLOTTA (*bewildered, does not dare to reply, stammers*):
    I—don't know—I was . . .

RICCARDO *(calmly, pointing to* JACOBSON, *attempting to help her):*
    He's asking whether the priest was here
    when you came, Carlotta.
DOCTOR *(infuriated):* Father, don't stoop so low!
    (Casually to CARLOTTA, *pointing to* RICCARDO.)
    Well then, when did your soulmate get here?
CARLOTTA: The Father—I don't know—I couldn't . . .

Although nothing really depends on her answer any more, the DOC-
TOR, *out of pleasure in tormenting her, forces her to her knees with
an iron grip and then bends her over so that she is almost on her
back. He applies this force so unexpectedly that she cries out.*

DOCTOR: Well—do you know or don't you?
CARLOTTA: I didn't look up, I was just—
    scrubbing the floor—I . . .
DOCTOR *(pulls her to her feet again, with smiling sadism):*
    Shall I send you where your family went?
    Look at the fires over there.
    And there—the fence—do you want me to
    chase you over there or over there?

At this casual mention of the end of her family CARLOTTA *collapses
psychically—this news is the last straw. Madness already in her
eyes, she whispers, an insane stammering.*

CARLOTTA: Dead—all dead—dead—all dead—dead . . .

While she stammers, the DOCTOR *says offhandedly—*

DOCTOR: Was he here first—or was it this one?
CARLOTTA *(looks at him in silence, her face wildly contorted.*
    At last she stammers): I don't know, I don't know, I don't
    know.

The DOCTOR *has let go of her. She retreats several steps toward the
guardroom while staring hypnotized at "the most cunning of
brutes" (Canaris's phrase for Heydrich)—his bestiality has now
come fully to the fore. Now she screams, screams like a woman in
labor, under anesthesia, all inhibitions gone. The actress may, if she
wishes, blurt out words at this point—perhaps the simplest, the
most cliche phrases might be used.*

    No—no—let me alone—no—don't . . .

At the first piercing outcry, which even takes the DOCTOR *aback, she flees in a single bound up the steps and into the hut. Her movement is so wholly natural, so utterly irrepressible, so lacking in the "alienation" of theater, that it completely smashes all our efforts heretofore to create theatrical stylization, to remove from actuality the atrocities of the Final Solution, which are still so close to us.*

CARLOTTA's *screams pass over into spastic laughter. She tears off her kerchief, lashes aimlessly about with it, and throws it away. Her eyes dart frantically over the men. Rosary in her hands, she rushes into the guardroom, her harsh laughter like the cries of an animal as she looks into* HELGA's *mirror. She crouches in a corner with the mirror, gasping in brief bursts of laughter and sobbing, and tries to put the rosary around her neck like a necklace. It slips from her hands. The* DOCTOR *has recovered. Mechanically, he opens his holster, murmuring—*

DOCTOR: Gone off her rocker.

He strides quickly and firmly into the hut to do what is always done with deportees whose nerves give out before gassing. Putting down the breviary, he picks up the rosary and holds it out to CARLOTTA. *An insane smile passes over her face, for he radiates that "most persuasive kindness" we have mentioned. Her madly flickering eyes look into his. She jumps up and tries to grasp his hand and the rosary. She utters a cry of release because she has found "him" again and wants to embrace him.*

CARLOTTA: Marcello! Marcello! *(Laughs madly.)* I was afraid
    you would never come back from Africa.
    It's so long, Marcello—you've been gone so long.
DOCTOR *(evading her embrace, with compelling tenderness)*:
    Come along—come now—not here.

She follows without hesitation. He does not touch her, merely extends his arm to her—the gesture lightly, gracefully suggesting that she come with him. He moves backward toward the door, holding her gaze with his eyes. All this happens very quickly.

CARLOTTA *(passing in front of him, already outside on the last step, anxiously)*: Marcello—Marcello!

Standing behind her in the doorway, he draws his pistol with an unexpectedly rapid movement and kills her with a bullet in the back of the neck. Without so much as a glance at the corpse, he replaces the pistol in the holster. At this moment, while the two guards are absorbed in what is happening, RICCARDO *stoops for* GERSTEIN's *pistol, picks it up, and aims at the* DOCTOR, *crying out—*

RICCARDO: Destroy him!

He is shot down by the submachine gun of the SS man standing behind him before he can release the safety catch or press the trigger. RICCARDO *drops to his knees, then slowly falls over backward. The guard picks up* GERSTEIN's *pistol. Grinning with the shock, he holds it out to the* DOCTOR. GERSTEIN *has covered his eyes with his hand for a moment.*

DOCTOR: Aimed at me? I guess he really meant it.
    Thank you, sergeant.
    (Bending over RICCARDO.*)*
    Hm, Father, shooting comes almost as hard as praying—
    in Auschwitz.
    Too bad, I was looking forward to
    debating with you for a few weeks more . . .
    Any nearer to God now?
RICCARDO *(straightens up, tries to say something, sinks back, murmurs almost inaudibly):* In hora mortis meae voca me.
DOCTOR *(mockingly, as he straightens up):*
    Amen. Did you really hear him calling—
    in the crematorium?
    (Kicks JACOBSON, *orders:)*
    Get up—on your way, to the campfire
    (points to RICCARDO:*)*
    and take that with you—go on, take it along.

JACOBSON *gets up.* GERSTEIN *has stooped over* RICCARDO *and opened the dying man's jacket, thus plainly showing whose side he is on. Without a word the* DOCTOR *pushes between* GERSTEIN *and* RICCARDO. JACOBSON, *on his knees, his hands under* RICCARDO's *arm, tries in vain to lift* RICCARDO.

GERSTEIN: He isn't dead. You are a physician—help him.
    (Shouts:) He's still alive!
DOCTOR *(without looking at* GERSTEIN, *coolly):*
    The fire is a good physician. It will burn out

the Jew *and* the Christian in him.
(Beckons to the GUARD *who saved him.)*
Take this man to the Commandant.
Watch out for him—I'll be along shortly.
GUARD: Yes, sir.

GERSTEIN, *after a last look at his friends, strides off swiftly to the left behind the hut, followed by the SS man. The other guard, with kicks and blows of his submachine gun, has tried to make* JACOBSON *stand up. But* JACOBSON, *exhausted and numbed with horror, remains in a half kneeling position,* RICCARDO's *head in his lap. The sound of the circular saw is heard, very close.*

DOCTOR *(with biting impatience):* You'll have to help the cripple!
(Points to CARLOTTA.*)* And get that cleared away too.
GUARD: Yes, sir.

Reluctantly, he takes RICCARDO's *shoulders,* JACOBSON *takes* RICCARDO's *feet. They go off right. The* DOCTOR *walks slowly to the left, where* GERSTEIN *was led away. After passing behind the windows of the guardroom, he remembers the* Spiritual Exercises, *returns, passes by* CARLOTTA's *body, enters the hut, leafs through the book, smiles, tucks it under his arm, and leaves the stage like a professor after a lecture.*

The unemotional voice of an announcer on tape reads:

"On October 28, 1943, Herr von Weizsäcker, Hitler's Ambassador to the Holy See, writes to the Foreign Office in Berlin":

Here, as the glow of the flames sinks lower and lower, a different voice continues, the deliberate, refined voice of a well-bred elder statesman:

"Although the Pope is said to have been importuned from various quarters, he has not allowed himself to be carried away into making any demonstrative statements against the deportation of the Jews. Although he must expect our enemies to resent this attitude on his part, he has nevertheless done all he could, in this delicate question as other matters, not to prejudice relationships with the German government. Since further action on the Jewish problem is probably not to be expected here in Rome, it may be assumed that this question, so troublesome to German-Vatican relations, has been disposed of.

"On October 25 the *Osservatore Romano*, moreover, published a semiofficial communiqué on the Pope's charitable activities in which the statement was made, in the style typical of this Vatican newspaper—that is to say, involved and vague—that the Pope extends his paternal solicitude to all men without distinction of nationality and race. There is no need to raise objections to its publication, since hardly anyone will understand the text as referring specially to the Jewish question."

The unemotional announcer speaks again. The fire is out, the stage dark; we see only the dead girl close to the footlights.

"And so the gas chambers continued to work for a full year more. In the summer of 1944 the so-called daily quota of exterminations reached its maximum. On November 26, 1944, Himmler ordered the crematoria to be blown up. Two months later the last prisoners in Auschwitz were freed by Russian soldiers."

CURTAIN

Translated by Richard and Clara Winston;
abridged by Margaret Herzfeld-Sander

HEINAR KIPPHARDT

In the Matter of
J. Robert Oppenheimer

Characters

J. ROBERT OPPENHEIMER, *physicist*

Personnel Security Board

GORDON GRAY, *Chairman*
WARD V. EVANS, *member*
THOMAS A. MORGAN, *member*

Counsel

ROGER ROBB, *counsel for the Atomic Energy Commission*
C. A. ROLANDER, *associate of Robb, security expert*
LLOYD K. GARRISON, *counsel for Oppenheimer*
HERBERT S. MARKS, *counsel for Oppenheimer*

Witnesses

MAJOR NICHOLAS RADZI, *Security Officer*
JOHN LANSDALE, *lawyer, formerly Security Officer*
EDWARD TELLER, *physicist*
HANS BETHE, *physicist*
DAVID TRESSEL GRIGGS, *Chief Scientist of the Air Force,*
    geophysicist
ISADOR ISAAC RABI, *physicist*

Part 1

The stage is open. Visible spotlights. White hangings separate the stage from the auditorium, sufficiently high for the following documentaries to be projected on them:

Scientists in battledress, looking like military personnel, are doing the count-down for test explosions—4-3-2-1-0 (in English, Russian, and French).

Cloud formations caused by atomic explosions unfold in great beauty, watched by scientists through dark filters.

On the wall of a house, radiation shadows of a few victims of the atomic explosion on Hiroshima.

The hangings open.

SCENE 1

Room 2022

A small ugly office; walls of whitewashed wooden boards. The room has been temporarily furnished for the purpose of the investigation. On a raised platform, back center, a table and three black leather armchairs for the members of the Board. Behind, on the wall, the Stars and Stripes. In front of the platform, floor level, the stenographers are seated with their equipment. On the right, ROBB and ROLANDER, counsel for the Atomic Energy Commission, are busying themselves with stacks of documents. Opposite ROBB and ROLANDER, on a raised platform, tables and chairs for OPPENHEI-MER'S counsel. In front of the platform, floor level, a small old leather sofa.

J. ROBERT OPPENHEIMER enters Room 2022 by a side door on the right. He is accompanied by his two lawyers. An official leads him diagonally across the room to the leather sofa. His lawyers spread out their materials. He puts down his smoking paraphernalia and steps forward to the footlights.

OPPENHEIMER: On the twelfth of April 1954, a few minutes to ten, J. Robert Oppenheimer, Professor of Physics at Princeton, formerly Director of the Atomic Weapons Laboratories at Los Alamos, and, later, Adviser to the Government on atomic matters, entered Room 2022 in Building T3 of the Atomic Energy commission in Washington, to answer questions put to him by a Personnel Security Board, concerning his views, his associations, his actions, suspected of disloyalty. The evening before this investigation, Senator McCarthy said in a television interview:

A huge picture of Joseph McCarthy is projected on the white screens at the back. OPPENHEIMER *goes to the leather sofa and fills his pipe. A voice shaking with agitation issues from the loudspeakers.*

MCCARTHY'S VOICE: If there are no Communists in our government, why do we delay the hydrogen bomb by eighteen months while our defense services report day after day that the Russians are feverishly stepping up on the H-bomb? Now they've got it! Now our monopoly is gone! When I tell America tonight that our nation may perish, it will perish because of that delay of eighteen months. And, I ask you, who is to blame? Were they loyal Americans or were they traitors, those who deliberately misled our government, who got themselves celebrated as atomic heroes, and whose crimes must at last be investigated.

The members of the Board enter by a small door, back center. Those present rise for a moment. Then everybody sits down.

GRAY: This Board has been appointed by the United States Atomic Energy Commission to investigate Dr. J. Robert Oppenheimer's continued eligibility for clearance. It is composed of the following members: Thomas A. Morgan, Ward V. Evans, and myself, Gordon Gray, Chairman. Counsel for the Atomic Energy Commission are Roger Robb and C. A. Rolander. Dr. Oppenheimer is represented by Lloyd K. Garrison and Herbert S. Marks. Dr. Oppenheimer is present as a witness in his own case. This inquiry is not a trial. It shall be regarded as strictly confidential.

MARKS: May I ask, Mr. Chairman, whether any of you saw the interview with Senator McCarthy last night?

GRAY: I did not see it. Did you, Mr. Morgan?

MORGAN [*looking up from his documents for a moment*]. McCarthy? No.

EVANS: I heard it on the radio. I was greatly surprised. I immediately thought of Oppenheimer.

MARKS: Did you hear the interview, Mr. Robb?

ROBB: No. Senator McCarthy would have to be clairvoyant if he alluded to our proceeding.

MARKS: He was interviewed by Fulton Lewis, Jr. I believe you represented that gentleman at various trials, Mr. Robb.

GRAY: Did you take his remarks as referring to yourself, Dr. Oppenheimer?

OPPENHEIMER: Five or six people called me up. Einstein said: "If I had the choice again I'd rather be a plumber or a peddlar, if only to enjoy some small measure of independence."

MARKS: I mention the interview because it makes me wonder if our proceedings can be kept private, Mr. Chairman.

GARY: We shall do our best. . . . It is my duty, Dr. Oppenheimer, to ask whether you are satisfied with the composition of the Board.

OPPENHEIMER: Yes. With one general reservation.

GRAY: What is your reservation?

OPPENHEIMER: The Board will examine the complex duties of a physicist in our times; therefore, I would have preferred the members to be scientists. Only Professor Evans is engaged in science, I believe.

EVANS: But I don't know anything about nuclear physics, either. Fortunately. You probably know that we had no choice in this matter here. We were appointed. I wouldn't have chosen it myself.

OPPENHEIMER: Neither would I, I guess.

MARKS: The profession of the members should perhaps be shown in the record.

GRAY: Very well, Mr. Marks. Ward V. Evans . . .

EVANS: Professor of Chemistry, Chicago.

GRAY: Thomas A. Morgan . . .

MORGAN: Chairman of the Board and President of the Sperry Gyroscope Company, atomic equipment. One of the sharks of Big Business. [*He laughs.*]

GRAY: Gordon Gray, newspaper editor, radio stations; former Secretary of the Army, Department of Defense.

MORGAN: Information concerning our income is not required?

MARKS: You wouldn't want to disclose yours, Mr. Morgan.

Slight laughter.

GRAY: I would like to ask Dr. Oppenheimer whether he wishes to testify under oath.

OPPENHEIMER. Certainly.

GRAY: You are not obliged to do so.

OPPENHEIMER: I know. [*He rises to his feet.*]

GRAY: Julius Robert Oppenheimer, do you swear that the testimony you are to give the Board shall be the truth, the whole truth, and nothing but the truth, so help you God?

OPPENHEIMER: I do.

GRAY: The proceeding may now commence. May I ask you to take the stand . . . Mr. Robb.

OPPENHEIMER *walks across to a swivel chair which faces the members of the Board. He sits down and lights his pipe.*

ROBB: You have been called the Father of the Atom Bomb, Doctor?

OPPENHEIMER: In magazines. Yes.

ROBB: You would not call yourself that?

OPPENHEIMER: It isn't a very pretty child—and it has about a hundred fathers, if we consider the basic research. In several countries.

ROBB: But the baby was ultimately born in Los Alamos, in the laboratories which you yourself had set up, and of which you were the Director from 1943 to 1945.

OPPENHEIMER: We produced that patent toy, yes.

ROBB: So you are not denying it, Doctor? [OPPENHEIMER *laughs.*] You produced it in a fantastically short time, you tested it, and then you dropped it on Japan, did you not?

OPPENHEIMER: No.

ROBB: You did not?

OPPENHEIMER: The dropping of the atom bomb on Hiroshima was a political decision—it wasn't mine.

ROBB: But you supported the dropping of the atom bomb on Japan. Or didn't you?

OPPENHEIMER: What do you mean by "supported"?

ROBB: You helped to select the targets, did you not?

OPPENHEIMER: I was doing my job. We were given a list of possible targets . . .

ROBB: Would you name them?

OPPENHEIMER: Hiroshima, Kokura, Nigata, Kyoto . . . [*Partial views of these cities are projected on the white screens at the back.*] . . . and we, as experts, were asked which targets would be most suitable for the dropping of the atomic bomb, according to the experience we had gathered from tests.

ROBB: Whom do you mean by "we," Doctor?

OPPENHEIMER: An advisory council of nuclear physicists, appointed for this purpose by the Secretary of War.

ROBB: Who was on that council?

OPPENHEIMER: Fermi, Lawrence, Arthur H. Compton, and myself.

Photographs of these scientists are projected on the screens.

ROBB: And you had to select the targets?

OPPENHEIMER: No. We supplied the scientific data as to the suitability of the targets.

ROBB: What kind of target did you consider to be the desired suitability?

OPPENHEIMER: According to our calculations, the area had to be at least two miles in diameter, densely built up, preferably with wooden buildings—because of the blast, and the subsequent wave of fire. Also, the selected targets had to be of a high military and strategic value, and unscathed by previous bombardments.

ROBB: Why, Doctor?

OPPENHEIMER: To enable us to measure exactly the effect of a single atomic bomb.

EVANS: These military considerations, I mean, after all, they were the business of the physicists, weren't they, at that time?

OPPENHEIMER: Yes. Because we were the only people who had the necessary experience.

EVANS: I see. I'm rather out of my depth here. How did you feel?

OPPENHEIMER: I asked myself that question, later. I don't know. . . . I was very relieved when the Secretary of War followed our suggestions and crossed the famous temple city, Kyoto, off the list. It was the largest and most vulnerable target.

ROBB: But you did not oppose the dropping of the atom bomb on Hiroshima?

OPPENHEIMER: We set forth arguments against . . .

ROBB: I am asking you, Doctor, whether *you* opposed it.

OPPENHEIMER: I set forth arguments against dropping it.

ROBB: Against dropping the atom bomb?

OPPENHEIMER: Yes, that's right. But I did not press the point. Not specifically.

ROBB: You mean to say that having worked day and night for three or four years to produce the atomic bomb, you then argued it should not be used?

OPPENHEIMER: No. When I was asked by the Secretary of War I set forth the arguments both for and against. I expressed my uneasiness.

ROBB: Did you not also determine the height, Doctor, at which the atomic bomb was to explode in order to produce the maximum effect?

OPPENHEIMER: We, as experts, were doing a job we were asked to do. But this does not mean that we thereby decided that the bomb should in fact be dropped.

ROBB: You knew of course, did you not, that the dropping of the atomic bomb on the target you had selected would kill thousands of civilians?

OPPENHEIMER: Not as many people as we thought, as things turned out.

ROBB: How many were killed?

OPPENHEIMER: Seventy thousand.

ROBB: Did you have moral scruples about that?

OPPENHEIMER: Terrible ones.

ROBB: You had terrible moral scruples?

OPPENHEIMER: I don't know anyone who would *not* have had terrible moral scruples after the dropping of the bomb.

ROBB: Isn't that a trifle schizophrenic?

OPPENHEIMER: What is? To have moral scruples?

ROBB: To produce the thing, to pick the targets, to determine the height at which the explosion has the maximum effect—and then to be overcome by moral scruples at the consequences. Isn't that a trifle schizophrenic, Doctor?

OPPENHEIMER: Yes. . . . It is the kind of schizophrenia we physicists have been living with for several years now.

ROBB: Would you elucidate that?

OPPENHEIMER: The great discoveries of modern science have been put to horrible use. Nuclear energy is not the atomic bomb.

ROBB: You mean it could be exploited industrially, and so forth?

OPPENHEIMER: It could produce abundance, for the first time. It's a matter of cheap energy.

ROBB: Are you thinking of a Golden Age, a Land of Cockaigne, that sort of thing?

OPPENHEIMER: Yes, plenty for all. It is our misfortune that people rather think of the reverse kind of uses.

ROBB: Whom do you mean by "people," Doctor?

OPPENHEIMER: Governments. The world is not ready for the new discoveries. It is out of joint.

ROBB: And you have come along "to set it right," as Hamlet says?

OPPENHEIMER: I can do no such thing. The world itself must do that.

MORGAN: Dr. Oppenheimer, do you mean to tell an old pragmatist like me that you made the atomic bomb in order to create some Land of Cockaigne? Did you not make it in order to use it and win the war with it?

OPPENHEIMER: We made it in order to prevent it being used. Originally, at any rate.

MORGAN: You spent two billion dollars of the taxpayers' money on the bomb in order to prevent it being used?

OPPENHEIMER: To prevent it being used by Hitler. In the end it turned out that there wasn't any German atomic bomb project. . . . But then we used it all the same.

ROLANDER: I beg your pardon, sir, but were you really not asked—at a certain stage in the development of the bomb—were you not asked whether it should be used against Japan?

OPPENHEIMER: We weren't asked *whether* it should be used, but only *how* it should be used in order to produce the maximum effect.

ROLANDER: Is that entirely correct, sir?

OPPENHEIMER: What do you mean?

ROLANDER: Did not the Secretary of War show you the so-called Franck Report, the memorandum by the physicists Szilard, Franck, and others? It strongly opposed the dropping of the bomb on Japan and recommended an internationally public demonstration of the bomb over a desert.

OPPENHEIMER: We were given it to read. That's right. Not officially, I believe.

ROBB: What did you say to that, Doctor?

OPPENHEIMER: That we were in no position to decide this question, that opinion was divided among us. We set forth our arguments—for, and against.

ROBB: Were you against?

OPPENHEIMER: Lawrence was against. I was undecided, I'm afraid. I think we said that the exploding of one of these things as a firecracker over a desert wasn't likely to be very impressive—and, probably, that the overriding consideration should be the saving of lives, by bringing the war to an end as soon as possible.

ROBB: Did this not mean, in effect, Doctor, that you were *against* a demonstration of the weapon—and *for* it being dropped without warning?

OPPENHEIMER: It most certainly did not mean that. No. We were physicists, not the military, not politicians. That was the time of very heavy fighting on Okinawa. It was a horrible decision.

ROBB: Did you write the official report on the effect of the bomb on Hiroshima?

OPPENHEIMER: According to the data supplied by Alvarez, yes; he flew in with the others, to measure the effect.

EVANS: Alvarez the physicist?

OPPENHEIMER: Yes. With new measuring instruments.

ROBB: Did you not state there that the dropping of the bomb had been a good thing, and very successful?

OPPENHEIMER: It was technically successful, yes.

ROBB: Oh, technically. . . . You are very modest, Doctor.

OPPENHEIMER: No, I am not.

ROBB: You are not?

OPPENHEIMER: We scientists have been on the brink of presumptuousness in these years. We have known sin.

ROBB: Good, Doctor. We shall speak of those sins.

OPPENHEIMER: I guess we don't mean the same thing.

ROBB: That is something we are going to find out, Doctor. . . . The reason I am digging up this old Hiroshima business is this: I want to find out why, at that time, you devoted yourself with such single-mindedness to your tasks, with a hundred-per-cent loyalty, I would say—and why, later, in the matter of the hydrogen bomb, you adopted an entirely different attitude.

OPPENHEIMER: It doesn't bear comparison, I think.

ROBB: It doesn't?

OPPENHEIMER: No.

ROBB: Would you have supported the dropping of a hydrogen bomb on Hiroshima, Doctor?

OPPENHEIMER: It would have made no sense at all.

ROBB: Why not?

OPPENHEIMER: The target was too small. . . . We were told that the atom bomb was the only means of bringing the war to an end quickly and successfully.

ROBB: You don't have to defend yourself, Doctor. Not on that count, anyway.

OPPENHEIMER: I know.

ROBB: Did the allegations contained in the letter of the Atomic Energy Commission surprise you?

OPPENHEIMER: They depressed me.

ROBB: What exactly depressed you, Doctor?

OPPENHEIMER: That twelve years' scientific work in the service of the United States should end in such allegations. . . . Twenty-three points in that letter deal with my associations with Communists or Communist sympathizers, associations going back more than twelve years. The letter contains only *one* new point. A most surprising one.

ROBB: Which point, Doctor?

OPPENHEIMER: That I strongly opposed the development of the hydrogen bomb, on moral and other grounds; that I turned other scientists against the hydrogen bomb; that I thereby considerably slowed down the development of the hydrogen bomb.

ROBB: In your opinion, Doctor, this allegation is not justified?

OPPENHEIMER: It is not true.

ROBB: Not true in any respect?

OPPENHEIMER: In no respect at all. Ever since our apprehensions concerning the monopoly of the hydrogen bomb have been proved right—ever since the two world powers have been facing each other like scorpions in a bottle—there have been people trying to persuade America that the blame lies with traitors.

ROBB: I would like, first of all, to deal with your former Communist associations, Doctor, taking the letter of the Atomic Energy Commission as the basis, and would like to have the letter set down in the record.

GARRISON: It would be appropriate for Dr. Oppenheimer's answering letter also to be set down in the record, Mr. Chairman.

GRAY: Very well, Mr. Garrison.

GARRISON: Furthermore, I would like to submit——

GRAY: Yes, please.

GARRISON: ——that allegations on which Dr. Oppenheimer was

cleared in previous security investigations should not be the subject of the present investigation.

ROBB: Objection.

GRAY: Would you sustain your objection, Mr. Robb?

ROBB: The Atomic Energy Commission wishes to have certain allegations re-investigated, Mr. Chairman, on the basis of evidence not available at previous investigations.

MARKS: May I ask, Mr. Robb, what new evidence you wish to present, for instance, as to Point Three of the letter?

EVANS: Which point, Mr. Marks?

MARKS: Point Three. It says there that sixteen years ago, in 1938, Dr. Oppenheimer was an honorary member of the West Coast Council of the Consumers' Union. What new evidence is now available?

ROBB: There is fairly new evidence in the matter of a closed Communist meeting at Dr. Oppenheimer's residence in 1941———

MARKS: I am asking you about Point Three———

ROBB: ———and a fairly new witness who has testified under oath to what Dr. Oppenheimer thinks fit to deny.

MARKS: Does that witness happen to be Paul Crouch?

ROLANDER: Mr. Chairman, I would like to ask Mr. Marks why he conjectures that the witness may be Paul Crouch.

MARKS: Paul Crouch figures rather excessively as a witness these days, Mr. Rolander. No investigation of anybody's loyalty without Paul Crouch, so to speak. It's his profession, I guess.

ROLANDER: Mr. Chairman, I would like to ask Mr. Marks whether, by some means or other, he has obtained information about Dr. Oppenheimer from secret F.B.I. files.

MARKS: No. Only you and Mr. Robb have such information. That's the difference between an investigation and a trial.

EVANS: I beg your pardon, it is rather bewildering, I am not used to this sort of thing. Mr. Rolander, who is this Paul Crouch? I have never heard his name before.

ROLANDER: Paul Crouch is a former Communist functionary who has turned his back on Communism.

EVANS: And he knows Dr. Oppenheimer?

MARKS: He knows Dr. Oppenheimer and he knows Malenkov, but I guess they don't know him!

EVANS: It would have surprised me.

Slight laughter.

MARKS: I believe, Mr. Robb, you haven't yet answered my question regarding Point Three.

ROBB: Indeed, I have not, Mr. Marks, as I uphold my objection for the following reasons: there is new evidence, and there are new rules governing clearance; furthermore, it appears to me that there is a connection between Dr. Oppenheimer's former associations and his attitude in the matter of the hydrogen bomb. I would therefore wish to retain the right to question him, and other witnesses, as to these matters. In his own interest as well.

GRAY: Objection sustained.

Change of lighting. ROBB *steps forward to the footlights. The hangings close.*

ROBB: People may think I am biased. They'd be wrong. When I started, Oppenheimer was my idol among the scientists of America, he was the Atom Bomb, he was—Oppie.

Then I studied his files—the material, four foot high, which had led the F.B.I. to conclude that Oppenheimer was "probably a camouflaged Soviet agent," and which caused President Eisenhower to give the immediate order to put "an impenetrable wall between Oppenheimer and all government secrets." Those files changed the idol into a sphinx.

Merits or no merits, we recently dismissed 105 officials of the State Department for less incriminating associations and less dangerous views. It was precisely in the most vital sphere of nuclear energy that we came across the new type of traitor—the traitor for ideological, ethical, and I don't know what other motives. How could I be entirely sure about Oppenheimer? I could not find the key to a number of contradictory facts in his life, I could not find the key to his attitude in the matter of the hydrogen bomb. But neither could I say: such and such facts are evidence of his disloyalty. They remained debatable, alongside other and equally debatable facts. I admit that particularly in the case of Oppenheimer I have come to realize the inadequacy of being strictly confined to facts in our modern security investigations. How clumsy and unscientific is our procedure when, over and above the facts, we do not concern ourselves also with the thoughts, the feelings, the motives which underlie those facts, and make them the subject of our inquires. It is the only method if we ever want to arrive at a conclusive judgment as to Oppenheimer's integrity.

Do we dissect the smile of a sphinx with butchers' knives? When the security of the free world depends on it, we must.

ROBB *returns to the stage itself.*

SCENE 2

The following text is projected on the hangings:

EXCERPT FROM THE PROCEEDINGS ON THE SECOND DAY:

GUILT THROUGH ASSOCIATION?

ROBB: Have you ever been a member of the Communist Party, Doctor?

OPPENHEIMER: No.

ROBB: Your wife?

OPPENHEIMER: At the time of her first marriage, yes. Up to 1936 or thereabouts.

ROBB: To whom was she married?

OPPENHEIMER: Joe Dallet.

ROBB: Was he a Communist?

OPPENHEIMER: He fell in the Spanish Civil War. I never knew him. . . . Yes.

ROBB: Was your brother Frank a member?

OPPENHEIMER: Until 1941.

ROBB: His wife, Jackie?

OPPENHEIMER: Yes

ROBB: Was there a time when you yourself were in pretty close agreement with certain Communist ideas, Doctor?

OPPENHEIMER: Sure. I've put it all down in my answering letter.

ROLANDER *continues the examination.*

ROLANDER: On page five of your letter, you use the expression "fellow traveler." What exactly do you mean by it?

OPPENHEIMER: I would call a person a fellow traveler when he agrees with certain parts of the Communist program and when he is willing to co-operate with Communists without himself belonging to the Party.

ROLANDER: In the sense of your definition, sir, were you a fellow traveler?

OPPENHEIMER: Yes.

ROLANDER: When?

OPPENHEIMER: From about 1936 onward. After 1939 I did far less "fellow traveling," and after 1942 practically none at all.

ROLANDER: As from 1942, you would no longer call yourself a fellow traveler?

OPPENHEIMER: No. Some vague sympathies remained.

ROLANDER: How would you explain the fact that your sympathies cooled off so fast, precisely in 1942?

OPPENHEIMER: They had already cooled off considerably at the time of the purge trials under Stalin, and I had practically no sympathies left when there was that pact between the Nazis and the Russians. It made me sick when I heard that the gifted German physicist, Houterman, and a hundred other arrested German Communists had been handed over to the Gestapo by the Soviets.

ROLANDER: And your sympathies revived again, did they not, when Russia became our ally?

OPPENHEIMER: I guess we all felt pretty relieved.

ROLANDER: But in 1942, when you were put in charge of Los Alamos, your sympathies had once again cooled off?

OPPENHEIMER: What do you mean?

ROLANDER: I am trying to discover your motives, sir.

OPPENHEIMER: Motives? In what respect?

ROLANDER: You broke off your connections with a number of Communist friends, sir.

OPPENHEIMER: Yes, because I was working on the atom bomb! In the New Mexico desert, under military security restrictions. That way, all personal connections were broken off.

ROBB: Not all of them, I believe, Doctor. . . . Was your former fiancée, Dr. Jean Tatlock, a member of the Communist Party?

OPPENHEIMER: Yes. Less from political than from romantic motives. She was a sensitive person, who profoundly despaired of the injustices in this world.

ROBB: How long was she a member of the Party?

OPPENHEIMER: It was an "on again, off again" affair. Right until her death, I think.

ROBB: How did she die, Doctor?

OPPENHEIMER: *(after a pause]* She killed herself. I believe F.B.I. agents have reported in detail how many days before that, and how long, I spent with her in such and such a hotel without informing the security authorities about our meeting.

ROBB: That is correct, Doctor. You spent the night with her, and————

OPPENHEIMER: What business is that of yours? What has it to do with my loyalty?

ROBB: *[in a friendly tone]*. Has it nothing to do with your loyalty, Doctor, when *you*, the man responsible for the atomic weapons project in Los Alamos, when *you* spend the night in a hotel with a Communist woman—without informing the security authorities?

OPPENHEIMER: That Communist woman happened to be my former fiancée who was going through a severe emotional crisis and who wished to see me. A few days later, she was dead.

ROBB: What did you talk about, the two of you?

OPPENHEIMER: I do not propose to tell you.

ROBB: You won't tell me?

OPPENHEIMER: No.

He rises from the swivel chair, the "witness stand," and walks across to the sofa. He lights his pipe.

ROBB: Let the record show that Dr. Oppenheimer has left the stand as a witness.

GARRISON: Mr. Chairman, I object to this line of questioning. It is immaterial to the proceedings, and it encroaches upon Dr. Oppenheimer's privacy. The matter of the meeting with Jean Tatlock has already been cleared up in previous security investigations.

GRAY: Objection sustained. . . . May I ask Dr. Oppenheimer to resume the stand as a witness.

OPPENHEIMER *resumes the stand.*

ROBB: The question was not put to you in an unfair spirit, Doctor.

OPPENHEIMER *glances at him, smoking his pipe. Change of lighting.* EVANS *steps forward to the footlights. The hangings close.*

EVANS: Perhaps I should have turned down this appointment, I probably should have, I am seventy years old. I cannot reconcile these interrogations with my idea of science; whose business are these private matters, what purpose do they serve, these humiliations? Is a humiliated man more loyal than a man who has not been humiliated? More devoted? It is now said in our universities: "Don't talk, don't write, don't move." If this continues, where is it going to lead us?

On the other hand, it was the physicists themselves who started the whole thing when they turned their profession into a military discipline. Oppenheimer in particular, Los Alamos was his idea. Take the dropping of the bomb, his explanations here. What more do they want? Do they need even greater submissiveness? I don't know, perhaps my liberal views are outmoded; perhaps science, too, must bow to the absolute claims of the state. Now that science has become so important. At any rate, I can see two kinds of development. The one is our increasing control over nature, our planet, other planets. The other is the state's increasing control over us, demanding our conformity. We develop instruments in order to pry into unknown solar systems, and the instruments will soon be used in electronic computers which reduce our friendships, our conversations, and thoughts to scientific data. To discover whether they are the right friendships, the right conversations, the right thoughts, which *conform*. But how can a thought be new, and at the same time conform? What is the difference between us and the dictatorships with their enforced conformity, if we go on as we do now? Perhaps I exaggerate. In one or two generations, scientists may take it for granted that they are functionaries. It makes me uneasy. I ask myself these questions as I listen to what is being said here. Is Oppenheimer only a beginning?

EVANS *returns to the stage itself.*

SCENE 3

The following text is projected on the hangings:

FROM THE PROCEEDINGS ON THE THIRD DAY:

ARE FORMER COMMUNIST SYMPATHIES COMPATIBLE WITH SECRET WAR PROJECTS?

ABOUT THE RELIABILITY OF PROFESSIONAL
WITNESSES.

ROBB: Dr. Oppenheimer, yesterday you confirmed that, for a time,
you were very closely associated with the Communist movement.

OPPENHEIMER: For a short time. Roughly, up to the end of the
Spanish Civil War. Fifteen years ago.

ROBB: In those days, you attended meetings, trade union meetings,
you had Communist friends, acquaintances, you belonged to a
number of organizations with Communist leanings, you read
Communist literature, you signed manifestoes, you paid out
fairly substantial sums of money which went through Communist channels———

OPPENHEIMER: I gave money for the men who fought Franco and
the Nazis in Spain. As you know, they depended on private support.

ROBB: You contributed up to three hundred dollars a month to
the cause of the Spanish Republic and the money went through
Communist channels?

OPPENHEIMER: If you had asked me for money to help that cause
I'd have given it to you also.

ROBB: But you gave it to Isaac Folkoff, the Communist functionary,
and you say in your answering letter to us, on page six, quote,
"At that time, I agreed with the Communist idea that a Popular
Front should be formed to oppose the spread of Fascism in the
world." What does that mean?

OPPENHEIMER: It means that I was greatly perturbed about conditions in Germany and Spain, and that I did not want anything
like that to happen here.

ROBB: What was it that perturbed you?

OPPENHEIMER: What perturbed me, Mr. Robb? That the world just
looked on, hands in pockets. I had relatives in Germany, Jews,
whom I was able to get across to this country, and they told me
what was happening there.

ROBB: Quite so, Doctor, but didn't you know at the time that it
was the tactics of the Communists to establish their rule everywhere by means of the so-called Popular Front?

OPPENHEIMER: Maybe it was their object. I myself did not see that
danger. I saw what came spreading across the world from Ger-

many, Italy, and Japan, and nobody did anything about it. That is how my sympathies started, and the manifestoes, and the donations. The best people of America put their names to the manifestos. Those were different times.

ROBB: What I am getting at, Doctor, is this: as you were in such complete agreement with the Communists at that time, why did you not join the Party?

OPPENHEIMER: Because I don't like to think the thoughts of others. It goes against my idea of independence.

ROBB: Have you never thought of becoming a member?

OPPENHEIMER: No.

ROBB: Did your friends never suggest it to you?

OPPENHEIMER: No.

ROBB: What is your explanation for that?

OPPENHEIMER: They must have known me well enough . . .

ROLANDER: Do you think it may possibly be Communist tactics, sir, to leave certain influential persons outside the Party because they would otherwise be less useful?

OPPENHEIMER: I don't know. I'm no expert.

ROLANDER: You do not regard yourself as very experienced in Communist affairs, sir?

OPPENHEIMER: No. By the time I started working on war projects, at Berkeley, my sympathies had almost completely cooled off.

ROBB: A closed Communist meeting takes place in a man's house. Does that point to "almost completely cooled-off sympathies," Doctor?

OPPENHEIMER: When is the meeting supposed to have taken place?

ROBB: So far, I did not speak of you.

OPPENHEIMER: I am sure you are referring to me.

ROBB: Since you are so sure: do you think it possible that on July 23, or thereabouts, in 1941, a closed Communist meeting was held in your house, at which a Communist functionary explained the new Party line?

OPPENHEIMER: No.

ROLANDER: Had you rented a house, 10 Kenilworth Court, in Berkeley, California, in July 1941, sir?

OPPENHEIMER: Yes.

ROLANDER: Do you know a man named Schneidermann?

OPPENHEIMER: Yes.

ROLANDER: Is he a Communist functionary?

OPPENHEIMER: Yes.

ROLANDER: How did you come to meet him?

OPPENHEIMER: I think I met him at Haakon Chevalier's house. At a literary meeting.

ROBB: Was Haakon Chevalier a frequent visitor at your house, in those days?

OPPENHEIMER: Yes.

ROBB: Was your pupil, Joseph Weinberg, a frequent visitor at your house, in those days?

OPPENHEIMER: Yes.

ROBB: It has been stated by two witnesses, Doctor, and the witnesses are prepared to testify under oath, that on July 23, or shortly after, you took part in a closed Communist meeting at 10 Kenilworth Court, in Berkeley, and that, at this meeting, Schneidermann explained the new line adopted by the Party as a consequence of Russia's entry into the war. According to the witnesses, there were present, among others: Haakon Chevalier, Joseph Weinberg, Dr. Oppenheimer, and Mrs. Oppenheimer.

OPPENHEIMER: That is not true.

ROLANDER: At that time, did you live in a Spanish-style bungalow which had colored wooden ceilings?

OPPENHEIMER: Yes.

ROLANDER: Was there a large candlestick of blue Venetian glass in your living room?

OPPENHEIMER: Yes.

ROLANDER: Was there a red wooden fairground horse standing by the fireplace?

OPPENHEIMER: Yes.

ROLANDER: These are some details of the furnishings as remembered by the witnesses. Maybe you have forgotten that meeting, sir?

MARKS: Mr. Chairman, may I ask Mr. Robb who these two witnesses are who remember candlesticks and fairground horses, and who wish to testify under oath that such a meeting took place?

ROBB: The witnesses are Paul Crouch and his wife.

EVANS: The same Crouch who has already been mentioned here?

ROBB: Yes, Dr. Evans.

MARKS: Mr. Chairman, I submit that the witness be called, to testify under oath.

ROLANDER: That is not possible, unfortunately.

GRAY: Why not?

ROLANDER: We ourselves would have liked to call the witnesses, Mr. Chairman, but the F.B.I. has not released them for our purposes here.

GRAY: I am sorry about that, Mr. Marks. Why did you want these witnesses called?

MARKS: I would have liked to show that their testimony is false, and that there are certain people who have a personal interest in that kind of testimony.

ROLANDER: Do you mean to say, sir, that the F.B.I. makes use of false testimony?

MARKS: That is not what I said. I do not know who the people are whose personal interests are involved here; I would have liked to question the witnesses about them. I only know that the testimony is false.

ROBB: I presume you will place your evidence for such knowledge before us, Mr. Marks.

MARKS: When is the meeting in Berkeley supposed to have taken place?

ROBB: In 1941. On July 23, or shortly after.

GARRISON: What exactly do you mean by that?

ROBB: Not before July 23, and not after July 30.

GARRISON: Did you have an opportunity to have this verified by the witnesses, Mr. Robb?

ROBB: Yes, recently.

MARKS *extracts a bundle of photostats from a file and takes it across to* GRAY.

MARKS: In that case, I would like to place evidence before the Board to the effect that from July 20 to August 10 Dr. Oppenheimer and his wife were not in Berkeley but in New Mexico. You will find here the names of the hotels where they stayed, and the names of the persons they met. I warned you about Paul Crouch, Mr. Robb. He isn't worth his witness fee.

ROBB: I see, Mr. Marks, that your office found it very important to prove Dr. Oppenheimer's absence at the time in question.

MARKS: Sure.

ROBB: Without previous knowledge of the allegations, I presume?

MARKS: We did it in the case of several longer journeys undertaken by Dr. Oppenheimer.

ROBB: I am perfectly convinced.

Change of lighting. MARKS *steps forward to the footlights. The hangings close.*

MARKS: Someday it will be realized, I hope, that it was not Oppenheimer who stood here before the Commission, but that it was our present-day security system which stood here. Oppenheimer is my friend; for many years, I have been General Counsel for the Atomic Energy Commission; I know the problems. If Oppenheimer is condemned here, our present-day security system will have passed judgment on itself, the subjugation of science to the military will have been proclaimed, and in their ranks there will be no room for independent spirits, for people who call a spade a spade.

If there had been no politics involved, if it had only been a matter of Oppenheimer himself, it would have been quite simple for the Atomic Energy Commission not to renew his contract—which expires in three months' time. Are the atomic secrets to vanish out of his head if his clearance is withdrawn? Lewis Strauss is the man whose first official action was to start these proceedings when he took over the Atomic Energy Commission—he is the same man who granted Oppenheimer's clearance in 1947. Now he cables the news of its suspension to the Air Force, the Army, and the Navy. Are these proceedings fair? The Board has access to secret F.B.I. files, but we are not allowed to see them. Oppenheimer cannot look at his own correspondence, his own reports; they have been confiscated and declared secret. I ask myself whether the course adopted by the defense is the right one; Oppenheimer wants us to follow this course, the defensive refutation of facts. But it is not a question of facts, or, if so, they are only a secondary matter. Why do we agree to have our battlefield here? Why don't we bring this issue out into the open, and place it before the whole body of scientists, before the public, whom it concerns? Are we waiting for the other side to make the attack—here, too? I do my utmost to convince Oppenheimer. His faith in the power of arguments makes him a worse witness than Joan of Arc, who could not read.

He returns to the stage itself.

SCENE 4

The following text is projected on the hangings:

FROM THE PROCEEDINGS ON THE FIFTH DAY:

WHERE DOES LOYALTY TO A BROTHER END, AND
WHERE TO THE STATE?

SHALL A MAN BE PERSECUTED FOR HIS OPINIONS?

MORGAN. What I am interested in, Dr. Oppenheimer, is the practical side. Not the opinions but the consequences. You had to find the scientists for the project at Los Alamos, didn't you?

OPPENHEIMER: Yes. I suggested people whom I considered qualified. The final decision rested with General Groves and with Colonel Lansdale, the Chief of Security.

MORGAN: In your opinion, is it appropriate that a Communist should work on a secret war project?

OPPENHEIMER: When? In those days, or now?

MORGAN: Let us say, now.

OPPENHEIMER: As a rule, no.

MORGAN: And in those days?

OPPENHEIMER: In those days, an exception to the rule would have seemed more feasible to me.

MORGAN: Why?

OPPENHEIMER: In those days, Russia was our ally; now she is our potential enemy.

MORGAN: In other words, it is the Communist Party's connection with Russia that makes it impossible to have a Communist working on a secret war project?

OPPENHEIMER: Obviously.

MORGAN: When did this become obvious to you?

OPPENHEIMER: '46, '47.

MORGAN: Let me ask you a blunt question, Dr. Oppenheimer. Did you not know in 1943 that the Communist Party was an instrument of espionage in this country?

OPPENHEIMER: No.

MORGAN: You never suspected it either, in those days?

OPPENHEIMER: No. The Communist Party was legal. The Russians were our lauded allies who had just beaten Hitler at Stalingrad.

MORGAN: I never lauded them, I believe.

OPPENHEIMER: But you never tipped me off, either. Nor did you tip off the government.

MORGAN: How would you know that?

OPPENHEIMER: As far as the practical side is concerned, Mr. Morgan, nobody was employed at Los Alamos who was known to be a member of the Communist Party.

MORGAN: And you never suggested such a person, Dr. Oppenheimer?

OPPENHEIMER: No.

MORGAN: Why not?

OPPENHEIMER: Because of the problem of divided loyalty.

MORGAN: Divided between whom?

OPPENHEIMER: It seemed incompatible to me for a man to work, on the one hand, on secret war projects which, on the other hand, he is expected to destroy, according to the program of his Party.

MORGAN: I see.

ROBB: With reference to Los Alamos, Doctor, what dangers did you envisage in such collaboration?

OPPENHEIMER: The danger of indiscretion.

ROBB: Is that just another word for espionage?

OPPENHEIMER: It means less than that. But it does imply danger.

ROBB: At any rate, you regarded a Communist as too great a security risk?

OPPENHEIMER: An active Party member, yes.

ROBB: And what about former Party members? What did you do when you had to recommend a physicist who was a former Party member?

OPPENHEIMER: When I knew that, and thought he was dangerous as far as the secret war project was concerned, I recommended him but added my reservations.

ROBB: What test did you apply to determine whether a former Party member was still dangerous?

OPPENHEIMER: I gave my personal impression of him. . . . It was very difficult to find qualified people. We were working under extremely hard, extremely unpleasant conditions.

ROBB: You have not answered my question, Doctor.

OPPENHEIMER: Would you repeat your question?

ROBB: What test did you apply, in those days, to satisfy yourself that a former Party member was no longer dangerous?

OPPENHEIMER: What test? Applied to whom? To my wife?

ROBB: Let us take your brother, who is a physicist like yourself. Tell us about the test you applied to convince yourself that you could trust him.

OPPENHEIMER: In the case of a brother you don't apply tests. At least I didn't. I knew my brother.

ROBB: Well, what convinced you that your brother was no longer dangerous?

OPPENHEIMER: I never regarded my brother as dangerous. The possibility that a member of the Communist Party might engage in espionage never meant to me that *every* Party member would actually engage in espionage.

ROBB: I see. Your brother was an exception to the rule you have just told me about?

OPPENHEIMER: No. I did not say that every Communist is in fact a security risk, but that it would be a good policy to make that rule. Joliot-Curie in France is an example of the opposite. He is a Communist, and he is in charge of the French atomic weapons program.

ROBB: The atom spies, Klaus Fuchs, Nunn May, and Pontecorvo are examples of a different kind?

Photographs of the three men are projected.

OPPENHEIMER. Yes.

EVANS [*interested, turning to* OPPENHEIMER]. I beg your pardon, did you know Klaus Fuchs?

OPPENHEIMER: Not very well. He only came with the British Delegation to Los Alamos. He was connected with the Department of Theoretical Physics, of which Hans Bethe was in charge.

EVANS: What kind of person was he?

OPPENHEIMER: Quiet, rather introvert, the son of a German pastor. He was crazy about driving cars, and drove with utter recklessness.

EVANS: I never understood his motives. Were they the usual kind of motives? Was he getting money from the Russians?

OPPENHEIMER: It seems he had rather pretentious ethical motives . . .

EVANS: Ethical motives? In what respect?

OPPENHEIMER: He told the British Secret Service he could not reconcile it with his conscience that the atom bomb should be left solely in the hands of a power which, he was afraid, might misuse the bomb. He rather fancied himself in the role of God, or the conscience of the world.

GRAY: Do such thoughts make any sense to you, Dr. Oppenheimer?

OPPENHEIMER: No. Not in that way.

EVANS: Do you think the Russians owe their atom bomb mainly to the information they received from Fuchs, or May, or others?

OPPENHEIMER: Not essentially. They got to know that we were working on it. Also, certain details about our plutonium bomb. As far as I know, our secret services discovered that the Russians were following a different line of research. That is why Fuchs could not answer the questions they put to him—because of the difference in research.

ROBB: May I continue, Mr. Chairman?

GRAY: Indeed, yes.

ROBB: When did your brother become a member of the Communist Party?

OPPENHEIMER: 1936 or 1937.

ROBB: And when did he leave the Party?

OPPENHEIMER: In the fall of 1941, I believe.

ROBB: That was when he went from Stanford to Berkeley, to work in the Radiation Laboratory, is that right?

OPPENHEIMER: Yes. Lawrence wanted him there, for unclassified work.

ROBB: But shortly after that, he was doing work on secret war projects?

OPPENHEIMER: About a year later.

ROBB: After Pearl Harbor?

OPPENHEIMER: Possibly.

ROBB: Did you, thereupon, inform the security authorities that your brother had been a member of the Communist Party?

OPPENHEIMER: Nobody asked me.

ROBB: Nobody asked you. Did you tell Lawrence or anyone else about it?

OPPENHEIMER: I told Lawrence that my brother's troubles at Stanford arose from his Communist connections.

ROBB: Doctor, I didn't ask you quite that question. Did you tell Lawrence or anybody else that your brother, Frank, had actually been a member of the Communist Party?

OPPENHEIMER: No.

ROBB: Why not?

OPPENHEIMER: I don't think it is my duty to ruin my brother's career when I have complete confidence in him.

ROBB: How did you reach the conclusion that your brother was no longer a member of the Party?

OPPENHEIMER: He told me.

ROBB: That was enough for you?

Oppenheimer. Sure.

ROBB: Do you know that at that time, and also quite a while later, your brother publicly denied he had ever been a Party member?

OPPENHEIMER: I know he denied it in 1947.

ROBB: Why, in your opinion, did he deny it?

OPPENHEIMER: He probably wanted to go on working as a physicist—and not as a farmer, as he has been forced to do since then.

ROBB: Do you approve of his conduct, Doctor?

OPPENHEIMER: I don't approve of it. I understand it. I disapprove of a person being destroyed because of his past or present opinions. That is what I disapprove of.

ROBB: We are speaking about work on secret war projects and about the possibly disagreeable measures we have to take in order to protect our freedom, Doctor.

OPPENHEIMER: I know. There are people who are willing to protect freedom until there is nothing left of it.

ROBB: In the case of your brother, would I be right in saying that your quite natural loyalty to him outweighed your loyalty to our security authorities?

OPPENHEIMER: I have explained that there was no such conflict of loyalties.

ROBB: According to your own testimony, you were of the opinion that it would be important for the security authorities to know whether somebody had been a member of the Communist Party. Yet, in the case of your brother, you concealed that fact from them, did you not?

OPPENHEIMER: I did not specifically conceal it. Nobody asked me.

ROBB: And you did not volunteer this information?

OPPENHEIMER: No.

ROBB: That is all I wanted to know, Doctor.

Change of lighting. ROLANDER *steps forward to the footlights. The hangings close.*

ROLANDER: People argue that we judge past events from our present point of view. Yes, that is so, for we are investigating whether Dr. Oppenheimer is a security risk *today*, when our enemies are the Communists, Russia, and not the Nazis, as in the past. Facts are very relative. For instance, in 1943 we certainly would not have told our most vital secrets to a man whose sympathies were with the Nazis, even if he was a genius; and now, in 1954, this is our attitude towards a man whose sympathies are with the Communists. Security measures are *realistic:* what has to be protected against whom, and in what situation. They have no claim to absolute justice and immaculate morality. They are *practical*. That is why I am disturbed by these ideological exercises here, this flogging of principles about the sacredness of privacy, a thing that dates back to the last century. We must examine quite soberly how strong Oppenheimer's sympathies were, how persistent they are, what consequences this had for us in the past, and whether we can afford such consequences in the future. . . . It is history itself—the possibility of the free world being destroyed—which makes our security measures rigorous and uncompromising.

I feel so old among these people who are older than me. Where they have their ideology I have a blind spot.

He returns to the stage itself.

SCENE 5

The following test is projected on the hangings:

FROM THE PROCEEDINGS ON THE SEVENTH DAY:

WHAT KIND OF PEOPLE ARE PHYSICISTS?

CAN A MAN BE TAKEN TO PIECES LIKE THE MECHANISM OF A FUSE?

ROLANDER: Speaking of secret war projects, sir, do you agree that, with a fellow traveler, there is a potentially greater danger of indiscretion?
OPPENHEIMER: Potentially, yes. It depends on the person.
ROLANDER: Is it a fact, Dr. Oppenheimer, that a considerable number of scientists in Los Alamos were fellow travelers?

OPPENHEIMER: Not very many. Less than at Berkeley, for instance. But in those days we'd have snatched a man from the electric chair if we needed him to get the thing going.

ROLANDER: What I cannot understand, sir, is this: why exactly was it the fellow travelers who were snatched from the electric chair in such numbers?

OPPENHEIMER: Because there were many physicists with left-wing views.

ROLANDER: How would you explain that?

OPPENHEIMER: Physicists are interested in new things. They like to experiment and their thoughts are directed toward changes. In their work and also in political matters.

ROLANDER: Many of your pupils were in fact Communists or fellow travelers, were they not?

OPPENHEIMER: A few of them, yes.

ROLANDER: Weinberg, Bohm, Lomanitz, Friedman?

OPPENHEIMER: Yes.

ROLANDER: And you recommended these young men for work at Berkeley or Los Alamos?

OPPENHEIMER: I recommended them as scientists, yes . . . Because they were good.

ROLANDER: Purely professionally. I see.

OPPENHEIMER: Yes.

ROLANDER: Many of your intimate friends and acquaintances— professional and otherwise—were also fellow travelers, were they not?

OPPENHEIMER: Yes. I don't find that unnatural. There was a time when the Soviet experiment appealed to all those who were dissatisfied with the state of the world which, I would agree, is certainly unsatisfactory. But now we view the Soviet experiment without any illusions; now Russia is facing us as a hostile world power. And so we condemn the hopes which many people had set on that experiment. . . . It seems to me unwise to condemn those hopes, and I feel it is wrong that people should be disparaged and persecuted because of their views.

ROLANDER: I do not wish to disparage anybody, sir. I merely pursue the question whether a physicist is a greater security risk when he has a certain number of friends and acquaintances who are former Communists or fellow travelers. Is he not in fact a greater security risk?

OPPENHEIMER: No.

ROLANDER: You think it is immaterial, nowadays too, how many acquaintances with Communist leanings———

OPPENHEIMER: I think that a man cannot be taken to pieces like a fuse mechanism. Such and such views: such and such security. Such a number of acquaintances who are fellow travelers: such a degree of security. These mechanical calculations are folly. If we had proceeded like that in Los Alamos, we'd never have employed the best people. We might perhaps have had a laboratory full of men with the most irreproachable views in the world, but I don't believe the thing would have worked. People with first-class ideas don't pursue a course quite as straight as security officers fondly imagine. You cannot produce an atomic bond with irreproachable, that is, conformist ideas. Yes-men are convenient, but ineffectual.

ROLANDER: What did you do, sir, when you heard in 1947 that Weinberg, Bohm, and others, were active Party members?

OPPENHEIMER: What do you mean?

ROLANDER: Did you break off all connections with them?

OPPENHEIMER: No.

ROLANDER: Why not?

OPPENHEIMER: Because it isn't exactly my idea of good manners.

ROLANDER: Is it your idea of security?

OPPENHEIMER: What?

ROLANDER: Did you recommend your own lawyer to Weinberg, sir?

OPPENHEIMER: It was my brother's lawyer, I believe.

ROLANDER: Did you give a party for Bohm?

OPPENHEIMER: I went to a farewell party given for him when he had been fired at Princeton and was going to Brazil.

ROLANDER: And you found it quite easy to reconcile such a demonstration of sympathy for active Communists with the duties of your high office, as the Advisor to the Government on atomic matters?

OPPENHEIMER: What has that to do with atomic matters? I gave some advice to old friends, and I said good-bye to them.

ROLANDER: Would you do the same again, today?

OPPENHEIMER: I should hope so.

ROLANDER: Thank you, sir.

GRAY: Any further questions to Dr. Oppenheimer?

EVANS *raises his hand.*

EVANS: I am surprised that there were actually so many physicists who were Reds. Perhaps it depends on the generation.

OPPENHEIMER: I would say they were Pink, not Red.

EVANS: I can't understand why these people, otherwise quite sensible, were so strongly attracted to radical political ideas. What kind of people are physicists?

OPPENHEIMER: You think they might be a bit crazy?

EVANS: I have no idea, maybe eccentric; how do they differ from other people?

OPPENHEIMER: I think they simply don't have so many preconceived notions. They want to probe into things that don't work.

EVANS: I have never read Marx and such people. I have never taken an interest in politics, as you obviously have.

OPPENHEIMER: I wasn't interested either. For a long time. In my childhood, nobody prepared me for such bitter and cruel things as I got to know later, during the great depression, when my students were hungry and couldn't find jobs, the same as millions of others. I realized that something is wrong with a world in which such things can happen. I wanted to discover the reasons for that.

EVANS: And that is why you read Communist books in those days, sociology, and that sort of thing?

OPPENHEIMER. Yes. Although I never understood Marx's *Kapital,* for instance. I never got beyond the first fifty pages.

EVANS: Oddly enough, I have never met anybody yet who understood it. Apart from Rockefeller, perhaps . . . [*Laughter from* MORGAN, MARKS, *and* ROBB.] . . . and my dentist who says every time he drills into a nerve: "Marx tells us this, and Marx tells us that." [*Laughter.*] To me, therefore, Marx is always associated with a specific pain in a nerve. [*Laughter.*]

OPPENHEIMER: That seems to be the case with many people.

EVANS [*laughing*]: Of all the known philosophers whose works are never read, he is the one who causes us most trouble. Look where it's got *you!*

OPPENHEIMER *laughs. The lighting changes.* MORGAN *steps forward to the footlights. The hangings close.*

MORGAN: I had a talk with Gray yesterday. He was very annoyed because the Secretary of War has intervened. And has stirred up the scientists, of course. Playing with fire. I said I felt that there was a bit too much general discussion of Oppenheimer's political background and opinions. That may be just the thing for Mc-Carthy, but not for those complicated highbrows, the physicists. We should make it clear to the scientists that we don't dictate such and such opinions to them, and that we don't intend to boot them out because they hold this or that opinion. But we must insist on a sharp dividing line between their subjective views and their objective work, because modern nuclear policy is possible only on that basis. This applies not only to science but also to industrial enterprise, to the modern state. That is why this Commission should not rest content with a documentation of Oppenheimer's political background, however astonishing it may be. Rather, we should find out whether, to our cost, he has wrongfully allowed that background, and those political, philo-sophical, moral views, to affect his work as a physicist and a government adviser. And whether this might be feared in the fu-ture. It is this aspect of the matter which makes his clearance an acute question, and this should be understood both by the public and by the physicists. No matter how extreme, the subjective views of a physicist are his own private affair as long as they don't interfere with his objective work. This dividing line bears upon the principles of our democracy.

He returns to the stage itself.

SCENE 6

The following text is projected on the hangings:

FROM THE PROCEEDINGS ON THE TENTH DAY:

WHAT IS ABSOLUTE LOYALTY?

IS THERE SUCH A THING AS HUNDRED-PER-CENT SECURITY?

ROBB: I see from my files that today is your fiftieth birthday, Doc-tor. I should like, for a moment, to lay aside the formality of these proceedings and wish you many happy returns.
OPPENHEIMER: Thank you. There is no need.

ROBB: May I ask, Doctor, whether you have already seen your birthday mail?

OPPENHEIMER: Some of it.

ROBB: Has Haakon Chevalier written to you?

OPPENHEIMER [*with a short contemptuous laugh*]: Yes, a greeting card.

ROBB: What does he write?

OPPENHEIMER: The usual good wishes. "In old friendship, ever yours, Haakon." No doubt you have a photostat copy of it.

ROBB [*smiling*]: You still regard him as your friend, don't you?

OPPENHEIMER: Yes.

ROBB: In your answering letter to the Atomic Energy Commission, on page twenty-two, you recount a conversation that you had with Chevalier in the winter of 1942–43. Where did that conversation take place?

OPPENHEIMER: At my house, in Berkeley.

EVANS: I beg your pardon, I'd just like to know a little more about this Chevalier; who was he, what kind of a person was he?

OPPENHEIMER: He was a member of the faculty.

EVANS: A physicist?

OPPENHEIMER: No. French literature.

EVANS: A Communist?

OPPENHEIMER: He has strong left-wing views.

EVANS: Red, or Pink?

OPPENHEIMIER: Pinkish-red.

EVANS: And as a person?

OPPENHEIMER: One of the two or three friends one has in a lifetime.

ROBB: In your letter, you give the gist of the conversation. Now I would like to ask you, Doctor, to tell us about the circumstances and, if possible, to give us a verbatim account of that conversation.

OPPENHEIMER: I can only give you the substance, not the exact wording. It is one of those things I have too often thought about . . . eleven years ago. . . .

ROBB: Very well, then.

OPPENHEIMER: One day, in the evening, Chevalier came to our house, with his wife, I think he came to us for dinner, or for drinks———

GRAY: Excuse me, was it he who had made the appointment?

OPPENHEIMER: I don't know. It was simply that one of us called up the other, and said: "Why not drop in."

GRAY: I think it is important, Dr. Oppenheimer, that you should give us the story as much in detail as possible.

OPPENHEIMER: All right. . . . They came to our house, we had a brandy, we talked about the latest news, possibly about Stalingrad—it was about that time. . . .

GRAY: Did Chevalier introduce the subject of Stalingrad?

OPPENHEIMER: I don't know, it may be that we talked about it on some other day, but I think it was on that particular evening. One thing is certain, anyway: when I went into the kitchen to mix some drinks Chevalier followed me there and told me that he had recently met Eltenton.

GRAY: Would you tell us, for the record, who Eltenton is?

OPPENHEIMER: A chemical engineer, an Englishman, who had been working in Russia for several years.

GRAY: Party member?

OPPENHEIMER. Closely associated. Whether he actually was a member?—I didn't know him all that well.

ROBB: What did Chevalier want from you?

OPPENHEIMER: I'm not sure whether he *wanted* anything. He told me that Eltenton was furious because we had left the Russians in the lurch, because we weren't opening up a second front, and didn't give them the technical information they needed, and that it was a bloody disgrace.

ROBB: Was this Chevalier's opinion?

OPPENHEIMER: He spoke about Eltenton. He said Eltenton had told him he knew certain ways and means of transmitting technical information to Soviet scientists.

ROBB: What ways and what means, Doctor?

OPPENHEIMER: Chevalier did not say what they were. I don't know whether Eltenton had said what they were. We did not discuss things, I mean, I just said: "But that is treason!" . . . I'm not sure, but, anyway, I said something to the effect that it was horrible and quite unspeakable. And Chevalier said he entirely agreed with me.

ROBB: Is that all that was said?

OPPENHEIMER: Then we talked about drinks, and about Malraux, I believe.

ROBB: Would you spell that name, Doctor?

OPPENHEIMER: M-a-l-r-a-u-x.

ROBB: Malraux? Who is he?

OPPENHEIMER: A French author. Chevalier translated his books.

ROBB: Is Malraux a Communist?

OPPENHEIMER: He used to be. Now he is the brain of de Gaulle.

ROBB: I have never heard his name.

GRAY: Did Chevalier know that, at Berkeley, work was being done on the development of the atomic bomb?

OPPENHEIMER: No.

ROBB: Did you use the word *treason*, Doctor?

OPPENHEIMER: It is such a hackneyed word, I could tell you the whole history of the word *treason*.

ROBB: Would you first answer my question?

OPPENHEIMER: I don't know.

ROBB: Did you regard it as treason?

OPPENHEIMER: What?

ROBB: To transmit secret information to the Russians?

OPPENHEIMER: Of course.

ROLANDER: Did you, thereupon, report the incident to your security authorities, sir?

OPPENHEIMER: No.

ROLANDER: Why not?

OPPENHEIMER: I didn't take that conversation very seriously. Just the way people talk, at parties.

ROBB: But six months later, Doctor, you took that conversation so seriously that you specially went from Los Alamos to Berkeley in order to draw the attention of the security authorities to it. Why?

OPPENHEIMER: Lansdale, the Chief Security Officer, had been in Los Alamos, and he had told me he was very worried about the situation at Berkeley.

ROBB: Do you agree with me, Doctor, when I say that his remark implied a fear of espionage?

OPPENHEIMER: That is right.

ROLANDER: Did he mention any names?

OPPENHEIMER: Lomanitz came up in the conversation. He had gossiped to people about things that were none of their business.

ROLANDER: Which people?

OPPENHEIMER: Of the C.I.O. union; that is why Eltenton came to my mind. Eltenton was rather active in the Scientists' and Engineers' Union.

ROBB: Did you tell Lansdale that you regarded Eltenton as a possible danger?

OPPENHEIMER: I first hinted at it to Johnson, the local Security Officer at Berkeley.

ROBB: Did you tell Johnson the story exactly as it happened?

OPPENHEIMER: No, I said little more than that Eltenton was somebody not to be trusted. He asked me why I said this. Then I invented a cock-and-bull story.

ROBB: You lied to him?

OPPENHEIMER: Yes. I thought that would be the end of the matter. But Johnson informed Radzi, his superior. Then I had an interview with both of them.

ROBB: Did you tell Radzi the truth?

OPPENHEIMER: I told him the same story, but more in detail.

ROBB: What in the story was not true?

OPPENHEIMER: That Eltenton had attempted to approach *three* members of the project, through intermediaries.

ROBB: Intermediaries?

OPPENHEIMER: Or through *one* intermediary.

ROBB: Did you disclose to Radzi the identity of the intermediary, Chevalier?

OPPENHEIMER: I only disclosed the identity of Eltenton.

ROBB: Why?

OPPENHEIMER: I wanted to keep Chevalier out of it, and myself too.

ROBB: In that case, why did you encumber him with contacting *three* members of the project?

OPPENHEIMER: Because I was an idiot.

ROBB: Is that your only explanation, Doctor? [OPPENHEIMER *makes a gesture.*] Didn't you realize that Radzi and Lansdale would move heaven and earth to discover the identity of the intermediary and the three members of the project?

OPPENHEIMER: I ought to have known.

ROBB: And didn't they move heaven and earth?

OPPENHEIMER. Yes. In the end, I promised Lansdale I would disclose the names if General Groves made that a military order. When Groves then commanded me to do so, I named Chevalier and myself.

ROBB: That is all [*Addressing himself to* GRAY.] I would now like to hear Major Radzi as a witness.

ROLANDER: When you told Major Radzi that "cock-and-bull story," sir, there was also something about microfilms, wasn't there, and about a man in the Russian Consulate?

OPPENHEIMER: I can't imagine. No.

ROLANDER: Thank you, sir.

GRAY: Now we have two witnesses, Major Radzi and Mr. Lansdale. Major Radzi is a witness called by Mr. Robb, and will be questioned first. [*An* OFFICIAL *ushers* MAJOR NICHOLAS RADZI *in, by the door to the right, and leads him to the witness stand.* RADZI *is in mufti. He bows slightly to the members of the Board.*] Nicholas Radzi, do you swear that the testimony you are to give the Board shall be the truth, the whole truth, and nothing but the truth, so help you God?

RADZI: I do. [*he seats himself.*]

GRAY: A few questions regarding your personal history. What do you specialize in?

RADZI: Counterespionage in relation to war projects. In particular, countering Communist agents.

GRAY: How long have you been engaged in that sort of work?

RADZI: Fourteen years.

GRAY: Did you receive special training for it?

RADZI: I received the kind of training the F.B.I. give *their* top people. Rather rigorous training. Since then, I've had some international experience.

GRAY: Could you tell us about one of your special assignments?

RADZI: Towards the end of 1943, I and my group had to find out whether the Germans were developing an atomic bomb. And I had to kidnap the German eggheads in question—before they were kidnaped by the Russians. I guess we did that rather well.

GRAY: Were you specially trained how to deal with scientists?

RADZI: Yes. I think I have a sort of knack for it. By now, I have a pretty shrewd idea how a nuclear physicist's mind works, and how to get at him.

GARRISON: Mr. Chairman, may I ask, for the record: what was the original profession of Mr. Radzi?

RADZI: Physical training instructor. [*Laughing.*] I was a natural boxer and quite a good football coach.

GARRISON: Mr. Chairman, may I ask Mr. Radzi whether it was his own wish to appear here as a witness?

GRAY: Major Radzi?

RADZI: No. I have been ordered here by my department.

GRAY: Well, you know of course, Major, that you must give nothing but your own testimony here, and that you are not to follow instructions you might possibly have been given. . . . You may question the witness, Mr. Robb.

ROBB: I would like to ask you, Major, what particular assignment brought you into contact with Dr. Oppenheimer in 1943?

RADZI: Well, yes, in May 1943 I was asked to investigate a possible case of espionage at Berkeley. We only knew that a man named Steve Nelson, a prominent Communist functionary in California, had attempted to secure information concerning the Radiation Laboratory. And that he had tried to get this information through a man of whom we only knew that his first name, or his code name, was Joe—and that Joe had come from New York, and had sisters living in New York. We started the investigation, and at first we thought the man was Lomanitz. That is why we wanted to remove him from the laboratory and push him off into the Army.

ROBB: But you were not able to do that? Why?

RADZI: Oppenheimer used his personal connections to keep Lomanitz at Berkeley. Then it turned out that Lomanitz was not identifiable with Joe. For a while, we thought it might be David Bohm. And, later, Max Friedman. Finally we discovered that Joe was Joseph Weinberg.

ROBB: What had that investigation to do with Dr. Oppenheimer?

RADZI: It seemed somewhat strange that everybody we suspected had some sort of connection with Dr. Oppenheimer. Whenever we trod on somebody's toes he was sure to turn to Dr. Oppenheimer for help.

ROBB: Thereupon, what steps did you take?

RADZI: We asked the F.B.I., in June 1943, to place Dr. Oppenheimer under investigation because of suspected espionage.

ROBB: Did you conduct that investigation?

RADZI: Yes.

ROBB: What did you discover?

RADZI: That Dr. Oppenheimer had probably been a member of the Communist Party and that he still had strong Communist leanings. Also, that he had associations with Communists such as David Hawkins and Jean Tatlock who, in turn, had contacts with Steve Nelson and, through Steve Nelson, possibly also with the Russians.

ROBB: Thereupon, what steps did you take, Major?

RADZI: We recommended to the Pentagon—to Mr. Lansdale, my superior—that Dr. Oppenheimer should be completely removed from any employment by the United States government. In case Dr. Oppenheimer was regarded as irreplaceable, we recommended them to use the pretext that he was endangered by certain Axis agents, whereupon he should have two bodyguards assigned to him—men specially trained by our department, who would watch him all the time. Much to our regret, neither Lansdale nor Groves accepted these recommendations.

ROBB: That happened quite some time before you had an interview with Dr. Oppenheimer, is that right?

RADZI: Two months before.

ROBB: In that case, did it not surprise you that Dr. Oppenheimer himself, in August, volunteered to give you some information about suspected espionage?

RADZI: Not particularly. It is quite a well-known reaction from people who have discovered that their personal affairs are being investigated.

ROSS: Do you recall your interview with Dr. Oppenheimer?

RADZI: Sure. I listened to the tape yesterday. . . . We made a recording of it in Lieutenant Johnson's office, at the time. [*He extracts a reel of tape from his briefcase.*] Here it is.

ROBB: May we hear it?

RADZI: Sure. It has been released by the F.B.I. [*He hands the tape to an* OFFICIAL *who fits it into a tape recorder.*]

ROBB [*to the* OFFICIAL]. Ready? Well, let us start.

The OFFICIAL *switches on the tape recorder. Projected on the screens: photographs of* RADZI *in summer uniform, and of Oppenheimer, 1943, young-looking, sunburned, in shirt and slacks. Alternative suggestion: the interview* RADZI-OPPENHEIMER-JOHNSON, *on an 8-mm. film, is projected, reasonably synchronized with the tape recording. The interview takes place on a hot August day at Los Alamos, in an office in an army hut.* OPPENHEIMER *in shirt and blue jeans, the officers in summer uniform.* JOHNSON, *seated at a small desk, surreptitiously manipulates a tape recorder.* RADZI *sees to it that the microphone is close to* OPPENHEMIER. *The whole film should look rather the worse for wear, in order to look like a genuine documentary. On no account must it give the impression of being a sound film.*

Tape recording:

RADZI: I am delighted, Dr. Oppenheimer, to meet you at last, and to be able to talk with you.

OPPENHEIMER: The pleasure is mine, Major.

RADZI: No, no. Doctor, on the contrary—you are one of the most important men in the world today, one of the most fascinating men, there's no doubt about it. Whereas we are only something like night watchmen. [*He laughs.*] I don't want to take up much of your precious time . . .

OPPENHEIMER: That's perfectly all right. Whatever time you want.

RADZI: . . . but Lieutenant Johnson told me yesterday you thought it possible that a certain group is interested in the project. He said you had been kind enough to give us this tip.

OPPENHEIMER: Yes, well, it is quite a while ago, and I have no first-hand knowledge, but I think it is true to say that a man, whose name I never heard, who was attached to the Soviet Consulate, has tried to indicate through intermediaries to people concerned in the project that he was in a position to transmit information, with no danger to anybody.

RADZI: Information for the Russians?

OPPENHEIMER: Yes. We all know how difficult the relations are between the two allies, and there are many people—those, too, who don't feel particularly friendly towards Russia—who think it is wrong that we deny the Russians certain technical information, radar, and so on, while they battle for their lives, fighting the Nazis.

RADZI: Yes, it sure is a problem. . . . Perhaps you know that I have Russian blood.

OPPENHEIMER: There may be some arguments for giving the Russians official information, but it is obviously quite out of the question to have such information moving out the back door.

RADZI: Could you give us a little more specific information as to how these approaches were made?

OPPENHEIMER: They were made quite indirectly, well, I know of two or three cases. Two or three of the people are with me at Los Alamos, and they are closely associated with me. That is why I feel I should give you only *one* name, which has been mentioned a couple of times, and this person may possibly be an intermediary. His name is Eltenton.

RADZI: Eltenton? Does he work on the project?

OPPENHEIMER: No. He is employed by the Shell Development Company. At least, he used to work there.

RADZI: Were these people contacted by Eltenton himself?

OPPENHEIMER: No.

RADZI: Through another party?

OPPENHEIMER: Yes.

RADZI: Would you tell us, please, through whom these contacts were made?

OPPENHEIMER: I don't think that would be right. I don't want to have people involved who have nothing to do with the whole thing. It wouldn't be fair. They confided in me, and they have been one-hundred-per-cent loyal. It's a question of trust.

RADZI: Obviously, we don't mistrust these people, Doctor—just as little as we mistrust *you*. [*He laughs*]. It would be absurd! But we must have the intermediary, so that we can get inside the network.

OPPENHEIMER: I wouldn't like to give you his name. I have implicit confidence in him. . . . But it is a very different matter when Eltenton comes and says he has good contacts with a man attached to the Russian Consulate, who has a lot of experience with microfilms or whatever the hell.

RADZI: Of course I am trying to get out of you everything I possibly can. Once we've licked blood—we bloodhounds [*He laughs.*]—we are persistent.

OPPENHEIMER: It is your duty to be persistent.

RADZI: At any rate, I'm glad you have such a positive attitude to our work. Certain scientists don't find that so easy.

OPPENHEIMER: Whom are you referring to?

RADZI [*laughs*]: I'm not referring to Niels Bohr—[*He laughs.*]—to whom I explained for three solid hours what he must *not* say. And then he said the whole lot within the first half-hour of a railway journey. [OPPENHEIMER *laughs.*] When we got him across from Denmark we had to drag him out of the plane, unconscious, because he had forgotten to work his oxygen mask which we had made him put on. We flew at an altitude of 36,000 feet. [*He laughs.*]

The OFFICIAL *switches off the tape recorder.*

EVANS [*turning to* OPPENHEIMER]: Was Niels Bohr with you at Los Alamos?

OPPENHEIMER: For a short time. Under a code name, like all of us. Nicolas Baker. He did not want to stay.

EVANS: Why not?

OPPENHEIMER: He was furious with us. He said we were turning science into an appendage of the military, and the moment we gave an atomic cudgel into their hands they'd let fly with it. It worried him a great deal.

EVANS: He was the most charming person I've ever known.

ROLANDER: Doesn't it emerge quite clearly from the tape recording, sir, that you spoke to Major Radzi of "a man in the Russian Consulate who had a lot of experience with microfilms"?

GARRISON: The exact words were, "with microfilms or whatever the hell."

ROLANDER: If you have a friend, sir, whom you regard as innocent, and you wish to protect him from the security authorities—why do you encumber him with the Russian Consulate, microfilms, and three contacts? I just can't see the reason for it.

OPPENHEIMER: Neither can I.

ROLANDER: You have no explanation?

OPPENHEIMER: Not an explanation that would sound logical.

ROBB: Do you have an explanation for Dr. Oppenheimer's behavior, Major Radzi?

RADZI: Sure. Dr. Oppenheimer told us the truth, at the time.

ROBB: You think that the story, which Dr. Oppenheimer called a cock-and-bull story here, is in fact true?

RADZI: Yes. And I think that his later attempt at minimizing it was the real cock-and-bull story. Dr. Oppenheimer told us about three genuine cases of people being contacted. This way, he wanted to secure our continued confidence in him, because he was afraid we might discover these contacts in the course of our investigations. But when our investigations weren't very successful he made light of the whole thing.

ROBB: Was that your opinion also at the time?

RADZI: Sure. I told Lansdale all about it.

ROBB: And Lansdale?

RADZI: The whole thing went up in blue smoke when Dr. Oppenheimer named Chevalier and himself. There was some more investigating, but finally the whole lot was thrown overboard.

ROBB: From your knowledge of F.B.I. files, and from your own experience in this matter, would you grant Dr. Oppenheimer his security clearance?

RADZI: I wouldn't have cleared him then, and I wouldn't clear him now.

ROBB: Were you alone in that opinion?

RADZI: I guess all security officers below the rank of Lansdale and General Groves shared that opinion.

ROBB: Thank you very much, Major.

GRAY: [*to* OPPENHEIMER's *counsel*]. Would you wish to cross-examine Major Radzi?

MARKS: Yes . . . I am going to ask you a psychological question, Mr. Radzi. Is Dr. Oppenheimer's personality easy to understand, or is it rather complicated?

RADZI: Extremely complicated. And extremely contradictory.

MARKS: In other words: one would have to know him very well in order to reach a conclusive judgment?

RADZI: Yes.

MARKS: How well do you know Dr. Oppenheimer?

RADZI: I know him very well, in so far as I know his file very well.

MARKS: How often have you talked with him?

RADZI: Once.

MARKS: Does one get to know a person better from his file or from actual conversation with him?

RADZI: In our work, I would give preference to files. They are the sum total of all the impressions of a man which one single person can't get, just by himself.

MARKS: How long have Dr. Oppenheimer's activities been under surveillance by the security authorities, in particular by the F.B.I.?

RADZI: Thirteen or fourteen years.

MARKS: During that time, was there any proof of Dr. Oppenheimer being indiscreet?

RADZI: No proof.

MARKS: Or disloyal?

RADZI: In the Chevalier business, there is no doubt that Dr. Oppenheimer's loyalty to a friend outweighed his loyalty to America.

MARKS: Did Chevalier prove to be innocent?

RADZI: It was not possible to prove that he was guilty.

MARKS: What happened to him?

RADZI: He was fired at Berkeley and he was of course put under surveillance.

MARKS: If Dr. Oppenheimer foresaw such consequences, would it not be understandable that he hesitated several weeks before naming him?

RADZI: No, not when the safety of the country is at stake. From a scientist of such stature, we must demand absolute loyalty.

MARKS: Do you know that, in 1946, F.B.I. investigated the Chevalier incident a second time?

RADZI: Yes.

MARKS: And that Mr. Hoover, the F.B.I. Chief, took an interest in it himself?

RADZI: Yes.

MARKS: And that Dr. Oppenheimer's clearance was granted, with no reservations?

RADZI: I'd have liked to see the man who'd have cast doubt on Dr. Oppenheimer's clearance in 1946, what with his prestige and influence! He was a god in those days.

MARKS: I have no more questions.

GRAY: Any further questions to Major Radzi: [*Evans indicates his wish to speak.*] Dr. Evans.

EVANS: What I have always wanted to hear from an expert, it interests me, is somewhat general. In your opinion, Mr. Radzi, with reference to a secret war project, is it possible to achieve one-hundred-per-cent security?

RADZI: No. It would be possible to have ninety-five-per-cent security if scientists and technicians were selected with proper care, and if they were taught some understanding of our problems.

EVANS: What do you mean?

RADZI: They should be made to realize that, nowadays, they are experts working within one vast enterprise. They have to do their own particular share of the work and then hand it over to the other experts, the politicians and the military, who then decide what is to be done with it. And we are the experts who make sure that there are no rubbernecks looking in. If we want to defend our freedom successfully, we must be prepared to forego some of our personal liberty.

EVANS: I don't know, it doesn't make me feel too good, but it was interesting to hear the views of an expert.

GRAY: Any further questions? Mr. Morgan.

MORGAN: Do you think that Dr. Oppenheimer's Communist sympathies had something to do with his attitude in the Chevalier incident?

RADZI: Beyond a doubt. Although I have come to the conclusion that Dr. Oppenheimer can give his undivided loyalty to only two things: science and his own career.

GARRISON: Do you regard Mr. Lansdale, your former superior, as an incompetent security expert, Mr. Radzi?

RADZI: No. He is the most competent amateur I've ever known. Perhaps he lacks toughness, which is vital in our business.

GRAY: If there are no further questions—may I thank you for having come here to help us. [*Radzi gets up and leaves the room.*] Would Mr. Lansdale now be asked to appear?

An OFFICIAL *leaves the room to fetch* LANSDALE.

ROBB: To complete the record, Dr. Oppenheimer. You maintained your good relations with Chevalier, is that right?

OPPENHEIMER: Yes.

ROBB: When did you last see him?

OPPENHEIMER: A few months ago, in Paris.

ROBB: Doctor, when did your friend, Haakon Chevalier, first discover that it was you who had reported his case to the security authorities?

OPPENHEIMER: I guess he will discover it now, from these proceedings.

EVANS: You have never told him, I mean, this is almost private, that you set the whole thing going?

OPPENHEIMER: No.

EVANS: Why not?

OPPENHEIMER: I guess he wouldn't have understood.

The OFFICIAL *who went to fetch* LANSDALE *opens the door and looks questioningly at* GRAY.

GRAY: Is Mr. Lansdale there? [*The* OFFICIAL *leads* LANSDALE *to the witness stand.*] Do you wish to testify under oath, Mr. Lansdale?

LANSDALE: I leave that to counsel or to the Board.

GRAY: The previous witnesses have testified under oath.

LANSDALE: Then let us keep it uniform.

GRAY: John Lansdale, do you swear that the testimony you are to give the Board shall be the truth, the whole truth, and nothing but the truth, so help you God?

LANSDALE: I do.

GRAY: Will you please take the stand. . . . You are at present working as a lawyer, Mr. Lansdale?

LANSDALE: Yes, in Ohio.

GRAY: Where did you study?

LANSDALE: Harvard.

GRAY: You were responsible for the security of the entire atomic
weapons project, were you not?

LANSDALE: During the war.

GRAY: You may question Mr. Lansdale as a witness, Mr. Garrison.

GARRISON: Was it up to you to grant Dr. Oppenheimer his clearance?

LANSDALE: Yes, or to refuse it. A difficult decision.

GARRISON: Why?

LANSDALE: In the opinion of the experts, Oppenheimer was the
only person who could make Los Alamos a reality. But, on the
other hand, the F.B.I. reports on him didn't look too good. The
F.B.I. recommended that Dr. Oppenheimer should be withdrawn from the project. Thus I had to arrive at a judgment of
my own.

GARRISON: How did you set about it?

LANSDALE: I had him placed under surveillance.

GARRISON: How was that done?

LANSDALE: We shadowed him, we opened his mail, we had his
phone calls monitored, we set him various traps—well, we did
all the nasty things that are usually done in such cases. And during that whole period I talked with him, and his wife, as often as
I possibly could. I think he rather liked me. At any rate, he talked
to me very frankly.

GARRISON: What was the purpose of these conversations?

LANSDALE: I wanted to find out what kind of a person he was,
what he thought, and *how* he thought. I had to reach my own
conclusion whether he was a Communist, as the F.B.I. suspected, or whether he was not.

GARRISON: What was your conclusion?

LANSDALE: That he was not a Communist, and that he should be
granted his clearance no matter what the F.B.I. reports said.

GARRISON: Dr. Oppenheimer has been rebuked here for having refused to disclose the identity of his friend, Chevalier. What is
your attitude in this matter?

LANSDALE: I thought it wrong and also rather naïve of him to imagine that he would get away with it, when he had *us* to deal with. His motives were that he regarded Chevalier as innocent and therefore wanted to protect him from trouble. Curiously enough, I always thought it was his brother, Frank, whom he wanted to protect, and General Groves thought the same.

GARRISON: Did his refusal endanger the security of the project?

LANSDALE: No. It just gave us a lot of extra work, that story he dished up to us. It was typical.

GARRISON: Typical of what?

LANSDALE: Scientists regard security officers either as extraordinarily stupid, or as extraordinarily cunning. And incompetent, in either case.

EVANS: Oh, how would you explain that?

LANSDALE: The scientific mind and the military security mind— well, it's like birds and rhinos sharing a ball game. Each thinks the other impossible, and both are quite right.

EVANS: Which are the rhinos?

LANSDALE: They are very nice animals.

GARRISON: Major Radzi has testified here that he still believes the true story to be the one about the three contacts, the microfilms, and the man at the Soviet Consulate.

LANSDALE: I know, but his views don't tally with the findings of our investigations.

GARRISON: Were those investigations concluded?

LANSDALE: They were concluded three times—in 1943, 1946, and 1950. I hope they will be concluded now, for the fourth time. The whole thing was just a lot of hot air.

GARRISON: If you had to decide now, today, whether to grant Dr. Oppenheimer his clearance, would you do so?

LANSDALE: By the same criteria which we used then, yes, certainly. I am not attempting to interpret the present ruling. Our criteria were: loyalty and discretion.

GARRISON: Thank you, Mr. Lansdale.

GRAY: Mr. Robb, do you wish to cross-examine Mr. Lansdale?

ROBB: Mr. Rolander will do so.

ROLANDER: As I understand it, sir, you are not offering any opinion as to whether or not you would clear Dr. Oppenheimer on the basis of presently existing criteria?

LANSDALE: These criteria are strange to me. I know them, but they appear strange to me. I do not wish to discuss their usefulness.

On the basis of my past experiences with Dr. Oppenheimer, I regard him as perfectly loyal and very discreet.

ROLANDER: His discretion was good?

LANSDALE: Very good.

ROLANDER: Does your idea of discretion include spending the night with a Communist woman?

LANSDALE: Mr. Rolander, if you should ever fall deeply in love with a girl who happens to have Communist views, and if she wants to see you because she is unhappy—then, I hope, you will go and comfort her, and leave your tape recorder behind.

ROLANDER: You have not answered my question, sir.

LANSDALE: The question concerning Jean Tatlock has been answered seventeen times, Mr. Rolander! Dr. Oppenheimer was under our surveillance. I have heard the tape recordings and I have destroyed the tapes.

ROLANDER: Why?

LANSDALE: Because there is a limit to everything, Mr. Rolander!

ROLANDER: I fail to understand you, sir.

LANSDALE: That's just too bad.

GRAY: I suggest we regard this whole matter as concluded, Mr. Rolander.

ROBB: Does the name Steve Nelson mean anything to you?

LANSDALE: Yes.

ROBB: Who was he?

LANSDALE: A Communist functionary from California of whom it was said that, towards the end of 1943 or thereabouts, he had discovered that we were working on atomic weapons.

ROBB: Through whom was he supposed to have made that discovery?

LANSDALE: It was said that the F.B.I. suspected he might have got that information through Jean Tatlock or Mrs. Oppenheimer. Our investigations————

ROBB: Would you confine yourself to my question, Mr. Lansdale.

LANSDALE: May I finish my sentence? Our investigations did not uncover any evidence to support that conjecture.

ROBB: On the basis of your investigations, could such a possibility be entirely excluded?

LANSDALE: We found nothing to go on.

ROBB: But you would not commit yourself to saying that such a possibility can be entirely excluded?

LANSDALE: Have it your own way.

ROBB: I would like to ask Dr. Oppenheimer a question.

GRAY: Very well.

ROBB: Would you call Steve Nelson an intimate acquaintance of yours?

OPPENHEIMER: No. He was an acquaintance of my wife's. He had been in Spain with her first husband. He came to see us two or three times when he was at Berkeley, till about 1942.

ROBB: What did you talk about when he was there?

OPPENHEIMER: No idea. About personal matters. He came with his wife, I think.

ROBB: Did Jean Tatlock know him well?

OPPENHEIMER: Superficially. There was nothing personal in their relationship.

ROBB: In that case, if Jean Tatlock had in fact visited him, Doctor, the assumption would be that the reasons were purely political, is that right?

OPPENHEIMER: I cannot answer that. "Would!" "Could!" "Should!"

ROBB: Admittedly, Doctor, it is a hypothetical question. I shall now put it this way: If, let us suppose, Jean Tatlock had, through somebody, discovered something about our atomic weapons project—we are only supposing it, of course—then, with your knowledge of her psychological make-up, would you entirely exclude the possibility that she might have confided this secret to Steve Nelson?

OPPENHEIMER: She did not discover anything through me.

ROBB: Would you see no connection whatever between such a hypothetical visit and her tragic end? [OPPENHEIMER *does not answer.*] I am asking you a question, Doctor.

OPPENHEIMER: I know. And I am not answering it.

ROBB: Mr. Chairman . . .

GARRISON: Mr. Chairman . . .

GRAY: On the basis of a previous objection by the defense, which was sustained, the question put by Mr. Robb is inadmissible. Mr. Lansdale is on the stand as a witness.

ROLANDER: You have said here, sir, that in your opinion the story dished up by Dr. Oppenheimer was typical.

LANSDALE: His attitude was typical.

ROLANDER: Typical of what?

LANSDALE: Of scientists.

ROLANDER: Dr. Oppenheimer has testified here that he lied to you and to Major Radzi. Is telling lies characteristic of scientists?

LANSDALE: It is characteristic of them that they want to decide for themselves what information I need and what I don't.

ROLANDER: My question was whether you think that scientists, as a group, are liars.

LANSDALE: I don't think people as a group are liars. But it is the tendency of brilliant people to regard themselves competent in matters in which they have no competence.

ROLANDER: At the time, sir, it was a question of investigating what you believed to be a serious case of suspected espionage. Is that right?

LANSDALE: Yes. Well, yes.

ROLANDER: And Dr. Oppenheimer knew this when he refused to disclose Chevalier's name to you?

LANSDALE: Yes.

ROLANDER: And you told him that his refusal seriously impeded your investigation?

LANSDALE: He was neither the first nor the last scientist who impeded my investigations.

ROBB: Mr. Lansdale, do you feel you have to defend Dr. Oppenheimer here?

LANSDALE: I am trying to be as objective as possible.

ROBB: Your last answer made me doubt it.

LANSDALE [*losing his self-control*]: The questions put by this young man make me doubt whether it is the truth that is to be discovered here! I am extremely disturbed by the current hysteria, of which these questions are a manifestation!

ROBB: You think these proceedings are a manifestation of hysteria?

LANSDALE: I think——

ROBB: Yes or no?

LANSDALE: I refuse to answer with "yes" or "no"! If you are going to continue in this way . . .

ROBB: What?

LANSDALE [*regaining his self-control*]: If you will allow me to finish, I shall gladly answer your question.

ROBB: Very well.

LANSDALE: I think that the current hysteria over Communism is a danger to our way of life and to our form of democracy. Lawful criteria are being obliterated by fear and demogoguery. What is being done today, what so many people are doing today, is looking at events which took place in 1941, 1942, and judging them in the light of their present feelings. But human behavior varies in the changing context of time. If associations in the thirties or forties are regarded in the same light as similar associations would be regarded today—then, in my view, it is a manifestation of the current hysteria.

ROBB: It is true, then, that you regard these proceedings as a manifestation of———

LANSDALE: Hell, I was told off, at the time, because I refused to allow the former political officer of the Lincoln Brigade to serve in our army—and then he was commissioned on direct orders from the White House! That's how it was then. What is the use of rehashing old stuff dating back to 1940 or 1943? That is what I mean by hysteria.

ROBB: How do you know that this Board is rehashing old stuff?

LANSDALE: I don't know. I hope I am wrong.

ROLANDER: Would it be true to say, sir, that the security officers below your own rank unanimously opposed the clearance of Dr. Oppenheimer?

LANSDALE: If I had judged by the F.B.I. reports alone, I would also have opposed it. But the success of Los Alamos, the atomic bomb—that was Dr. Oppenheimer.

ROLANDER: Thank you, sir.

GRAY: Any further questions to the witness? Mr. Morgan.

MORGAN: Mr. Lansdale, when you reached the conclusion that Dr. Oppenheimer was not a Communist, what was your definition of a Communist?

LANSDALE: A person who is more loyal to Russia than to his own country. You will note that this definition has nothing to do with philosophical or political ideas.

MORGAN: What was the alignment of Dr. Oppenheimer's political ideas?

LANSDALE: They were extremely liberal.

MORGAN: Do you think this can always be differentiated from Red itself?

LANSDALE: In many cases, no.

MORGAN: If I understood you correctly: contrary to Major Radzi, you do not think that Dr. Oppenheimer has discredited himself by his behavior in the Chevalier incident?

LANSDALE: No.

MORGAN: I am an old businessman, a pragmatist. May I ask you a hypothetical question?

LANSDALE: Please do.

MORGAN: Let us assume you are the president of a large bank.

LANSDALE: Gladly!

MORGAN: Would you employ a man at your bank who is on intimate terms with safecrackers? Would you employ him as the manager of your bank?

LANSDALE: If he is first-class.

MORGAN: Well, let us say you have such an excellent bank manager. . . . One day, a friend of this bank manager comes to see him, and he says: "I know some efficient fellows who'd be very interested in robbing your bank. Nothing can go wrong. All you have to do is disconnect the alarm system for a while." Your bank manager rejects the proposition; let us assume he uses strong words. Supposing he does not report this incident to you for six months—and he reports it only in connection with, let us say, some bank robbery in Chicago—would this not surprise you?

LANSDALE: I would ask him why he had waited so long before telling me.

MORGAN: Supposing he says to you: "The man who approached me about it is a good friend of mine; I didn't take it seriously; I'm sure he himself has nothing to do with it; that's why I didn't want to get him into trouble. But, because of that Chicago business, I want to draw your attention to the guy who took the initiative in the whole thing, at the time." Would you not urge him to tell you also the name of his friend?

LANSDALE: I guess I would. Of course I'd also try to discover whether it was a serious matter or idle talk.

MORGAN: Now let us suppose he tells you the story in this way: "My friend told me at the time that the fellows he knew intend to break into quite a number of banks, using all the latest gadgets." Would you not have reached the conclusion that the police ought to be informed of this?

LANSDALE: Yes.

MORGAN: Well, your bank manager is now put under pressure to disclose the name of his friend. He comes to you and says: "Mr. Lansdale, I recently told you a story about my friend and those

other fellows. Tear gas, submachine guns, and so forth. Well, it
was just a cock-and-bull story. Nothing in it is true. I merely
wanted to protect my friend from trouble." Would you not ask
yourself: why? What is behind it? Does one protect ones friend
by telling an extraordinary cock-and-bull story about him?

LANSDALE: I certainly would have asked myself these questions. But
I wouldn't have done so twelve years later, when it turned out
that none of those fellows had actually robbed a bank.

MORGAN: Do you know all the banks in America, Mr. Lansdale?

LANSDALE: The one you refer to is a bank I know quite well. The
analogy does not fit.

MORGAN: I agree it is crude. Crude thinking is one of my most
profitable faculties.

GRAY: Any further questions to Mr. Lansdale? Yes, Mr. Evans.

EVANS: I already asked Mr. Radzi. I wasn't satisfied with his answer; perhaps the fault lies with the question itself: With reference to a secret war project, is there such a thing as one-hundred-
per-cent security?

LANSDALE: No.

EVANS: Why is that so?

LANSDALE: In order to have one-hundred-per-cent security, we
would have to abandon all the freedoms we want to defend. It
can't be done.

EVANS: What, in your opinion, can be done, then, to ensure a country the maximum amount of security?

LANSDALE: We must see to it that we have the best ideas and the
best way of life.

EVANS: I'm no expert, but I feel I'd also have formulated it along
these lines. . . . It isn't easy.

LANSDALE: No.

EVANS: That is all.

GRAY: Thank you very much, Mr. Lansdale.

LANSDALE *rises to his feet.*

EVANS: One more question perhaps, just as nonprofessional or
naïve as my last one. When I look at the results of this strict
secrecy, of these security ramifications on all sides, I mean, we
are sitting rather uncomfortably on this powder keg of a world,
everywhere, I think the question arises whether these secrets
might not be safeguarded best of all by being made public?

LANSDALE: What do you mean?

EVANS: By re-establishing the age-old right of the scientists to publish the results of their researches, or maybe even demanding it of them?

LANSDALE: This is such a remote and utopian dream, Dr. Evans, that even children are forbidden it. . . . The world is divided into sheep and goats, and we are all the slaughterhouse.

EVANS: As I said before, I'm no expert.

GRAY: Thank you very much, Mr. Lansdale. [LANSDALE *leaves the room*]. Today's session is concluded, and we will now take a recess. We shall next deal with Dr. Oppenheimer's attitude in the matter of the hydrogen bomb. May I ask Mr. Garrison and Mr. Robb for the list of their witnesses.

SCENE 7

The members of the Board and counsel for both parties occupy their usual places. OPPENHEIMER *is on the witness stand. The Chairman,* GORDON GRAY, *steps forward to the footlights.*

GRAY: I've been afraid it might happen, and now it has. The *New York Times* has published the letter of the Atomic Energy Commission and Oppenheimer's reply to the allegations. The letters were released by Oppenheimer's counsel in order to counteract a subversive campaign against Oppenheimer. Now the case of J. Robert Oppenheimer dominates the headlines and public discussion all over America.

With a resigned gesture, he returns to his seat.

Voices reciting the following headlines issue from a loudspeaker. Simultaneous with the voices, five photographs of OPPENHEIMER *are successively projected, very different from each other, the facial expression in each corresponding with the headline that goes with it.*

VOICES ISSUING FROM THE LOUDSPEAKER:

The man who rated his personal friendships higher than loyalty to his country. [*Corresponding photo.*]

The man who betrayed his friends because of his loyalty to his country. [*Corresponding photo.*]

The martyr who fought against the development of the hydrogen bomb on moral grounds. [*Corresponding photo.*]

The ideological traitor who destroyed America's nuclear monopoly.
[*Corresponding photo.*]

Oppenheimer, an American Dreyfus Case. [*Corresponding photo*].

End of projection of photographs.

Part 2

The stage is open, as before. The following documentaries are projected on the hangings, with a simultaneously spoken text:

PROJECTION	SPOKEN TEXT
October 31, 1952. Test explosion of the first hydrogen bomb in the Pacific.	Test explosion of Mike, the first hydrogen bomb, in the Pacific.
The island of Elugelab sinks into the ocean.	The island of Elugelab, Atoll Eniwetok, sinks into the ocean.
President Truman speaks. Applause from a large crowd.	President Truman announces the American monopoly of the hydrogen bomb.
August 8, 1953. Test explosion of the first Russian hydrogen bomb.	Test explosion of the first Russian hydrogen bomb in Soviet Asia.
Minister President Malenkov speaks. Applause from a large crowd.	Minister President Malenkov declares: "The United States no longer holds the monopoly of the hydrogen bomb."
An American fleet of bombers. A Soviet fleet of bombers.	In the present state of nuclear balance, the high commands of the two big world powers keep their strategic A- and H-bomber fleets in the air.

The hangings close.

SCENE 2

The following text is projected on the hangings:

THE PROCEEDINGS ENTER A DECISIVE STAGE.

LOYALTY TO A GOVERNMENT.

LOYALTY TO MANKIND.

ROBB: We would now like to deal with your attitude in the matter of the hydrogen bomb, Doctor.

OPPENHEIMER: All right.

ROBB: I quote from the letter by the Atomic Energy Commission, page six, at the bottom: "It was further reported that in the fall of 1949, and subsequently, you strongly opposed the development of the hydrogen bomb; (1) on moral grounds, (2) by claiming that it was not feasible, (3) by claiming that there were insufficient facilities and scientific personnel to carry on the development, and (4) that it was not politically desirable." Is this statement true?

OPPENHEIMER: Partly. With reference to a specific situation in the fall of 1949, and to a specific technical program.

ROBB: Which parts of it are true, Doctor, and which are not?

OPPENHEIMER: I made that clear in my answering letter.

ROBB: I would like to have it clearer still.

OPPENHEIMER: Let us try.

ROBB: I have a report here, from the General Advisory Committee of which you were the Chairman. It dates back to October 1949, and it is in answer to the question whether the United States should, or should not, initiate a crash program for the development of the hydrogen bomb. Do you remember that report? [*He hands* OPPENHEIMER *a copy.*]

OPPENHEIMER: The majority report. I wrote it myself.

ROBB: It says there—Mr. Rolander will read it out to us . . .

ROLANDER: "The fact that there are no limits to the destructiveness of this weapon makes its very existence a danger to humanity as a whole. For ethical reasons, we think it wrong to initiate the development of such a weapon."

OPPENHEIMER: That is from the minority report which was written by Fermi and Rabi.

ROLANDER: It says here, in the majority report: "We all hope that the development of this weapon can be avoided. We are all agreed that it would be wrong at the present moment for the United States to initiate an all-out effort toward the development of this weapon."

ROBB: Does this not mean, Doctor, that you were against the development of the hydrogen bomb?

OPPENHEIMER: We were against *initiating* its development. In an exceptional situation.

ROBB: What was exceptional about the situation in the fall of 1949, Doctor?

OPPENHEIMER: The Russians had exploded their first atomic bomb, Joe I, and we reacted with a nation-wide shock. We had lost our monopoly of the atomic bomb, and our first reaction was: we must get a hydrogen bomb monopoly as quickly as possible.

ROBB: That was quite a natural reaction, was it not?

OPPENHEIMER: Maybe natural, but not sensible. The Russians then also developed the hydrogen bomb.

ROBB: Were we not in a much better position, technically?

OPPENHEIMER: Perhaps, but in Russia there are only two targets suitable for a hydrogen bomb, Moscow and Leningrad, whereas we have more than fifty.

ROBB: One more reason to get ahead of the Russians, or is it not?

OPPENHEIMER: It seemed wiser to me to try for an international declaration of renunciation of that terrible weapon. With a third world war, fought with hydrogen bombs, there would be no victors and no vanquished any more but only the destruction of ninety-eight per cent or a hundred per cent of mankind.

MORGAN: A declaration of renunciation without controls? I think, Dr. Oppenheimer, you were the Scientific Adviser of our government when Gromyko declared in Geneva, in 1946, that he could not agree to any kind of control whatsoever. And, in those days, we had the monopoly of the atom bomb.

OPPENHEIMER: Yes, I felt very depressed at the time.

MORGAN: Why should the Russians be more obliging in 1949?

OPPENHEIMER: The ability to extinguish all life upon earth is a new attribute. The writing on the wall has appeared for mankind.

MORGAN: In Cyrillic lettering, too, Doctor?

OPPENHEIMER: Since we had the fall-out of the Russian hydrogen bomb analyzed, yes. We should have knocked before opening the door to the horrible world in which we now live. But we preferred to break the door down. Although it gave us no strategic advantage.

MORGAN: Did you feel competent to decide strategic questions? Was that your function?

OPPENHEIMER: The greater part of our report gave our assessment of whether a serviceable hydrogen bomb could be made, and how long it would take.

ROBB: How did you assess it?

OPPENHEIMER: We doubted the practicability of the technical propositions we had at that time—they proved impracticable indeed.

ROBB: Did this not mean that the hydrogen bomb was to be shelved until some better ideas emerged?

OPPENHEIMER: No. We recommended a research program.

ROBB: In other words, the project of the hydrogen bomb was in a bad way?

OPPENHEIMER: The first model looked pretty bad. Miserable. Otherwise we wouldn't have spoken of five years' development.

ROBB: Was the prognosis correct?

OPPENHEIMER: For that model?

ROBB: For the hydrogen bomb?

OPPENHEIMER: No. There were some brilliant ideas in 1951, and we tested Mike, the first hydrogen bomb, in October 1952.

ROBB: The test was very successful, was it not?

OPPENHEIMER: Yes. The island of Elugelab in the Pacific disappeared within ten minutes. Nine months later, the Russians had their hydrogen bomb. It was superior to our own model.

EVANS: In what respect, Dr. Oppenheimer?

OPPENHEIMER: The Russians had exploded the so-called "dry" hydrogen bomb which weighed much less than ours because it needed no cooling devices.

EVANS: Was that very essential, strategically?

OPPENHEIMER: Sure. The Russians could appear above us with their hydrogen bombs at any time, while we could only retaliate with atom bombs. Our first models were so heavy that we could get them to a target only by ox cart.

ROBB: Wouldn't the Russians have produced their hydrogen bomb in any case?

OPPENHEIMER: Possibly. We did not attempt to prevent an armaments race in that sphere. I think we paid too high a price for our short-lived monopoly.

ROBB: Couldn't we have had the hydrogen bomb much earlier, and wouldn't our position have been very different, if we had initiated the crash program in 1945?

OPPENHEIMER: We didn't have the facilities.

ROBB: In 1942, you already foresaw the possibility of developing a thermonuclear bomb, is that right?

OPPENHEIMER: We would have developed it if we could. We would have developed any kind of weapon.

ROBB: I do not know whether this is classified or not—but when we speak of a hydrogen bomb we mean a bomb with ten thousand times the power of the atomic bomb, is that right?

OPPENHEIMER: Roughly speaking, yes. Very powerful anyway.

ROBB: It would be no exaggeration to say: ten thousand times as powerful?

OPPENHEIMER: I believe there are no limits to its power. According to our calculations, the lethal zone of a medium-sized model has a diameter of about 360 miles.

ROBB: When you first went to Los Alamos, would you have had moral scruples about developing such a weapon?

OPPENHEIMER: In 1942? No. My scruples came much later.

ROBB: When? When did you start having moral scruples about developing the hydrogen bomb?

OPPENHEIMER: Let us leave the word "moral" out of it.

ROBB: All right. When did you start having scruples?

OPPENHEIMER: When it became clear to me that we would tend to *use* the weapon we were developing.

ROBB: After Hiroshima?

OPPENHEIMER: Yes. And I said it had not been *our* decision that the bomb should be dropped.

ROBB: I am not saying that it was. You only selected the targets, and you had strong scruples after the dropping of the atomic bomb?

OPPENHEIMER: Yes. Terrible ones. We all had terrible scruples.

ROBB: Wasn't it those terrible scruples, Doctor, which prevented you from initiating an all-out hydrogen bomb program in 1945?

OPPENHEIMER: No. when the production of the hydrogen bomb seemed feasible in 1951 we were fascinated by the scientific ideas, and we produced it in a short time, regardless of scruples. That is a fact. I'm not saying it is a good fact.

ROBB: Did you do any scientific work on the hydrogen bomb?

OPPENHEIMER: Not any practical work.

ROBB: In what way did you contribute?

OPPENHEIMER: In an advisory capacity.

ROBB: Would you give us an example?

OPPENHEIMER: In 1951, I called a conference of the leading physicists. It was very fruitful. We were enthusiastic about the new possibilities, and many physicists returned to Los Alamos.

ROBB: Who was it who had the brilliant ideas?

OPPENHEIMER: Teller, mainly. Neumann's calculating machines played a part in it. Bethe and Fermi contributed.

ROBB: Did you return to Los Alamos?

OPPENHEIMER: No.

ROBB: Why not?

OPPENHEIMER: I had other work to do. . . . My scientific contributions in the thermonuclear field were negligible.

ROLANDER: [*extracts a document from his files*]. I have a patent here, sir, for an invention appertaining to the hydrogen bomb. You applied for it in 1944.

OPPENHEIMER: Together with Teller?

ROLANDER: Yes. You were granted the patent in 1946.

OPPENHEIMER: That's right. It was a detail. . . . I had forgotten we followed the matter up.

ROBB: You refused Teller's request to come to Los Alamos, saying you wished to remain neutral in regard to the hydrogen bomb?

OPPENHEIMER: It is possible.

ROBB: That you wished to remain neutral?

OPPENHEIMER: That I said something to that effect. There was a time when Teller wanted to pursue the hydrogen bomb program at any price. I had to consider the arguments for and against—at least until the President himself ordered the crash program.

ROBB: But you refused to return to Los Alamos, even after the President's decision?

OPPENHEIMER: Yes.

ROBB: Don't you think, Doctor, that it would have made a great impression on many scientists if you had rolled up your sleeves and had taken charge of the hydrogen bomb program yourself?

OPPENHEIMER: Maybe. I did not think it right.

ROBB: You did not think it right to produce the hydrogen bomb, even after the President's decision?

OPPENHEIMER: I did not think it right to take the responsibility for the program. I was not the right man for the job.

ROBB: That is not what I asked you, Doctor.

OPPENHEIMER: I feel you did.

ROBB: You did not think it right to produce the hydrogen bomb, even after the President's decision?

OPPENHEIMER: I always regarded it as a dreadful weapon, and that it would be better if it did not exist. But I supported the crash program.

ROBB: In what way?

OPPENHEIMER: In an advisory capacity.

ROBB: Any other way?

OPPENHEIMER: I recommended a number of young scientists, my pupils, to Teller.

ROBB: Did you talk to them? Did you make them feel enthusiastic about the program?

OPPENHEIMER: Teller talked to them, I don't know whether he made them enthusiastic.

ROBB: Didn't you say, Doctor, that you were enthusiastic about the program in 1951?

OPPENHEIMER: I was enthusiastic about the fascinating scientific ideas.

ROBB: You thought the scientific ideas for the development of the hydrogen bomb were fascinating and wonderful—and you thought of the possible result, the hydrogen bomb itself, as horrible. Is that right?

OPPENHEIMER: I think that's right. It isn't the fault of the physicists that brilliant ideas always lead to bombs nowadays. As long as that is the case, one can have a scientific enthusiasm for a thing and, at the same time, as a human being, one can regard it with horror.

ROBB: I see you are capable of it, Doctor. It surprises me.

GRAY: Would you not say, Dr. Oppenheimer, that such an attitude might imply something like divided loyalty?

OPPENHEIMER: Divided between whom?

GRAY: Loyalty to a government—loyalty to mankind.

OPPENHEIMER: Let me think. . . . I would like to put it this way: if governments show themselves unequal to, or not sufficiently equal to, the new scientific discoveries—then the scientist *is* faced with these conflicting loyalties.

GRAY: If you are facing such a conflict, Dr. Oppenheimer, and it obviously did happen in the case of the hydrogen bomb, to which loyalty would you give the preference?

OPPENHEIMER: In every case, I have given undivided loyalty to my government, without losing my uneasiness or losing my scruples, and without wanting to say that this was right.

ROBB: You do not want to say that it is right to give one's undivided loyalty to the government in every case?

OPPENHEIMER: I don't know. I think about it. But I have always done it.

ROBB: Does this apply also to the hydrogen bomb program?

OPPENHEIMER: Yes.

ROBB: You mean to say you actively supported it after the President's decision?

OPPENHEIMER: Yes, although my grave doubts remained.

ROBB *extracts a document from his files.*

ROBB: But you say in a television interview—Mr. Rolander will read it out to us . . .

He gives ROLANDER *the sheet of paper and places a copy on the Chairman's table.*

ROLANDER: I quote: "Early history tells us about the annihilation of individual tribes, individual races, individual nations. Now mankind as a whole can be annihilated by man. To the rational mind, this is now a probability unless we develop the new forms of political co-existence which are needed on this earth. That apocalyptic possibility is very real in our lives. We know it, but we suppress our knowledge. It does not seem immediate to us. We imagine there is still time. But we do not have much time left."

ROBB: Does that sound as though you supported the hydrogen bomb program, Doctor?

OPPENHEIMER: It had nothing to do with that program. When I gave the interview we had already tested our first models, and so had the Russians.

ROLANDER: That is not so, sir. You gave the interview before the presidential election of 1952, when we actually had the monopoly.

ROBB: I think this makes a difference. It was at the time, was it not, when the war in Korea had ended and when our bases in Asia seemed extremely vulnerable?

OPPENHEIMER: It was at a time when quite a number of people were seriously discussing the idea of a preventive war, yes.

ROBB: Did *you* discuss that idea?

OPPENHEIMER: Well, we were asked to give our opinion on a technical problem, and we reached a negative conclusion.

MORGAN: A question of conscience, Dr. Oppenheimer: if it had looked pretty good from a technical point of view, would you have confined yourself to a technical opinion only?

OPPENHEIMER: I don't know—I hope not. No.

ROBB: Doesn't it emerge quite clearly from our conversation here, Doctor, that you had strong moral scruples about the hydrogen bomb, and that you still have them today?

OPPENHEIMER: I have already asked you to leave the word "moral" out of it. It confuses the issue. I had, and I have, grave scruples about this dreadful weapon actually being used.

ROBB: And that is why you were against the development of the hydrogen bomb. Is that right?

OPPENHEIMER: I was opposed to taking the initiative in its development.

ROBB: Doctor, in the report of the General Advisory Committee, which you yourself wrote—and in the appendix, which you approved—did you not state quite clearly, I quote: [*He reads it out.*] "We believe a hydrogen bomb should never be produced."

OPPENHEIMER: That referred to the program at the time.

ROBB: What did you mean by "never"?

OPPENHEIMER: I did not write the appendix.

ROBB: But you signed it, did you not?

OPPENHEIMER: I believe what we meant to say, what I meant to say, was that it would be a better world if there was no hydrogen bomb in it.

ROBB: What was your reaction when, in spite of it, the President ordered the crash program?

OPPENHEIMER: I offered to resign from the General Advisory Committee.

ROBB: As a protest?

OPPENHEIMER: I guess a man has to take the consequences when he has been overruled on a crucial issue.

ROBB: You felt you had been overruled when the order was given to initiate the crash program?

OPPENHEIMER: We had advised against it. Yes.

ROBB: When the hydrogen bomb was to be tested in October 1952, would it be true to say that you opposed that test?

OPPENHEIMER: "Opposed" is too strong. I was in favor of postponement.

ROBB: Why?

OPPENHEIMER: It was shortly before the presidential election, and I did not think it right to involve the new President with the responsibility for the hydrogen bomb. He should make his own decision.

ROBB: Were there any other reasons in favor of postponement?

OPPENHEIMER: The Russians would have got a lot of information out of the test.

ROBB: Any other reasons?

OPPENHEIMER: It would most certainly have buried our hopes for disarmament negotiations, particularly or hopes for a test ban.

ROBB: But, in spite of your recommendations, the hydrogen bomb was tested in October 1952?

OPPENHEIMER: Yes.

ROBB: If, in the style of our newspaper columnists, we were to speak of the Father of the Hydrogen Bomb—whom would you call that?

OPPENHEIMER: Teller has been called that.

A photograph of TELLER *is projected.*

ROBB. You yourself would lay no claim to that title?

OPPENHEIMER: Oh, no.

ROBB: Thank you, Dr. Oppenheimer.

GRAY: Any further questions to Dr. Oppenheimer? . . . Mr. Morgan.

MORGAN: I have only one question, Dr. Oppenheimer. When a country spends enormous sums of money on research, is it to be denied the right to do with results of that research as it thinks fit?

OPPENHEIMER: Since certain results of research can be used to destroy human civilization as a whole, such a right has become questionable.

MORGAN: Does this not mean that you want to limit the national sovereignty of the United States in this particular sphere?

OPPENHEIMER: When things have gone so far that mathematicians have to calculate whether a certain test might not burn up the whole atmosphere—well, then national sovereignties begin to look slightly ridiculous. The question is, what authority is independent and powerful enough to prevent nations, or groups of nations, from committing suicide? How is such an authority to be established?

MORGAN: Do you think the United States should make an effort towards reaching some understanding with Soviet Russia?

OPPENHEIMER: If the Devil himself were on the other side, one would have to reach an understanding with the Devil.

MORGAN: But you do draw a sharp distinction between the preservation of life as such and the preservation of a life that is worth living?

OPPENHEIMER: Oh, yes. And I have great faith in the ultimate power of common sense.

EVANS: I would like to refer back to the moral scruples, so often mentioned here, and to the contradiction in forging ahead with something and, at the same time, being afraid of the result. When did you first feel this contradiction?

OPPENHEIMER: When we exploded the first atom bomb in the Alamogordo desert.

EVANS: Would you elucidate that?

OPPENHEIMER: When I saw that ball of fire, two passages, in the Bhagavad-Gita came to my mind. One was:

> *The radiance of a thousand suns*
> *which suddenly illuminate the heavens*
> *all in one moment—thus*
> *the splendor of the Lord.*

And the other:

> *And I am Death, who taketh all,*
> *who shatters worlds. . . .*

EVANS: How can you tell whether a new idea is really important?

OPPENHEIMER: I know it from the profound awe I feel.

GRAY: If there are no further questions I would like to thank Dr. Oppenheimer for his patience. [OPPENHEIMER *leaves the witness stand and walks across to the sofa.*] We now have the witnesses who have been called by Mr. Robb and Mr. Garrison. Dr. Teller has already been waiting some time. Therefore, I think, we should hear him first, and Mr. Griggs afterwards.

An OFFICIAL *leaves the room to fetch* TELLER.

GARRISON: If possible, Mr. Chairman, we would prefer to call Dr. Bethe as a witness after Dr. Teller.

GRAY: Indeed it is possible. Can you get in touch with Dr. Bethe?

GARRISON: He is waiting in his hotel. It wouldn't take more than five minutes. Here is his telephone number.

He hands another OFFICIAL *a slip of paper, and the* OFFICIAL *leaves the room. The first* OFFICIAL, *returning, appears at the door with* TELLER.

GRAY: If Dr. Teller is ready, may we ask him to take the stand as a witness. Dr. Teller, do you wish to testify under oath?

TELLER: Yes.

TELLER *rises to his feet.*

GRAY: Edward Teller, do you swear that the testimony you are to give the Board shall be the truth, the whole truth, and nothing but the truth, so help you God?

TELLER: I do.

GRAY: Mr. Robb, you may question the witness.

ROBB: Dr. Teller, it was already at Los Alamos that you were working on the problem of thermonuclear development?

TELLER: Yes.

ROBB: Did you frequently discuss the thermonuclear problems with Dr. Oppenheimer?

TELLER: Very frequently. Ever since we met at Berkeley, in the summer of 1942. We investigated the feasibility of a thermonuclear program.

ROBB: Whom do you mean by "we"?

TELLER: Oppenheimer had gathered together the best people in that field. Among them, Fermi and Bethe. The idea of reproducing the miracle of solar energy by a fusion of lightweight atoms filled us all with enthusiasm.

ROBB: Was Dr. Oppenheimer enthusiastic?

TELLER: Very. And he has the ability to rouse others to enthusiasm.

ROBB: Did a thermonuclear program seem feasible to you then?

TELLER: For a time, it seemed easier than it actually turned out to be. We encountered serious difficulties at Los Alamos. I think I myself discovered some of them.

ROBB: Could you tell us about some of the difficulties, without violating any secrecy?

TELLER: One of them was that we needed the heat of an ordinary atomic bomb to get a hydrogen bomb going. Later we discovered how to generate the required heat in a different way. Another difficulty was that our conventional calculating machines proved inadequate. And so forth.

ROBB: In spite of all this, would it have been possible to produce the hydrogen bomb at Los Alamos during the war?

TELLER: No. I rather fancied the idea, it was my baby, but parents are shortsighted.

ROBB: In your opinion, when were there the faculties to initiate an all-out hydrogen bomb program?

TELLER: In 1945. I remember, after "Trinity," that we——

EVANS: What is that?

TELLER: "Trinity" was the code name for the atomic bomb test in Alamogordo.

EVANS: "Trinity"?

TELLER: Yes. . . . I remember that, afterwards, we wanted to develop the hydrogen bomb in a very vigorous fashion—the most outstanding people, like Fermi and Bethe, under Oppenheimer's direction.

ROBB: After the first atomic bomb test?

TELLER: Yes.

ROBB: Was work on the development in fact stepped up?

TELLER: No. In a very short time, it all came to a standstill.

ROBB: Why?

TELLER: After the dropping of the atom bombs on Japan, the whole plan was practically abandoned.

ROBB: Why?

TELLER: Because, after Hiroshima, Dr. Oppenheimer thought it was not the time to pursue such a program any further.

ROBB: Did he say that to you?

TELLER: I remember a conversation with Oppenheimer, Fermi——

ROBB: Was Fermi of the same opinion?

TELLER: Yes. . . . I should add, however, that this was in consonance with the general mood of the physicists. Hiroshima had been a great shock for many of them. The mood in those days was something like a hangover.

ROLANDER: Did Dr. Oppenheimer say that the best thing to do would be to give Los Alamos back to the Indians?

TELLER: He is said to have made that remark, I don't know whether he actually made it.

ROBB: Would it have been possible, at Los Alamos, to initiate a crash program for the hydrogen bomb by the end of the war?

TELLER: It is my firm belief that we would have been in a position to initiate an energetic hydrogen bomb program. If Dr. Oppenheimer had stayed on at Los Alamos, if he had supported that program, other highly capable people would also have participated—at least as many people as we had recruited in 1949 under much more difficult conditions.

ROBB: In that case, we would have had the hydrogen bomb sooner?

TELLER: I am convinced of that.

ROBB: When, according to your estimate, could we have had the hydrogen bomb?

TELLER: It is very difficult to assess when that would have been possible if things had taken a different course. To conjecture about the past is almost as difficult as to make predictions about the future, except that it is less risky to do so.

ROBB: Let us try, all the same.

TELLER: If we had initiated the program in 1945 we would probably have had the hydrogen bomb in 1948.

ROBB: Before the Russians had their atomic bomb?

TELLER: Presumably.

ROBB: It has been said here, Doctor, that the ultimate success of the program was the result of a brilliant discovery which you made in 1951. Is that so?

TELLER: If such excellent people as Fermi, Bethe, and others, had gone after the program in 1945 they'd probably have had the same brilliant idea, or other brilliant ideas. Then we'd have had the hydrogen bomb as early as 1947.

ROBB: You mean: "If one doesn't seek, one doesn't find." Is that right?

TELLER: Brilliant ideas can be organized. They are not tied up with particular individuals.

GRAY: What would have been the advantages of having the hydrogen bomb in, let us say, 1947?

TELLER: You will know that better than I do, from the vantage point of the War Department. It would have saved us the débâcle in China and, presumably, a few other disasters. We would have kept our number one position in relation to the Communists, and that is a comfortable position, I should think.

MARKS: Do you know, Dr. Teller, that our secret services found out that the Russians had reached roughly the same stage in research as we had, in 1945?

TELLER: Yes. That is why I wanted the hydrogen bomb, while other people were playing around with disarmament illusions.

MARKS: By other people you mean the government at that time, don't you?

TELLER: The government, the physicists, public opinion. It was enough to drive one to despair.

ROBB: When did you leave Los Alamos?

TELLER: In February 1946. There was no point in staying there. I accepted a teaching post at the University of Chicago and went back only occasionally to Los Alamos, as a consultant.

ROBB: Would you tell us about the work being done on thermonuclear development at Los Alamos between 1945 and 1949?

TELLER: It was virtually at a standstill. It was resumed only in 1949 when the Russians had exploded their atom bomb.

ROBB: Did you then talk with Oppenheimer?

TELLER: Yes. Frankly, I was staggered.

ROBB: Why?

TELLER: In those days, I had so little to do with war projects that I only read in a newspaper about the Russian atom bomb. I decided that I must devote myself entirely to an effective hydrogen bomb program, no matter what the odds. I called up Dr. Oppenheimer, and I said: "For God's sake what's going to happen now?" And I asked for his advice. Do you know what he said? He said: "Keep your shirt on!"

ROBB: What did you conclude from that advice?

TELLER: That a hydrogen bomb program could only be undertaken against his wishes, and that it would be a big problem considering Oppenheimer's influence.

ROLANDER: Did you discuss it further?

TELLER: Yes.

ROLANDER: On what occasion?

TELLER: I discussed things with Bethe. We had to get a team together, and I had strong hopes that Bethe would agree to take charge of the hydrogen bomb program.

ROLANDER: When was that?

TELLER: At the end of October.

ROBB: 1949?

TELLER: Yes. Shortly before the General Advisory Committee decided against the crash program. I insisted so much that Bethe finally made up his mind to come to Los Alamos, even though he had strong reservations, at least that was my impression. In the middle of all this, Oppenheimer called us up and invited us to Princeton. I said to Bethe: "After you've talked with Oppenheimer you won't come."

ROLANDER: Did Dr. Bethe come to Los Alamos?

TELLER: No. Only much later.

ROLANDER: Do you think it was due to Dr. Oppenheimer's influence that Dr. Bethe didn't come when you first asked him to?

TELLER: Yes. When we left Oppenheimer's office, Bethe said: "You can be quite satisfied, I'm still coming." Two days later he called me up, and he said: "Edward, I've thought it over. I'm not coming."

ROLANDER: Do you know whether Dr. Bethe had in the meantime again talked with Dr. Oppenheimer?

TELLER: I guess he had.

ROBB: Did Dr. Oppenheimer bring forward any moral or political arguments against the program?

TELLER: He quoted the arguments of other people, for and against; for instance, there was a letter from Conant which said: "The hydrogen bomb—only over my dead body."

ROBB: When the General Advisory Committee decided against the crash program, would you say that this decision was due to Dr. Oppenheimer?

TELLER: That would be going too far.

ROBB: Was the assessment of the technical side of the program correct?

TELLER: It was not correct in so far as it overlooked the great possibilities of development, which we were soon able to verify.

ROBB: Do you think it possible that the technical snags rather suited some of the members?

TELLER: Not consciously, I don't think.

ROBB: Unconsciously?

TELLER: That is too vague a question.

ROBB: What effect did the report have on the physicists who were working on the hydrogen bomb?

TELLER: Rather a paradoxical one. When I saw the report, and ten or twelve others were also shown it, on Oppenheimer's suggestion, I thought it was sure to be the end of the program. To my surprise, there was a psychological reaction of defiance among those who participated in the program.

ROBB: You mean the report infuriated them, and they were more than ever determined to continue their work?

TELLER: Yes, it made them indignant that their work was supposed to be immoral as soon as it was making good progress.

ROBB: Did Dr. Oppenheimer support the crash program when it had finally been ordered by the President?

TELLER: I can't remember any such support, on the contrary.

ROBB: When you say "on the contrary" you mean he continued to oppose the crash program?

TELLER: I mean that the further recommendations of the General Advisory Committee served as a brake rather than encouragement.

ROLANDER: Would you give us some examples?

TELLER: The second laboratory. We wanted to concentrate the program at Livermore; the General Advisory Committee was against it. We wanted to develop reactor work for our purposes at Oak Ridge; the General Advisory Committee concentrated it in Chicago. We needed more money because only the experimental approach could bring us nearer a solution; Oppenheimer recommended further theoretical research without tests. All this did not further our work, but impeded it.

ROBB: Did you have any discussions with Dr. Oppenheimer during that time?

TELLER: A few.

ROBB: How would you describe his attitude?

TELLER: Reserved and neutral. He told me that himself when I asked him for advice about the recruitment of capable people.

ROBB: Did he give you the advice you asked for?

TELLER: I wrote to all the people he had suggested; none of them came. . . . But I should add that Dr. Oppenheimer's attitude to the program changed at a later stage.

ROBB: When was that?

TELLER: In 1951, after our first tests. Then he called a meeting of the General Advisory Committee and all the experts, in Princeton. I went to that meeting, with considerable misgivings because I expected some further obstacles. But Oppenheimer was actually delighted with our new theoretical discoveries, and he said he'd never have opposed the program if those wonderful ideas had come earlier.

ROBB: Did he then support the program?

TELLER: Not to my knowledge, but he may of course have assisted without my noticing it.

ROBB: A question to you as an expert: if Dr. Oppenheimer were to go fishing for the rest of his life, what effect would that have on the further atomic energy program?

TELLER: Do you mean if he did similar work to what he did at Los Alamos, or similar to what he did after the war?

ROBB: Similar to what he did after the war.

TELLER: After the war, Dr. Oppenheimer mainly served on committees and, judging from my own experience, I would say that all committees can go fishing without affecting the work of those who are actually doing the work.

ROBB: These are my questions. Thank you for having given us your valuable time.

GRAY: Do you wish to cross-examine the witness, Mr. Garrison?

GARRISON: Mr. Marks has some questions.

MARKS: Dr. Teller, in your opinion, has Dr. Oppenheimer been disloyal to the United States?

TELLER: Until I am given proof to the contrary, I shall believe that he wanted to act in the best interests of the United States.

MARKS: You regard him as perfectly loyal?

TELLER: Subjectively, yes.

MARKS: Objectively?

TELLER: Objectively, he has given wrong advice which was injurious to this country.

MARKS: Is the loyalty of a man, who gave great service, to be doubted because he came forward with advice which was later regarded as having been wrong?

TELLER: No, but it is to be questioned whether he continues to be the right kind of adviser.

MARKS: But you know that the subject of the present inquiry is whether Dr. Oppenheimer has been loyal, whether he can be trusted, whether he might not be a security risk?

TELLER: It wasn't I who proposed that these matters should be inquired into.

MARKS: Do you regard Dr. Oppenheimer as a security risk?

TELLER: His actions after the war appeared to me confused and complicated, and I personally would feel more secure if the vital interests of this country did not rest in his hands.

GARRISON: What do you understand by "security risk"?

TELLER: That there are well-founded doubts as to the discretion, the character, or the loyalty of a person.

GARRISON: In the sense of this definition, do you regard Dr. Oppenheimer as a security risk?

TELLER: No. . . . But I am no expert on questions of security.

MARKS: Do you think that his former left-wing sympathies affected his attitude in the matter of the hydrogen bomb?

TELLER: I think a man's attitude is always affected by his philosophy. But I do not know Dr. Oppenheimer well enough to analyze this.

MARKS: Could you tell us about Dr. Oppenheimer's philosophy?

TELLER: No. To me, it seemed contradictory. It surprised me how effectively he had preserved his illusion that people, if patiently taught, might in the end achieve some political common sense. For instance, on the question of disarmament.

MARKS: You do not share that belief?

TELLER: I am convinced that people will learn political common sense only when they are really and truly scared. Only when the bombs are so big that they can destroy everything there is.

MARKS: If your advice should ever prove to have been wrong, would that disqualify you from serving the United States as a scientist?

TELLER: No, but I would no longer be the right man to occupy the leading position.

MARKS: Would you think it right if, because of it, your clearance were suspended?

TELLER: No.

MARKS: You know that Dr. Oppenheimer's clearance has been suspended until the final decision at these proceedings?

ROBB: I don't think it was suspended because he gave wrong advice!

MARKS: That is not what I said, Mr. Robb.

ROBB: But you are suggesting it, Mr. Marks.

MARKS: Dr. Teller, if it were up to you to grant Dr. Oppenheimer his clearance, would you do so?

TELLER: As I have no cognizance of possible reasons against it, yes, I would do so.

MARKS: These are my questions.

GRAY: Dr. Evans.

EVANS: What bothers me is this: is enthusiasm a good quality in a man who works on a weapons project?

TELLER: Without enthusiasm, we wouldn't have had the atom bomb in 1945, and neither would we have the hydrogen bomb.

EVANS: Good. Or, rather, not good, maybe. What I mean to say is this: is enthusiasm just as good a quality in a man who has to advise the government?

TELLER: I don't know. You have already heard that I have a poor opinion of committees. I am not competent to judge. I only know that Dr. Oppenheimer would have helped us a great deal even if he had simply gone to Los Alamos and sat there in his office, twiddling his thumbs. He would have helped by the weight of his prestige alone.

EVANS: Should a man be reproached for not having shown any enthusiasm for a given thing—in our case, for the hydrogen bomb?

TELLER: No, he shouldn't. But one can state it as a fact, and one can inquire into the reasons for it.

EVANS: Have you never had any moral scruples about the hydrogen bomb?

TELLER: No.

EVANS: How did you mange to come to terms with that problem?

TELLER: I never regarded it as *my* problem.

EVANS: You feel that one can produce something, produce a hydrogen bomb, or something like that, and then say: "It isn't *my* problem what is to be done with it, run along and cope with it yourselves." Is that your attitude?

TELLER: It is not a matter of indifference to me, but I cannot possibly foresee the consequences, the full range of practical uses for a hydrogen bomb!

EVANS: Isn't it possible to foresee quite well the range of practical uses for a hydrogen bomb?

TELLER: No. It may be a good thing—and we all hope for it—if the hydrogen bomb were never used. And maybe in twenty or thirty years' time the face of the earth will be beneficially changed by the principle on which the bomb was developed—artificially generated solar energy, the cheapest and most powerful energy we have ever known.

EVANS: God grant that it be so, Dr. Teller.

TELLER: For instance, when Hahn in Germany first succeeded in splitting uranium he never thought that the energy thus released might be used for producing explosions.

EVANS: Who was the first to think of it?

TELLER: Oppenheimer. And it was a constructive thought which only naïve people call immoral.

EVANS: Would you explain this to an older colleague?

TELLER: Discoveries in themselves are neither good nor evil, neither moral nor immoral, but merely factual. They can be used or misused. This applied to the internal-combustion engine, and it applies to nuclear energy. By painful experience, man has always learned in the end how best to use them.

EVANS: You say this although, judging from what you stated before, you have no great faith in common sense?

TELLER: I have faith in facts, which may in the end even produce common sense, occasionally.

EVANS: I have recently read in the newspapers about a terrible accident which was caused by one of our hydrogen bomb tests . . .

TELLER: Bikini?

EVANS: Yes, recently, twenty-three Japanese fishermen were seriously affected by radiation. One of them is already dead.

TELLER: Yes, that's right.

EVANS: How could such a thing happen?

TELLER: Their trawler drifted into a radioactive blizzard because the wind suddenly shifted from north to south, unfortunately.

EVANS: How did you react to this news about the fishermen?

TELLER: We set up a commission to study all the effects. And we were able to make considerable improvements in the meteorological forecasts for our tests.

EVANS: What kind of people are physicists?

TELLER: You mean: do they beat their wives, do they have hobbies, that kind of thing?

EVANS: I mean: do they differ from the other people? I asked Dr. Oppenheimer the same question.

TELLER: What was his answer?

EVANS: That they were just like other people.

TELLER: Sure. They need a little bit more imagination and a little bit better brains, for their job. Apart from that, they are just like other people.

EVANS: I have been asking myself this question ever since I've been sitting on this Board. . . . Thank you very much.

GRAY: Perhaps you would like to ask Dr. Teller some questions, Dr. Oppenheimer?

OPPENHEIMER [*haughtily*]: No. [OPPENHEIMER *and* TELLER *look at each other for a moment.*] No.

GRAY: Then I would like to thank you for your evidence, Dr. Teller, which has touched upon some essential points, I think.

TELLER: May I make a general explanatory statement?

GRAY: Of course.

TELLER: I think it is necessary to say something about our problems. All great discoveries had, at first, a devastating effect on the state of the world and on its image in our minds. They shattered it and introduced new conditions. They forced the world to move forward. But this was possible only because the discoverers were not afraid of the consequences of their discoveries, no matter how terrifying these were to all those who wanted to preserve the world as it was, and hang a big notice on it, saying: Please do not disturb.

This was the case when the earth was discovered to be a planet among other planets; and this is the case now that we have been able to reduce matter, seemingly so complicated, to only a few elements which can be transformed and which release immeasurable energies.

If we preserve with our work, regardless of the consequences, we shall force man to adjust to these new energies, and to put an end to that state of the world in which he was half free, half enslaved! God alone knows whether this might not happen through a nuclear war—which would be terrible, like any other war, but, limited or unlimited, would not necessarily mean more suffering than in former wars, and which would probably be shorter though more violent.

If we shrink from the temporary aspect of discoveries, their powers of destruction—and I find this is the reaction of many a physicist—we'll get stuck halfway, and we'll be overwhelmed by the difficulties which our discoveries brought into the world.

Because of my relentless logic, my people regard me as an incorrigible warmonger, I know that, I read that in the newspapers; but I hope the time will come when I shall be called a peace monger, when the unspeakable horror of our destructive weapons will have discredited war as the classic means of realizing political aims, for ever.

EVANS: In case of survival, Dr. Teller, as they call it in the insurance business. But, supposing your prognosis turned out to be wrong, we perhaps ought to consider that mankind would have no chance of correcting the mistake. This is something new. Maybe even a physicist can't simply let it go at that.

TELLER: I don't think I do.

GRAY: Was that the explanatory statement you wished to make?

TELLER: Yes.

GRAY: Very well. Thank you.

TELLER *bows slightly to the Board and leaves the room.*

GRAY: The next witness is Dr. Bethe. . . . Has he arrived?

GARRISON: I'll have a look.

GARRISON *walks toward the door when the* OFFICIAL *enters with* BETHE. BETHE *stops in the front of the witness stand.*

GRAY: Hans Bethe, do you swear that the testimony you are to give the Board shall be the truth, the whole truth, and nothing but the truth, so help you God?

BETHE: I do.

GRAY: Will you please take the stand. . . . When did you come to America, Dr. Bethe?

BETHE: In 1935. About the same time as Teller.

GRAY: Where did you originally come from?

BETHE: Munich. I spent a short time in England, and then I taught nuclear physics here, until I went to Los Alamos.

GRAY: You may question the witness, Mr. Garrison.

GARRISON: Were you in charge of the Theoretical Physics Department at Los Alamos?

BETHE: Until the end of the war, yes.

GARRISON: Did Dr. Teller work in your department?

BETHE: Yes.

GARRISON: How did you get on with him there?

BETHE [*smiling*]: Not at all. Edward Teller is a friend of mine, but it is very difficult to work with him.

GARRISON: Why?

BETHE: Edward is a highly gifted guy, full of brilliant ideas which he pursues with dogged fanaticism, until he drops them. Then he spends whole nights playing the piano, until he again gets some brilliant ideas, and he demands every time that one should be just as enthusiastic as he is, himself. I am not saying this to belittle him, he is a genius, but he needs some other person to sort out his ideas for him. In the end it was better to forego his services than to have a whole team disrupted.

GARRISON: What do you mean by "forego his services"?

BETHE: We decided to relieve him of all the work on our own program because he was interested in nothing but the hydrogen bomb. Although we needed him badly.

GARRISON: Who took Teller's place?

BETHE: Klaus Fuchs.

GARRISON: Was there considerable tension between Dr. Teller and Dr. Oppenheimer at Los Alamos?

BETHE: They didn't like each other. Teller often complained that his work was not sufficiently appreciated, and that Oppenheimer was not sufficiently enthusiastic about it. But Oppenheimer had to co-ordinate a huge laboratory towards producing the atom bomb, and Edward was wrong to complain.

GARRISON: Was there any work done on thermonuclear development at Los Alamos?

BETHE: Oppenheimer had directed a whole group of people from my division to work on it—among them, Teller.

GARRISON: Did you work together well with Dr. Oppenheimer?

BETHE: I think we have been good friends ever since we met at the University of Göttingen in 1929.

GARRISON: Were there sufficient facilities for a hydrogen bomb program by the end of the war?

BETHE: Certainly not. Because I was coming here today, I checked with Fermi, to make sure. He was of the same opinion.

GARRISON: After the atom bomb test at Alamogordo, was there a plan to start a large-scale hydrogen bomb program?

BETHE: We discussed the possibilities. We realized we only had sufficient resources for an intensified research program. There was a plan for an intensified research program.

GARRISON: Dr. Teller has testified here that the plan for a hydrogen bomb program was abandoned only after Hiroshima, and that the reasons for abandoning it were the moral scruples of the scientists, in particular Dr. Oppenheimer. Is that right?

BETHE: No. The scientific ideas were frustrated because there were neither sufficient technical facilities nor sufficient personnel. . . . But it is true to say that Hiroshima made a great difference to us.

GARRISON: What effect did Hiroshima have on the physicists at Los Alamos?

BETHE: We had been working for several years under rigorous military conditions, and none of us had really stopped to think of those consequences. But Hiroshima put us face to face with the consequences—and, from then on, nobody could work on these weapons without being aware that they would actually be used.

GARRISON: Thereupon, what did you do?

BETHE: I left Los Alamos and went to Ithaca, where I taught physics. . . . I think it is well known that a number of scientists, including myself, appealed to the President and to the public, and I think it was the right thing to do.

GARRISON: Did you return to Los Alamos later on?

BETHE: Yes. After the outbreak of the war in Korea. I worked there until we tested the hydrogen bomb.

GARRISON: During that time, did you have moral scruples about working on the hydrogen bomb?

BETHE: Very strong ones. I still have them now. I have helped to create the hydrogen bomb, and I don't know whether it wasn't perhaps quite the wrong thing to do.

GARRISON: Why, then, did you go back to Los Alamos?

BETHE: The armaments race towards the H-bomb was in full swing, and I became convinced that we ought to be the first to have that dreadful weapon—if it could be produced at all. Yet, when I went to Los Alamos, I hoped that its production would prove impossible.

GARRISON: Dr. Teller has testified here that you wanted to take charge of the hydrogen bomb program at an earlier date, and it was due to Dr. Oppenheimer that you changed your mind. Is that right?

BETHE: I suppose Teller meant the talk we had with Oppenheimer, after the Russian atom bomb.

GARRISON: Before that visit, had you promised Teller that you would go to Los Alamos?

BETHE: I was undecided. On the one hand, I was very impressed by some of the ideas, and it was tempting to be able to work with the new calculating machines which had been released only for war projects. On the other hand, I was deeply troubled because I doubted that the H-bomb would solve any of our problems.

GARRISON: Did Dr. Oppenheimer speak against the hydrogen bomb?

BETHE: He presented us with facts, arguments, points of view. He appeared to be just as undecided as I was myself. I was very disappointed.

GARRISON: Did you say to Teller afterwards that you would go to Los Alamos?

BETHE: Yes.

GARRISON: Why did you change your mind about it?

BETHE: Because I could not rid myself of my doubts. I spent a whole night talking with my friends, Weisskopf and Placzek, both of them eminent physicists, and we agreed that after a war with hydrogen bombs, even if we were to win it, the world would no longer be the world which we wanted to preserve, and that we would lose all the things we were fighting for, and that such a weapon should never be developed.

GARRISON: Is it known to you that Dr. Oppenheimer turned other physicists against the hydrogen bomb?

BETHE: No.

MORGAN: Why, then, did he make the General Advisory Committee's secret report accessible to the leading physicists who were working on the program, Dr. Bethe?

BETHE: Oppenheimer? He did it on instructions from Senator McMahon.

GARRISON: Would you tell us who is Senator McMahon?

BETHE: He headed the Senate Committee on Atomic Matters, and was one of the apostles of the H-bomb.

GARRISON: Do you think that because of Dr. Oppenheimer's attitude the development of the hydrogen bomb was decisively delayed, possibly for a matter of years?

BETHE: No. It was Teller's brilliant idea which made its production possible.

GARRISON: In Dr. Teller's opinion, you, or Fermi, or others, might have had the same brilliant idea if the program had been started earlier. Is that feasible?

BETHE: I don't know. I don't think the discovery of the Theory of Relativity, or something of that order, is made every day.

GARRISON: Why did Teller not manage to get a sufficient number of capable people for the program?

BETHE: Probably one of the reasons was the general uneasiness about it, and another reason was Teller himself. He is a wonderful physicist, but even his friends will have asked him: "All right,

Edward, you'll get the acts together, but who is going to run the show?"

GARRISON: Did Dr. Oppenheimer oppose the crash program after the President had given the order to initiate it?

BETHE: After that, Oppenheimer only discussed how the H-bomb was to be made. Contrary to myself, who questioned its political usefulness.

GARRISON: What was his attitude to security requirements at Los Alamos?

BETHE: Many of us regarded him as too pro-government. That was my criticism too.

GARRISON: Dr. Bethe, you told us that you and Dr. Oppenheimer are good friends?

BETHE: Yes.

GARRISON: If Dr. Oppenheimer had to face a conflict of loyalties in which he would have to choose between you and the United States—to which loyalty, do you think, would he give the preference?

BETHE: Loyalty to the United States. I hope it will never come to that.

GARRISON [*with a look at* GRAY]: Thank you very much, Dr. Bethe.

GRAY *looks questioningly at* ROBB. ROLANDER *makes a gesture to indicate that he wishes to cross-examine* BETHE.

GRAY: Mr. Rolander.

ROLANDER: How long did Fuchs work in your division, Dr. Bethe?

BETHE: A year and a half.

ROLANDER: Did he work well?

BETHE: Very well.

ROLANDER: Did you ever notice that he behaved incorrectly in matters of security?

BETHE: No.

ROLANDER: Did you ever consider him a security risk?

BETHE: No.

ROLANDER: But it turned out that he had transmitted secret information to the Russians?

BETHE: Yes. . . . May I ask what you wish to imply?

ROLANDER: No, sir, since you are the witness, and not I! . . . When Dr. Teller visited you in Ithaca and asked you to take charge of the program, did you discuss the amount of your monthly salary?

BETHE: Yes. Teller made me an offer, and I asked for more.

ROLANDER: How much did you ask?

BETHE: Five thousand dollars a month.

ROLANDER: Did Teller agree to that?

BETHE: Yes.

ROLANDER: Does a man demand a higher salary when he is undecided whether to accept the job?

BETHE: In my case, yes. Good ideas are expensive. I like to eat well.

ROLANDER: I have an article here, from the periodical *Scientific American*; it dates back to the beginning of 1950. There you write: "Are we supposed to convince the Russians of the value of the individual by killing millions of them? If we fight a war with H-bombs, and win it, history will not remember the ideals we fought for but the method we used to enforce them. That method will be compared to the war techniques employed by Genghis Khan." Did you write that?

BETHE: I think it sounds sensible. The article was confiscated at the time because it was supposed to have given away important armaments secrets.

ROLANDER: You wrote that article a few weeks after you had turned down Teller's proposition?

BETHE: I think so.

ROLANDER: Yet, a couple of months later, you went to Los Alamos to develop the hydrogen bomb?

BETHE: Yes. . . . The article you've just read expresses the opinions I still have today.

ROLANDER: Your opinions today?

BETHE: Yes. We can justify the development of the hydrogen bomb only by preventing it being used.

ROLANDER: Thank you, Dr. Bethe.

GRAY: If I understand you correctly, you think it was wrong to develop the hydrogen bomb?

BETHE: I do.

GRAY: What should we have done instead?

BETHE: We ought to have come to an agreement by which nobody was allowed to produce this damned thing, and any breach of the agreement would mean war.

GRAY: Do you think there would have been the slightest chance of such an agreement in those days?

BETHE: Presumably it would have been easier to come by than to do the things we now have to do.

GRAY: What are you referring to?

BETHE: It seems the two power blocs haven't got much time left to decide whether to commit a double suicide with each other, or how to get that thing out of this world again.

GRAY [*to* ROBB]: Any further questions?

ROBB *shakes his head.* EVANS *raises his hand.*

EVANS: I would like to ask you something as an expert. Dr. Teller said here that a nuclear war, even if unlimited, would not necessarily mean more sufferings than in former wars. What is your opinion?

BETHE: That I can't bear to listen to such nonsense. I beg your pardon.

EVANS: That's all right.

GRAY: Thank you for having come here, Dr. Bethe.

BETHE: I considered it my duty. [*He rises to his feet.*] May I ask Dr. Oppenheimer to call me up at my hotel when he has finished here?

OPPENHEIMER: How long shall we still be here, Mr. Chairman?

GRAY: We have a big program behind us, we can recess until tomorrow . . . Mr. Robb?

ROBB: As Mr. Griggs is already waiting, I would like to ask for a few minutes for Mr. Griggs.

MARKS: In that case, may we also hear Dr. Rabi?

GRAY: Very well . . . Would you call Dr. Griggs, please?

An OFFICIAL *leaves the room to fetch* GRIGGS.

OPPENHEIMER [*to* BETHE]: We might eat together.

BETHE: Fine.

BETHE *leaves the room. Immediately afterward,* GRIGGS *enters.*

GRAY: Dr. Griggs, do you wish to testify under oath?

GRIGGS: Yes. My name is simply Griggs, David Tressel Griggs.

GRAY: David Tressel Griggs, do you swear that the testimony you are to give the Board shall be the truth, the whole truth, and nothing but the truth, so help you God?

GRIGGS: I do.

GRAY: Would you please take the stand. . . . Was it your own wish to testify here as a witness?

GRIGGS: I was ordered by the Air Force to come here.

GRAY: I should point out to you that you are only allowed to give your own personal views here.

GRIGGS: Of course.

GRAY: What is your present position?

GRIGGS: Chief Scientist of the Air Force.

GRAY: What is your special field?

GRIGGS: Geophysics.

GRAY: The witness may now be questioned.

ROBB: I would like to ask you, Mr. Griggs, whether you know Dr. Oppenheimer's attitude in the matter of the hydrogen bomb?

GRIGGS: Yes. We saw all the estimates and reports submitted by him.

ROBB: How would you describe his attitude?

GRIGGS: In the course of observation and analysis, I finally came to the conclusion that there was a silent conspiracy among some prominent scientists, a conspiracy directed against the hydrogen bomb. This group endeavored to prevent or delay the development of the hydrogen bomb, and it was led by Dr. Oppenheimer.

ROBB: Is this your private opinion, or is it shared by others?

GRIGGS: It is my own opinion, and it is the opinion also of Mr. Finletter, the Secretary of the Air Force, and of General Vandenberg, the Chief of Staff of the Air Force.

ROBB: What were the facts which convinced you?

GRIGGS: For a long time I was puzzled by the actions of Dr. Oppenheimer and some others. Then, one day, I found a clue to it all.

ROBB: When was that?

GRIGGS: In 1951, there was a conference on strategy, on the so-called Vista Project. The subject of the discussions was whether the emphasis should in future be on a strategic H-bomber fleet, or on a strengthening of the air defenses, the warning systems, anti-aircraft missiles, and so forth. A kind of electronic Maginot Line, purely defensive and very costly. The Air Force had decided on an H-bomber fleet.

ROBB: And Oppenheimer?

GRIGGS: I am coming to that. . . . One day, when the two opposing parties were not yet clearly defined, and when I had just attacked those who were in favor of air defense, Dr. Rabi went to the blackboard and wrote the word ZORC on it.

ROBB: ZORC? What is the meaning of ZORC? Would you spell it, please.

GRIGGS: Z-O-R-C. These are the initials of a group consisting of Zacharias, Oppenheimer, Rabi, and Charlie Lauritzen. They advocated world disarmament.

ROBB: Why did Rabi write this word on the blackboard?

GRIGGS: In my opinion, in order to indicate to his supporters which side they were to take in the discussions at the conference.

MARKS: Mr. Robb, may I ask the witness a question?

ROBB: You will have an opportunity to ask Mr. Griggs any question you like when you cross-examine him, Mr. Marks! [*To* GRIGGS.] How did the conference end?

GRIGGS: On three major points, the recommendations of the conference were entirely opposed to the line taken by the Air Force, and this part of the recommendations had been written by Dr. Oppenheimer himself.

ROBB: Have you observed other activities of the Oppenheimer group?

GRIGGS: Yes. A story was being spread among the scientists that Mr. Finletter had said in the Pentagon: "If we had such-and-such a number of hydrogen bombs, we could rule the world." . . . This was meant to prove that we had irresponsible warmongers at the head of the Air Force.

ROBB: Did you speak to Dr. Oppenheimer about it?

GRIGGS: Yes. I challenged him, and asked whether he himself had told that story. He said he had heard the story but didn't take it seriously. I said that I myself took it very seriously indeed because it was designed to spread lies, for a definite purpose. Dr. Oppenheimer asked me whether this meant that I doubted his loyalty, and I said, Yes, that was exactly what I meant.

ROBB: What was his reaction to this?

GRIGGS: He said that I was a paranoiac, and simply walked away! Later I understood well enough why Dr. Oppenheimer, in Princeton, praised the technical side of the program but boycotted the second laboratory although the Air Force was willing to provide the money for it. I understood the obstacles which Teller complained about. Particularly when I had read the F.B.I. report.

ROBB: Do you think there is a connection between his left wing associations and his attitude in the matter of the hydrogen bomb?

GRIGGS: I am convinced of that.

ROBB: Do you regard Dr. Oppenheimer as a security risk?

GRIGGS: Yes, a very serious one.

ROBB: Thank you, Mr. Griggs.

GRAY: Mr. Marks?

OPPENHEIMER *makes an emphatically negative gesture to* MARKS.

MARKS: Dr. Oppenheimer wishes his counsel to refrain from cross-examining Mr. Griggs. The members of the Board will not construe this as an indication of agreement.

GRAY: Any questions to Mr. Griggs? . . . Yes, Dr. Evans.

EVANS: Were there many people present when Rabi wrote those four letters, the secret code, on the blackboard?

GRIGGS: Quite a number.

EVANS: And they all saw it?

GRIGGS: Yes. They reacted to it.

EVANS: In what way?

GRIGGS: In various ways. Some of them laughed.

EVANS: Mr. Griggs, if you belonged to a group of conspirators, and you wanted to communicate something to your fellow conspirators, would you think it wise to write it on a blackboard?

GRIGGS: I did not say it was wise. I have never taken part in a conspiracy myself.

EVANS: Neither have I, but I think I'd rather have gone to my confederates and said to them: we'll do this in such-and-such a way.

GRIGGS: The one doesn't exclude the other. The fact is: Rabi wrote ZORC on the blackboard.

EVANS: You said so, yes.

GRAY: Any further questions? . . . May I thank you for having come here, Mr. Griggs. [GRIGGS *bows stiffly to* GRAY, *and leaves the room.*] We shall now call Dr. Rabi.

MARKS: I believe he is already here.

DR. I. I. RABI *enters and takes the witness stand.*

GRAY: Do you wish to testify under oath, Dr. Rabi?

RABI: Certainly.

GRAY: I must ask your full name.

RABI: Isador Isaac Rabi.

GRAY: Isador Isaac Rabi, do you swear that the testimony you are to give the Board shall be the truth, the whole truth, and nothing but the truth, so help you God?

RABI: I do . . . [*Wryly.*] . . . and I know that the penalties for perjury are dire.

GRAY: You may question the witness, Mr. Marks.

MARKS: Dr. Rabi, what is your present occupation?

RABI: I am the Higgins professor of physics at Columbia University.

MARKS: What official positions do you have with the government?

RABI: Let me see if I can add them all up. Chairman of the General Advisory Committee, member of the Scientific Advisory Committee which is supposed in some way to advise the President, member of a whole lot of boards, research development laboratories, and so on. I added them up once and it amounted to 120 working days last year, so you might well ask what time I spend at Columbia.

MARKS: I won't take up much of your time.

RABI: If I get away from here early enough, I must see Chairman Strauss of the Atomic Energy Commission.

MARKS: On behalf of Dr. Oppenheimer?

RABI: Yes, certainly. But even more on behalf of U.S. security. To tell you frankly, I have very grave misgivings as to the nature of this charge and the general public discussion it has aroused. Important security information absolutely vital to the United States may bit by bit inadvertently leak out. I myself am confused about what is classified and what is not.

GRAY: I should point out, Dr. Rabi, that we regard the proceedings as a matter confidential in nature between the Commission and Dr. Oppenheimer. The Commission will make no public release of matters pertaining to these proceedings.

RABI: I hope not. It makes your hair stand on end to hear high officers and people in Congress say some of the things they say. A man like Oppenheimer knows when to keep his mouth shut. But the papers and magazines skirt around very important security information. Bits and pieces can be put together. I am very much worried about that.

GRAY: There will be no public release of matters pertaining to these proceedings.

A cover of the hearing transcript and a headline bearing date of publication is projected on the screens.

MARKS: Now, Dr. Rabi, how long have you known Dr. Oppenheimer?

RABI: Since 1928 or '29. We worked together all through the war.

MARKS: Do you know him intimately?

RABI: Yes, whatever the term may mean. I think I know him quite
well.

MARKS: Would you describe for us what took place in 1949 with
the General Advisory Committee regarding going ahead with the
thermonuclear, the H-bomb program?

RABI: As I recollect it now—it is five years ago—Dr. Oppenheimer,
who was then Chairman, called us together and started very solemnly to consider, *not* whether we should make the bomb, but
whether there should be a crash program to develop what was
then a very vague thing. Different people had different thoughts
on it: I myself took the dimmest technical view. Others were
more optimistic, but technically we really did not know what we
were talking about. . . . Also, there was the military and political
question.

MARKS: So the General Advisory Committee did not deal solely
with technical aspects of the program?

RABI: There were technical, military, and the combination of mili-
tary-political questions. We felt—I am talking chiefly about myself—that to protect American lives was worth anybody's while,
but that a crash program for an H-bomb should not be at the
expense of continental defense. First we have the H-bomb, then
they have it; you can't just go in and slug it out with a punching
arm like the H-bomb with no defense guard. And politically, this
was not just a weapon, it was very much more. We felt it was
essential, but a crash program was just a sort of horseback thing.
We didn't even know whether this thing contradicted the laws
of physics.

MARKS: You didn't know what?

RABI: Whether it contradicted the laws of physics.

MARKS: In other words, it could have been altogether impossible?

RABI: It could have been altogether impossible . . . the thing we
were talking about. I want to be specific.

MARKS: You have spoken of differences of opinion. Could you explain?

RABI: One group felt that this projected weapon was just no good
as a weapon, not technically, but militarily. The possible targets

were very few in number and so on. Dr. Fermi and I felt that the whole discussion raised an opportunity for President Truman to make some political gesture which would strengthen our moral position should we decide to go ahead with it.

GRAY: With respect to the development of the hydrogen bomb and the issue of who was for and who was against, was it your impression that Dr. Oppenheimer was unalterably opposed to the development?

RABI: No. I distinctly remember Dr. Oppenheimer saying he would be willing to sign statements by both groups.

GRAY: Both groups?

RABI: Yes. There was no difference as far as a crash program was concerned. Both groups thought that was not in order.

GRAY: Subsequent to the President's decision to go ahead with the bomb, would you say Dr. Oppenheimer encouraged the program and assisted with it?

RABI: Yes, sir.

EVANS: Did you think it was appropriate for the General Advisory Committee to speak about these rather nontechnical but more political, diplomatic, and military considerations?

RABI: It would be very hard for me to tell you now why we thought it was appropriate, but we thought so.

MARKS: If you can, Dr. Rabi, what was the connection between the reluctance you have just described at Los Alamos in 1949 and a later meeting in 1951?

RABI: That was an entirely different meeting. At that meeting we really got on the beam because a new invention had occurred.

MARKS: Are you referring to Dr. Teller's discovery?

RABI: I wouldn't call it Dr. Teller's discovery. Dr. Teller had a very important part in it, but I would not make a personal attribution.

MARKS: Do you believe Dr. Oppenheimer was responsible for any delay between 1949 and 1951?

RABI: There has been all this newspaper stuff about delay. Dr. Oppenheimer and I first discussed this project as early as 1943, but it wasn't until 1951 we had a situation you could really talk about, know what to calculate, and so on.

MARKS: Are you familiar with the term "ZORC," Dr. Rabi?

RABI: Isn't everyone? *Fortune* magazine gave that term some notoriety.

MARKS: When was that in relation to the Vista Conference?

RABI: I don't remember exactly. Several months before, I know that, because Zacharias made a joke of it at that meeting by writing it on the blackboard.

MARKS: Zacharias? Who was he?

RABI: Scientific Adviser to the Navy, a first-class nuclear physicist.

MARKS: It has been testified here that it was you, Dr. Rabi, who wrote *ZORC* on the board.

RABI: Not at all. It was Zacharias. Everyone had a good laugh at the expense of *Fortune*.

MARKS: Are you sure the article mentioning ZORC was published *before* the conference?

RABI: Weeks before. And they didn't mention it. They *invented* it.

MARKS: Dr. Rabi, this board has the function of advising the Commission on Dr. Oppenheimer's security clearance. Do you feel you know Dr. Oppenheimer well enough to comment on this issue?

RABI: Dr. Oppenheimer is a man of upstanding character. He is a loyal individual, not only to the United States, which of course goes without saying in my mind, but also to his friends and to his organizations. He is a very upright character, a very upright character.

MARKS *indicates he is finished.*

ROBB: Dr. Rabi, you said you and Dr. Oppenheimer had your first discussion about the H-bomb in 1943?

RABI: From our very first contact at Los Alamos.

ROBB: And from 1943 on—even after the President's directive in 1950 that the bomb should be built—the progress was . . . negligible?

RABI: It was just a ball of wax. The President says go do something that nobody knows how to do. Just because he says something should appear at this end, doesn't mean it's going to appear just like that.

ROBB: Is it not true that while you and Dr. Oppenheimer were opposed to the crash program, other scientists were enthusiastic about it?

RABI: Oh yes. They were all keyed up to go bang into it.

ROBB: But you and Dr. Oppenheimer resisted.

RABI: Not the H-bomb as it exists. The thing that Oppenheimer and I—and others—were opposed to crash is not the H-bomb as it now is; it was something that has not been made, probably never will be made, and we don't know to this day whether the thing would function anyway.

ROBB: Why did the development of something functional take so long?

RABI: The human mind! It takes time to get rid of ideas that were, and probably are, no good.

ROBB: Dr. Rabi, you have read the F.B.I. file on Dr. Oppenheimer?

RABI: I may say that the record is not something I wanted to see.

ROBB: No, I understand that.

RABI: In fact, I disliked the idea extremely of delving into the private affairs in this way of a friend of mine.

ROBB: Certainly. Doctor, did it surprise you to learn that the man you have here, today, called "upright" and "loyal" had lied to the security authorities when there was serious suspicion of espionage?

RABI: It did surprise me at the time. I thought he behaved foolishly.

ROBB: If you had been in Dr. Oppenheimer's place, would you have lied to the security authorities—the same as he did?

RABI: The Lord alone knows.

ROBB: But I am asking *you*.

RABI: I don't think I would have done anything more than Oppenheimer did unless I thought the man who contacted me was just a poor jackass and didn't know what he was doing.

GRAY: I should like to ask another question, Dr. Rabi. As of today, would you expect Dr. Oppenheimer's loyalty to the country to take precedence over loyalty to an individual or some other institution?

RABI: I just don't think that anything is higher in his mind or heart than loyalty to his country. I must say I think that our generation, Dr. Oppenheimer's and my other friends, created American physics . . . that between the years 1929 and, say, 1939 we made it to the top of the heap. And it wasn't just because certain refugees came out of Germany. But because of what we did here. This was a conscious motivation. And Oppenheimer's school of theoretical physics was a tremendous contribution. I don't know how we could have carried out the scientific part of the war without the contributions of the people who worked with Oppenheimer at Los Alamos. It was really a miracle of a laboratory, just a miracle of a place.

GRAY: Would you expect Dr. Oppenheimer today to follow the course of action he followed in 1943 with regard to the Chevalier incident?

RABI: At the present time if a man came to him with a proposal like that, I think Oppenheimer would clamp him into jail.

GRAY: You are saying that in your judgment Dr. Oppenheimer has changed?

RABI: He has learned. He was always a loyal American. There was no doubt in my mind as to that. But he has learned more about the way you have to live in the world as it is now.

EVANS: Let me ask you a question that has nothing particularly pertinent to the proceedings. We have a mutual friend, George Pegram. I wonder if you know if he is still active?

RABI: Wonderfully. He is seventy-eight, doing two men's work.

EVANS: I wish you would tell him Dr. Evans asked about him.

RABI: I would be delighted to.

EVANS: Thank you.

MARKS: Dr. Rabi, would you be confident or would you not be confident that today Oppenheimer would resolve the question of his responsibility to the country or the public in a way you would?

RABI: I think he would be very conscious of his position not to impair his usefulness to the United States. I think he is just a much more mature person than he was then.

MARKS: That is all.

GRAY: You understand, Dr. Rabi, that these proceedings are not in the nature of a trial? And that we do not bring a verdict.

RABI: But your opinion will have the same weight. I think this business of suspending Dr. Oppenheimer's clearance is very unfortunate. It doesn't seem to me the kind of thing called for against a man who accomplished what he accomplished. We have a whole series of A-bombs. This is just a tremendous achievement. What more do you want? Mermaids? If the end of the road is this kind of hearing—which can't help but be humiliating—then where have we come?

GRAY: Let me thank you for your views, Dr. Rabi. And for taking the time to come here today.

RABI *exits.*

Change of lighting. The hangings close.

SCENE 3

The following text is projected on the hangings:

IN THE MORNING OF MAY 6, 1954, THE COMMISSION
CONCLUDED THE INTERROGATION OF WITNESSES.
FORTY WITNESSES HAD TESTIFIED IN THE MATTER OF
J. ROBERT OPPENHEIMER. THE RECORD OF THE
HEARINGS RAN TO 3,000 TYPEWRITTEN PAGES.

THE INTERROGATION OF THE WITNESSES WAS
FOLLOWED BY THE SPEECHES FOR THE PROSECUTION
AND FOR THE DEFENSE.

GRAY: I call on Mr. Robb to place his summing-up before the Board. The same right is granted to counsel for the defense, and Mr. Marks will avail himself of that right. Thereafter, the Board will recess in order to reach a final decision, as it has been instructed to do. Mr. Robb.

ROBB: Mr. Chairman, members of the Board. In the course of the three and a half weeks during which Dr. Oppenheimer has been before us, there has been recorded here the life story of an eminent physicist, the contradictions, the conflicts, and I confess I have been moved by it. I feel its tragic aspect. None of us has any doubt of Dr. Oppenheimer's great merits, and only a few would be able to resist the charm of his personality. However, it is our arduous duty to examine whether the safety of this country, in a field as important as nuclear energy, rests secure in his hands. Unfortunately, our security is at present threatened by the Communists who aim at establishing their form of government all over the world. According to his own testimony, Dr. Oppenheimer has for a long period of his life been in such close sympathy with the Communist movement that it is difficult to say in what respect he actually differed from a Communist. His nearest relatives, the majority of his friends and acquaintances, were either Communists or fellow travelers. He attended Communist meetings, he read Communist newspapers, he donated sums of money and belonged to a great number of camouflaged Communist organizations. I have no doubt that, to begin with, he was impelled by admirable motives, by a desire for social justice, by a dream of an ideal world. However, in the course of these proceedings, my conviction grew that Dr. Oppenheimer never abandoned his Communist sympathies, even when his enthusiasm had cooled, even when, disappointed, he turned away from the political manifestations of Communism in Russia.

His Communist sympathies were apparent when Communist physicists, recommended by Dr. Oppenheimer, gained key positions in work on secret war projects; they were apparent when, using his very considerable influence, he had these men retained on the war projects even though they were distrusted; and they finally were apparent in the Eltenton-Chevalier incident when he hesitated for half a year before he reported a serious suspicion of espionage, and when he deliberately lied to the security authorities, and when he placed his loyalty to a Communist friend above his loyalty to the United States.

It has been argued here that this incident belongs to the past, and that Dr. Oppenheimer has proved his absolute loyalty by his great services in connection with the atom bomb. I cannot share this view, although I do not dispute his merits in relation to Los Alamos. Rather, I see in his actions after the war, and particularly in the matter of the hydrogen bomb, the same manifestation of the same old Communist sympathies.

According to many testimonies, Dr. Oppenheimer was equally enthusiastic about the atom bomb *and* the hydrogen bomb as long as the enemy was Nazi Germany. But when it became clear that there were not only right-wing but also left-wing dictatorships that threatened us, and when Russia became our potential enemy, his scruples about the hydrogen bomb grew ever stronger, and he advocated internationalization of nuclear energy although it had been due entirely to our atom-bomb monopoly that we succeeded in stopping the Russians in Europe and Asia.

According to his own testimony, Dr. Oppenheimer felt profoundly depressed when it proved impossible to come to any agreement with the Russians. But he did not draw the conclusion from it which would have been in the best interests of the United States: the conclusion that the development of the hydrogen bomb should be stepped up before the Russians had their own atomic bomb.

Even when our danger was brought home to us in no uncertain manner by the existence of the Russian bomb, he used his considerable influence to oppose the crash program for the hydrogen bomb, and he yet again advocated negotiations with Soviet Russia in order to prevent the development of such a weapon. When, in spite of it, the order was given to initiate the crash program, and although he was fascinated by the brilliant new scientific ideas for the development of the hydrogen bomb, he still persevered in recommending a long-term research program; and when the date had already been fixed for the first test, he tried to postpone it in order not to jeopardize any disarmament negotiations.

We have heard several witnesses stating here that they found the discrepancy between his words and his actions inexplicable. Some of them—for instance, Major Radzi, William Borden, and Mr. Griggs—had come to the conclusion that a particularly subtle kind of treason lay at the root of it. But whoever had the opportunity to observe Dr. Oppenheimer for three and a half weeks, as we did, and whoever is as impressed with his personality as we are, will realize that this man is no common traitor. I am convinced that Dr. Oppenheimer wanted to serve the best interests of the United States. But his actions after the war, his obvious failure in the matter of the hydrogen bomb, were in fact injurious to the interests of this country—indeed, according to Dr. Teller's most convincing exposition, we could already have had the hydrogen bomb four or five years earlier if Dr. Oppenheimer had supported its development.

What is the explanation for such a failure in a man so wonderfully gifted, a man whose diplomatic acumen, whose sagacity have been praised here so often?

This is the explanation: Dr. Oppenheimer has never entirely abandoned the utopian ideals of an international classless society. He has kept faith with them consciously or unconsciously, and this subconscious loyalty could only in this way be reconciled with his loyalty to the United States. It is in this contradiction that his tragedy lies, and it is a lasting tragedy which prevents him from serving the best interests of the United States in that difficult sphere—even though he honestly wishes to do so. This is a form of treason which is not known in our code of law; it is ideological treason which has its origins in the deepest strata of the personality and renders a man's actions dishonest against his own will.

I speak of lasting tragedy because, in the course of these proceedings, Dr. Oppenheimer has never once availed himself of the opportunity to dissociate himself from his former political ideas and from his Communist associations. On the contrary, he has kept up these associations throughout the war, and after, and still has some of these personal associations even now. Neither has he ever recognized how wrong his actions have been, and he has not regretted them. And when we heard him saying here that, in the age of nuclear energy and weapons of mass destruction, the world needs new forms of human, economic, political coexistence—then I see in those words also a projection of his old ideals.

What America in fact needs today is a strengthening of her economic, military, and political power.

We have reached a point in our history when we must recognize that our freedom has its price, and historical necessity does not permit us to give any discount to anybody, even if he is a man who has rendered great service. This does not mean that we forget his past services; indeed, we respect them. It is my conviction, taking all facts into account, that Dr. Oppenheimer is *not* eligible for security clearance.

GRAY: Thank you, Mr. Robb. The Board will now hear counsel for the defense. Mr. Marks.

MARKS: Mr. Chairman, Dr. Evans, Mr. Morgan, Mr. Robb has spoken of the great merits and the tragic aspects of my client. I take this sympathy to be an admission that no facts have emerged in these proceedings which would impugn Dr. Oppenheimer's loyalty.

It is generally known that in the thirties Dr. Oppenheimer had strong leanings towards radical left-wing and Communist ideas, that he had friends who were Communists, and that he belonged to some organizations which had Communist sympathies. In those days, this was the attitude of many, if not most, intellectuals; and their social criticism corresponded to our policy of the New Deal, which introduced a greater measure of social justice in our country. What we have learned here about Dr. Oppenheimer's associations was already to be found in the questionnaires which Dr. Oppenheimer filled in before he started working on secret war projects, and those facts were fully known to the high and highest committees which granted Dr. Oppenheimer his clearance in 1943 and 1947. The material which the F.B.I. collected about Dr. Oppenheimer, and to which we have been denied access, was also known to the relevant committee already in 1947. I presume Mr. Robb would not have hesitated to acquaint us with that material if it had contained well-founded charges which are unknown to us. Likewise, the security authorities had full cognizance of Dr. Oppenheimer's conduct in the matter of Eltenton-Chevalier. That matter was cleared up before, and Mr. Robb has failed to present us with any fresh evidence. There was no conflict of loyalties, since Dr. Oppenheimer regarded Chevalier as innocent and Chevalier in fact proved to be innocent. Although it was realized that there had been no such thing as attempted espionage, Dr. Oppenheimer did not hesitate to say that his conduct had been foolish, and nobody will doubt that his conduct today would be different from what it was in 1942.

There remains the question whether Dr. Oppenheimer endangered the security of the United States by opposing the hydrogen bomb program, against his better judgment, and with disloyal intent. It is not a matter of whether his advice was good or bad, but whether it was honest advice, and whether it was given in the best interests of the United States, or not.

Many experts have here testified to their opinion that Dr. Oppenheimer's advice was good advice when he submitted that the development of the hydrogen bomb should be prevented by means of an international agreement. He anticipated, and apprehended, the balance of fear which paralyzes us today. But other experts, such as Teller and Alvarez, had different views, and they carried their point. They sharply criticized his proposals, but even the determined advocates of the hydrogen bomb did not doubt that he had wanted to serve the best interests of America with his advice. Dr. Teller has complained here that Dr. Oppenheimer had not been sufficiently enthusiastic about the hydrogen bomb and that it was his lack of enthusiasm which delayed the hydrogen bomb for a matter of years. But how is a man to feel enthusiastic when he fears that such a weapon may in fact weaken America and imperil our whole civilization? How is a man to feel enthusiastic when he is confronted with a program which is technically not feasible and which is a program for a weapon that has all the strategic and political arguments against it? What would Dr. Teller say if he were reproached for his lack of enthusiasm for the atomic bomb during the war, and if it were pointed out to him that his place had therefore been taken by Klaus Fuchs, and thus it was his, Teller's fault that atomic secrets had been given away? He would be quite right to consider this absurd, and the myth about the delay of the hydrogen bomb because of Dr. Oppenheimer's lack of enthusiasm is equally absurd.

It was in the light of his best judgment that Dr. Oppenheimer expressed an adverse opinion on a bad crash program. He was in complete agreement there with the foremost experts in the country. When, in spite of it, the order was given to initiate the crash program and when new ideas for the hydrogen bomb made its production feasible, he no longer discussed its political usefulness but supported the program to the best of his abilities. I do not see how any man's attitude could be *more* correct and *more* loyal than that.

Where are those dishonest actions which contradict his words? Where are the facts to bear out the allegation that Dr. Oppenheimer has been disloyal, that he cannot be trusted, that he endangers the security of the United States? Is the "closed Communist meeting" alleged by Mr. Crouch, is the "silent conspiracy" alleged by Mr. Griggs, such a fact? Was it traitorous conduct when Dr. Oppenheimer did not toe the line of Air Force enthusiasts in the weapons rivalry over the defense of the country? Dr. Oppenheimer had to advise the American government, and not the Air Force. He had to think of America, and not of the priority of one kind of weapon over another.

We may doubt the wisdom of his advice, and this is quite in order if his advice is no longer required, but we cannot cast doubt upon the loyalty of a man because we doubt the wisdom of his advice.

If we were to follow Mr. Robb's suggestion and introduced here the concept of ideological treason, a category which is not known in our code of law, we would destroy not only the scientific career of a great American but would destroy also the very foundations of our democracy.

I agree with Mr. Robb when he says that freedom has its price. Dr. Oppenheimer himself, in a newspaper article he wrote in defense of one of his colleagues, had the following to say about the price of freedom:

"Political opinion, no matter how radical or how freely expressed, does not disqualify a scientist from a high career in science; it does not impugn his integrity nor his honor. We have seen in other countries criteria of political orthodoxy applied to ruin scientists, and to put an end to their work. This has brought with it the attrition of science. It has been part of the destruction of freedom of inquiry, and of political freedom itself. This is no path to follow for a people determined to stay free."

GRAY: Thank you, Mr. Marks. The Board will now recess. We shall let you know the date of the final session. I thank all those present for their participation. In particular, I thank Dr. Oppenheimer.

OPPENHEIMER: Thank you, sir. [*The lighting changes.* OPPENHEIMER *steps forward to the footlights. The hangings close.*] On May 14, 1954, a few minutes to ten, physicist J. Robert Oppenheimer entered, for the last time, Room 2022 of the Atomic Energy Commission in Washington in order to hear the final decision of the Board, and to make a concluding statement. [OPPENHEIMER *returns to the stage itself.*]

SCENE 4

The following text is projected on the hangings:

THE FINAL DECISION

The members of the Board, OPPENHEIMER, *and counsel for both parties occupy their usual places.* GRAY *takes a report from a folder and rises to his feet to read it aloud.*

GRAY: After due consideration of all the facts the majority of this Board—the members Thomas A. Morgan and Gordon Gray jointly diverging from the conclusions reached by the member Ward V. Evans—propose to submit to the Atomic Energy Commission their final decision in the matter of J. Robert Oppenheimer, as follows:

"Although we consider Dr. Oppenheimer's numerous Communist associations in the past a grave indictment, and although Dr. Oppenheimer made the regrettable decision to continue some of those associations up to the present day, we find no indication of disloyalty as far as his present associations are concerned.

"Dr. Oppenheimer's attitude in the Eltenton-Chevalier incident appears to us a weightier matter. There, in a serious case of suspected espionage, he deliberately lied to the security authorities in order to protect a friend whose Communist background was well known to him, and thus he placed himself outside the rules which govern the conduct of others. It is not important whether it was in fact a case of attempted espionage; what is important is that he believed in the possibility of it being such. The continued falsification and false statements point to disquieting defects of character.

"Loyalty to our friends is one of the noblest qualities. But if a man puts his loyalty to friends above what may reasonably be considered his duties to his country and its security system, this is, beyond a doubt, incompatible with the interests of his country.

"As to Dr. Oppenheimer's attitude in the matter of the hydrogen bomb, we find it ambiguous and disquieting. If Dr. Oppenheimer had given the program his enthusiastic support, organized endeavor would have begun sooner, and we would have had the hydrogen bomb at a considerably earlier date. This would have increased the security of the United States. We believe that Dr. Oppenheimer's negative attitude in the matter of the hydrogen bomb stemmed from his strong moral scruples, and that his negative attitude had an adverse effect on other scientists. Although we have no doubt that he gave his advice with loyal intent and to the best of his ability, we note a deplorable lack of faith in the United States government, a lack of faith which is exemplified by his endeavor to prevent the development of the hydrogen bomb by means of international agreements, and is further exemplified by his demand for a guarantee that we shall not be the first to use that weapon.

"We find that his conduct gives rise to considerable doubt as to whether his future participation in a national defense program would be unequivocally compatible with the requirements of the country's security, if he persisted in such conduct.

"Summing up our doubts, and with reference to evidence of his basic defects of character, we conclude that Dr. Oppenheimer can no longer claim the unreserved confidence of the government and of the Atomic Energy Commission, a confidence which would have found expression in the granting of his security clearance.—Gordon Gray. Thomas A. Morgan."

Appendix by Gordon Gray:

"In my view, it would have been possible for us to reach a different conclusion if we had been permitted to judge Dr. Oppenheimer independently of the rigid rulings and criteria now enforced upon us."

I now call on Dr. Evans to read his minority report.

GRAY *sits down.* EVANS *picks up a sheet of paper and holds it close to his eyes in order to read it aloud.*

EVANS: "After due consideration of the facts laid here before us, I regard Dr. Oppenheimer as absolutely loyal, I do not consider him a security risk, and I see no reason why his security clearance should be withheld.

"My arguments are as follows: Dr. Oppenheimer's former Communist associations, including also his attitude to Chevalier, go back to a time *before* the great services he rendered the United States. Dr. Oppenheimer has never made a secret of those associations, and all the charges brought here against him were already known when, lastly in 1947, he was granted his security clearance. I am troubled by the phenomenon that an assessment of the *same* facts should change when there is a change in the political climate.

"In the discussions about the hydrogen bomb, it was not only Dr. Oppenheimer's right but his duty to express his own opinion. His views in this complicated matter were well founded; they coincided with the views of many of the foremost experts, and it is by no means certain whether his advice was not the best advice after all. When we inquire into a man's loyalty, however, it is not a matter of whether his advice was sound but whether it was honest. Moral and ethical reservations about the development of a weapon are not necessarily injurious to the interests of America, and it is common sense to consider in good time the consequences of a development which is fraught with so many possible repercussions.—Ward V. Evans."

GRAY: It thus is evident that the majority of the Personnel Security Board of the Atomic Energy Commission recommend that Dr. Oppenheimer shall not be granted his security clearance. [*To* OP-PENHEIMER's *counsels.*] You may request the Atomic Energy Commission to review that recommendation. I now give Dr. Oppenheimer the opportunity he requested for a few concluding words. Dr. Oppenheimer.

OPPENHEIMER *rises to his feet.*

OPPENHEIMER: When, more than a month ago, I sat for the first time on this old sofa I felt I wanted to defend myself, for I was not aware of any guilt, and I regarded myself as the victim of a regrettable political conjunction. But when I was being forced into that disagreeable recapitulation of my life, my motives, my inner conflicts, and even the absence of certain conflicts—my attitude began to change. I tried to be absolutely frank, and this is a technique one must relearn when one has not been frank with people for many years of one's life. As I was thinking about myself, a physicist of our times, I began to ask myself whether there had not in fact been something like ideological treason, a category of treason Mr. Robb proposed should be considered here. It has become a matter of course to us that even basic research in the field of nuclear physics is top secret nowadays, and that our laboratories are financed by the military and are being guarded like war projects. When I think what might have become of the ideas of Copernicus or Newton under present-day conditions, I begin to wonder whether we were not perhaps traitors to the spirit of science when we handed over the results of our research to the military, without considering the consequences. Now we find ourselves living in a world in which people regard the discoveries of scientists with dread and horror, and go in mortal fear of new discoveries. And meanwhile there seems to be little hope that people will soon learn how to live together on this ever smaller planet, and there is little hope that, in the near future, the material side of their lives will be enhanced by the new beneficent discoveries. It seems a thoroughly utopian idea that atomic energy, which can be produced everywhere equally easily and equally cheaply, would be followed by other benefits for all; and that the electronic brains, originally developed for the great weapons of destruction, would in future run our factories and thus restore the creative quality to man's work. Our lives would be enriched by material freedom which is one of the prerequisites of happiness, but such hopes are not borne out by the reality we have now to live with. Yet they are the alternatives to the destruction of this earth, a destruction we fear and are unable to imagine. At these crossroads for mankind we, the physicists, find that we have never before been of such consequence, and that we have never before been so completely helpless. As I was looking at my life here I realized that the actions the Board hold against me were closer to the idea of science than were the services which I have been praised for.

Contrary to this Board, therefore, I ask myself whether we, the physicists, have not sometimes given too great, too indiscriminate loyalty to our governments, against our better judgment—in my case, not only in the matter of the hydrogen bomb. We have spent years of our lives in developing ever sweeter means of destruction, we have been doing the work of the military, and I feel it in my very bones that this was wrong. I shall request the Atomic Energy Commission to review the decision of the majority of this Board; but, no matter what the result of that review may be, I will never work on war projects again. We have been doing the work of the Devil, and now we must return to our real tasks. Rabi told me a few days ago that he wants to devote himself entirely to research again. We cannot do better than keep the world open in the few places which can still be kept open.

The hangings close.

The following text is projected on the hangings:

ON DECEMBER 2, 1963, PRESIDENT JOHNSON PRESENTED J. ROBERT OPPENHEIMER WITH THE ENRICO FERMI PRIZE FOR SERVICES RENDERED ON THE ATOMIC ENERGY PROGRAM IN CRUCIAL YEARS.

THE RECOMMENDATION FOR THE CONFERMENT WAS SUBMITTED BY EDWARD TELLER, THE PRIZE WINNER OF THE PREVIOUS YEAR.

CURTAIN

Translated by Ruth Speirs

HEINER MÜLLER

Hamletmachine

1
Family Scrapbook

I was Hamlet. I stood at the shore and talked with the surf
BLABLA, the ruins of Europe in back of me. The bells tolled the
state-funeral, murderer and widow a couple, the councillors goose-
stepping behind the highranking carcass' coffin, bawling with badly
paid grief WHO IS THE CORPSE IN THE HEARSE/ABOUT WHOM
THERE'S SUCH A HUE AND CRY/'TIS THE CORPSE OF A GREAT/GIVER
OF ALMS the lane formed by the populace, creation of his statecraft
HE WAS A MAN HE TOOK THEM ALL FOR ALL. I stopped the funeral
procession, I pried open the coffin with my sword, the blade broke,
yet with the blunt reminder I succeeded, and I dispensed my dead
procreator FLESH LIKES TO KEEP THE COMPANY OF FLESH among
the bums around me. The mourning turned into rejoicing, the re-
joicing into lipsmacking, on top of the empty coffin the murderer
humped the widow LET ME HELP YOU UP, UNCLE, OPEN YOUR LEGS,
MAMA. I laid down on the ground and listened to the world doing
its turns in step with the putrefaction.
I'M GOOD HAMLET GI'ME A CAUSE FOR GRIEF*
AH THE WHOLE GLOBE FOR A REAL SORROW*
RICHARD THE THIRD I THE PRINCE-KILLING KING*
OH MY PEOPLE WHAT HAVE I DONE UNTO THEE*
I'M LUGGING MY OVERWEIGHT BRAIN LIKE A HUNCHBACK
CLOWN NUMBER TWO IN THE SPRING OF COMMUNISM
SOMETHING IS ROTTEN IN THIS AGE OF HOPE*
LET'S DELVE IN EARTH AND BLOW HER AT THE MOON*
Here comes the ghost who made me, the ax still in his skull. Keep
your hat on, I know you've got one hole too many. I would my

---

*The lines with an asterisk are in English in the German text.

mother had one less when you were still of flesh: I would have been spared myself. Women should be sewed up—a world without mothers. We could butcher each other in peace and quiet, and with some confidence, if life gets too long for us or our throats too tight for our screams. What do you want of me? Is one state-funeral not enough for you? You old sponger. Is there no blood on your shoes? What's your corpse to me? Be glad the handle is sticking out, maybe you'll go to heaven. What are you waiting for? All the cocks have been butchered. Tomorrow morning has been canceled.

SHALL I

AS IS THE CUSTOM STICK A PIECE OF IRON INTO

THE NEAREST FLESH OR THE SECOND BEST

TO LATCH UNTO IT SINCE THE WORLD IS SPINNING

LORD BREAK MY NECK WHILE I'M FALLING FROM AN

ALEHOUSE BENCH

Enters Horatio. Confidant of my thoughts so full of blood since the morning is curtained by the empty sky. YOU'LL BE TOO LATE MY FRIEND FOR YOUR PAYCHECK/NO PART FOR YOU IN THIS MY TRAGEDY. Horatio, do you know me? Are you my friend, Horatio? If you know me how can you be my friend? Do you want to play Polonius who wants to sleep with his daughter, the delightful Ophelia, here she enters right on cue, look how she shakes her ass, a tragic character. HoratioPolonius. I knew you're an actor. I am too, I'm playing Hamlet. Denmark is a prison, a wall is growing between the two of us. Look what's growing from that wall. Exit Polonius. My mother the bride. Her breasts a rosebed, her womb the snakepit. Have you forgotten your lines, Mama. I'll prompt you. WASH THE MURDER OFF YOUR FACE MY PRINCE/AND OFFER THE NEW DENMARK YOUR GLAD EYE. I'll change you back into a virgin mother, so your king will have a bloodwedding. A MOTHER'S WOMB IS NOT A ONE-WAY STREET. Now, I tie your hands on your back with your bridal veil since I'm sick of your embrace. Now, I tear the wedding dress. Now, I smear the shreds of the wedding dress with the dust my father turned into, and with the soiled shreds your face your belly your breasts. Now, I take you, my mother, in his, my father's invisible tracks. I stifle your scream with my lips. Do you recognize the fruit of your womb? Now go to your wedding, whore, in the broad Danish sunlight which shines on the living and the dead. I want to cram the corpse down the latrine so the palace will choke in royal shit. Then let me eat your heart, Ophelia, which weeps my tears.

2
The Europe of Women

Enormous room.* Ophelia. Her heart is a clock.

OPHELIA (CHORUS/HAMLET):

I am Ophelia. The one the river didn't keep. The woman dangling from the rope. The woman with her arteries cut open. The woman with the overdose. SNOW ON HER LIPS. The woman with her head in the gas stove. Yesterday I stopped killing myself. I'm alone with my breasts my thighs my womb. I smash the tools of my captivity, the chair the table the bed. I destroy the battlefield that was my home. I fling open the doors so the wind gets in and the scream of the world. I smash the window. With my bleeding hands I tear the photos of the men I loved and who used me on the bed on the table on the chair on the ground. I set fire to my prison. I throw my clothes into the fire. I wrench the clock that was my heart out of my breast. I walk into the street clothed in my blood.

3
Scherzo

The university of the dead. Whispering and muttering. From their gravestones (lecterns), the dead philosophers throw their books at Hamlet. Gallery (ballet) of the dead women. The woman dangling from the rope. The woman with her arteries cut open, etc. . . . Hamlet views them with the attitude of a visitor in a museum (theatre). The dead women tear his clothes off his body. Out of an upended coffin, labeled HAMLET 1, step Claudius and Ophelia, the latter dressed and made up like a whore. Striptease by Ophelia.

OPHELIA: Do you want to eat my heart, Hamlet? *Laughs.*

HAMLET: *Face in his hands.* I want to be a woman. *Hamlet dresses in Ophelia's clothes, Ophelia puts the make-up of a whore on his* face, Claudius—now *Hamlet's father*—*laughs without uttering a sound, Ophelia blows Hamlet a kiss and steps with Claudius/ HamletFather back into the coffin. Hamlet poses as a whore. An angel, his face at the back of his head: Horatio. He dances with Hamlet.*

Voice(s): *From the coffin.* What thou killed thou shalt love. *The dance grows faster and wilder. Laughter from the coffin. On a swing, the madonna with breast cancer. Horatio opens an umbrella, embraces Hamlet. They freeze under the umbrella, embracing. The breast cancer radiates like a sun.*

4
Pest in Buda/Battle for Greenland

Space 2, as destroyed by Ophelia. An empty armor, an ax stuck in the helmet.
Hamlet:
The stove is smoking in quarrelsome October
A BAD COLD HE HAD OF IT JUST THE WORST TIME*
JUST THE WORST TIME OF THE YEAR FOR A REVOLUTION*
Cement in bloom walks through the slums
Doctor Zhivago weeps
For his wolves
SOMETIMES IN WINTER THEY CAME INTO THE VILLAGE
AND TORE APART A PEASANT
He takes off make-up and costume.

THE ACTOR PLAYING HAMLET:
I'm not Hamlet. I don't take part any more. My words have nothing to tell me anymore. My thoughts suck the blood out of the images. My drama doesn't happen anymore. Behind me the set is put up. By people who aren't interested in my drama, for people to whom it means nothing. I'm not interested in it anymore either. I won't play along anymore. *Unnoticed by the actor playing Hamlet, stagehands place a refrigerator and three TV-sets on the stage. Humming of the refrigerator. Three TV-channels without sound.* The set is a monument. It presents a man who made history, enlarged a hundred times. The petrification of a hope. His name is

interchangeable, the hope has not been fulfilled. The monument is toppled into the dust, razed by those who succeeded him in power three years after the state funeral of the hated and most honored leader. The stone is inhabited. In the spacy nostrils and auditory canals, in the creases of skin and uniform of the demolished monument, the poorer inhabitants of the capital are dwelling. After an appropriate period, the uprising follows the toppling of the monument. My drama, if it still would happen, would happen in the time of the uprising. The uprising starts with a stroll. Against the traffic rules, during the working hours. The street belongs to the pedestrians. Here and there, a car is turned over. Nightmare of a knife thrower: Slowly driving down a one-way street towards an irrevocable parking space surrounded by armed pedestrians. Policemen, if in the way, are swept to the curb. When the procession approaches the government district it is stopped by a police line. People form groups, speakers arise from them. On the balcony of a government building, a man in badly fitting mufti appears and begins to speak too. When the first stone hits him, he retreats behind the double doors of bullet-proof glass. The call for more freedom turns into the cry for the overthrow of the government. People begin to disarm the policemen, to storm two, three buildings, a prison a police precinct an office of the secret police, they string up a dozen henchmen of the rulers by their heels, the government brings in troops, tanks. My place, if my drama would still happen, would be on both sides of the front, between the frontlines, over and above them. I stand in the stench of the crowd and hurl stones at policemen soldiers tanks bullet-proof glass. I look through the double doors of bullet-proof glass at the crowd pressing forward and smell the sweat of my fear. Choking with nausea, I shake my fist at myself who stands behind the bullet-proof glass. Shaking with fear and contempt, I see myself in the crowd pressing forward, foaming at the mouth, shaking my fist at myself. I string up my uniformed flesh by my own heels. I am the soldier in the gun turret, my head is empty under the helmet, the stifled scream under the tracks. I am the typewriter. I tie the noose when the ringleaders are strung up. I pull the stool from under their feet, I break my own neck. I am my own prisoner. I feed my own data into the computers. My parts are the spittle and the spittoon the knife and the wound the fang and the throat the neck and the rope. I am the data bank. Bleeding in the crowd. Breathing again behind the double

doors. Oozing wordslime in my soundproof blurb over and above the battle. My drama didn't happen. The script has been lost. The actors put their faces on the rack in the dressing room. In his box, the prompter is rotting. The stuffed corpses in the house don't stir a hand. I go home and kill the time, at one/with my undivided self.
Television The daily nausea Nausea
Of prefabricated babble Of decreed cheerfulness
How do you spell GEMÜTLICHKEIT
Give us this day our daily murder
Since thine is nothingness Nausea
Of the lies which are believed
By the liars and nobody else
Nausea
Of the lies which are believed Nausea
Of the mugs of the manipulators marked
By their struggle for positions votes bank accounts
Nausea A chariot armed with scythes sparkling with punchlines
I walk through streets stores Faces
Scarred by the consumers battle Poverty
Without dignity Poverty without the dignity
Of the knife the knuckleduster the clenched fist
The humiliated bodies of women
Hope of generations
Stifled in blood cowardice stupidity
Laughter from dead bellies
Hail Coca Cola
A kingdom
For a murderer
I WAS MACBETH
THE KING HAD OFFERED HIS THIRD MISTRESS TO ME
I KNEW EVERY MOLE ON HER HIPS
RASKOLNIKOV CLOSE TO THE
HEART UNDER THE ONLY COAT THE AX FOR THE
ONLY
SKULL OF THE PAWNBROKER
In the solitude of airports
I breathe again I am
A privileged person My nausea
Is a privilege
Protected by torture

Barbed wire Prisons
Photograph of the author.
I don't want to eat drink breathe love a woman a man a child an animal anymore.
I don't want to die anymore. I don't want to kill anymore.
Tearing of the author's photograph.
I force open my sealed flesh. I want to dwell in my veins, in the marrow of my bones, in the maze of my skull. I retreat into my entrails. I take my seat in my shit, in my blood. Somewhere bodies are torn apart so I can dwell in my shit. Somewhere bodies are opened so I can be alone with my blood. My thoughts are lesions in my brain. My brain is a scar. I want to be a machine. Arms for grabbing Legs to walk on, no pain no thoughts.

TV screens go black. Blood oozes from the refrigerator. Three naked women: Marx, Lenin, Mao. They speak simultaneously, each one in his own language, the text:

THE MAIN POINT IS TO OVERTHROW ALL EXISTING CONDITIONS . . .*

The Actor of Hamlet puts on make-up and costume.

HAMLET THE DANE PRINCE AND MAGGOT'S FODDER STUMBLING FROM HOLE TO HOLE TOWARDS THE FINAL HOLE LISTLESS IN HIS BACK THE GHOST THAT ONCE MADE HIM GREEN LIKE OPHELIA'S FLESH IN CHILDBED AND SHORTLY ERE THE THIRD COCK'S CROW A CLOWN WILL TEAR THE FOOL'S CAP OFF THE PHILOSOPHER A BLOATED BLOODHOUND'LL CRAWL INTO THE ARMOR

He steps into the armor, splits with the ax the heads of Marx, Lenin, Mao. Snow. Ice Age.

5
Fiercely Enduring Millennia in the Fearful Armor

The deep sea. Ophelia in a wheelchair. Fish, debris, dead bodies and limbs drift by.

---

*English-language productions could use the entire quote from Karl Marx: Introduction to *Critique of Hegel's Philosophy of Law.*

OPHELIA:

While two men in white smocks wrap gauze around her and the wheelchair, from bottom to top.

This is Electra speaking. In the heart of darkness. Under the sun of torture. To the capitals of the world. In the name of the victims. I eject all the sperm I have received. I turn the milk of my breasts into lethal poison. I take back the world I gave birth to. I choke between my thighs the world I gave birth to. I bury it in my womb. Down with the happiness of submission. Long live hate and contempt, rebellion and death. When she walks through your bedrooms carrying butcher knives you'll know the truth.

The men exit. Ophelia remains on stage, motionless in her white wrappings.

END

Translated by Carl Weber

Copyright Acknowledgments

Titles Available in
The German Library

All titles available from Continuum International
370 Lexington Avenue, New York, NY 10017
www.continuumbooks.com

Titles Available in The German Library

Titles Available in The German Library

Titles Available in The German Library